MICHAEL RABIN

MICHAEL RABIN

AMERICA'S VIRTUOSO VIOLINIST

ANTHONY FEINSTEIN

AMADEUS
PRESS

An Imprint of Hal Leonard Corporation

Amadeus Press
An Imprint of Hal Leonard Corporation
7777 West Bluemound Road
Milwaukee, WI 53213

Trade Book Division Editorial Offices
33 Plymouth St., Montclair, NJ 07042

Paperback edition published in 2011 by Amadeus Press

Originally published in hardcover in 2005 by Amadeus Press

All interior photographs not otherwise credited are from the collection of Bertine Lafayette.

ISBN: 978-1-57467-199-5

Printed in the United States of America

The Library of Congress has cataloged the hardcover edition as follows:

Feinstein, A. (Anthony), 1956-
  Michael Rabin: America's virtuoso violinist / by Anthony Feinstein.
      p. cm.
  Includes bibliographical references and index.
  ISBN 1-57467-109-X
  1. Rabin, Michael, 1936-1972. 2. Violinists--United States--Biography. I. Title.

ML418.R113F44 2005
787.2'092--DC22

2005007925

www.amadeuspress.com

FOR KALLY

"The heart can do anything."
— MOLIÈRE

CONTENTS

CHAPTER 1
NATURE AND NURTURE

"Life," remarked Samuel Butler, "is like giving a concert on the violin while learning to play the instrument."[1] One does not have to be a violinist to appreciate the wisdom of Butler's words, although a few lessons in one's youth will surely have sharpened a person's insight. For mastering the violin, that infernally beautiful and bewitching instrument, the devil's accomplice, presents formidable challenges. It is a good metaphor for life.

When seen in the context of the career of Michael Rabin, Butler's insight takes on a poignancy. There were few violinists in the twentieth century who mastered the instrument so completely, who were able to conquer the daunting technical challenges posed and use this remarkable mechanical proficiency as the bedrock on which to launch a meteoric career. To his renowned teacher, Ivan Galamian, who over a long career molded the talents of many of today's great virtuoso violinists, Michael was the star, a violinist *sans pareil*, "without weakness, none."[2] But when it came to life and the fragile passage of wunderkind to mature adult, Michael's trajectory was less certain. It was life, not the fiendish tenths, octaves, and double-harmonics so beloved of Paganini and subsequent generations of virtuosos, that presented Michael with his greatest challenge.

This disconnect between a rare and wonderful talent frugally granted to only a handful in any one generation and a fulfilling personal life comfortably at home in society was, for most of his adult years, painfully apparent. Such were the insuperable demands of an itinerant existence prematurely foisted upon him that Michael's career derailed at a point where a brilliant future was his for the taking. Feted nationally and internationally as America's great, homegrown violin virtuoso, Michael had a rare talent that allowed him equal access to a stage for the most part dominated by foreign celebrities, the Jaschas, Mischas, and Toschas of Gershwin's witty song that spoke to the hopes of immigrant parents for their first-generation offspring.[3] Michael was the local kid who made good, the child who arrived on the stage of Carnegie Hall direct from the Upper West Side of Manhattan, spared the circuitous and potentially hazardous migrations of many of the previous generation's violin greats.

By his late teens, Michael had the musical world at his feet. His inability to seize the moment was a personal tragedy and, for his legion of admirers, a source of lingering sadness and regret. A little more than a decade later, his sudden death prematurely ended a career revival and sparked a flurry of rumor, innuendo, and misinformation. That he died during a period of greater personal happiness adds to the pathos. And yet it would be a mistake for his life to be viewed as simply yet another example of precocious talent unfulfilled. The disappointments of his later years must be viewed within the context of a series of remarkable professional triumphs and a small but influential recorded legacy that has assured him a place in the pantheon of violin greats — if not quite at the summit attained by his boyhood idol Heifetz, then one rung lower, safely ensconced alongside another revered figure who, among all the fellow virtuosos of that era, came closest to befriending him: Zino Francescatti.

MICHAEL JOSEPH RABIN was born into a family blessed by Apollo, for in the perennial nature-versus-nurture debate, both sides were well represented. His parents were two talented professional musicians whose temperaments could not have been more different. George Rabinowitz was born in New York City on December 21, 1898, the son of Romanian immigrants Jacob Rabinowitz and Sarah Lazar. He was the second eldest of nine children. In late life, George recalled that he had been born on the Lower East Side next to a synagogue. One of his earliest memories was of being taken to the place of worship by his father and his rapture at listening to a choir of five or six singers rehearse: "I couldn't get enough of them. I used to hear them rehearse on the fourth floor and I was drawn to their music. A year later I sang with them at the temple. It opened up my feelings for music."[4]

Music was clearly important to the Rabinowitz family. Although Sarah did not play an instrument, she developed the physical mannerism of simulating vibrato, compensating for her lack of formal training with a rich musical imagination.[5] Four years before George's arrival, she gave birth to

Clara in Bucharest on July 16, 1894. George in turn was followed by Rose and Jean, the two sisters each separated by an interval of four years. Two years after Jean, Norman was born, followed by the youngest Rabinowitz, Grace. Three children did not survive into adulthood — Minnie, Esther, and Sigmund — the latter, according to family legend, a talented cellist who fell down a flight of stairs after being tickled by a maid and died from the injuries sustained.

The turn of the century was a hectic time for the Rabinowitz family. USA census data reveal that Sarah Lazar and her daughter Clara emigrated from Romania in 1905. This, if accurate and taken in conjunction with George's date and place of birth, suggests that Sarah, and probably Jacob, traveled back and forth between Romania and New York at least once before Jacob was financially secure enough to set up his family's permanent move to the New World.

"Our family was poor," reminisced George, "and we couldn't afford to buy any musical instruments. So we went to the Third Street Music School and they gave me a violin for free to play. I went for lessons there for two years."[6]* An undisclosed misdemeanor brought an end to this arrangement, and the teacher left under a cloud. George was promptly found a substitute pedagogue, who, for seventy-five cents a lesson, continued his tuition in a church across the way from the school. Meanwhile, Clara was making rapid progress on the piano. In time Jean would learn the cello, Rose the violin, and Grace the piano, and as young adults, the three siblings performed as the Rabinowitz piano trio, making radio broadcasts and giving concerts during the summers at resorts in the Catskills.

Neither Rose nor Jean was able to sustain a musical career, despite their obvious talent, and by 1930 Rose was working as a typist in a glassware factory, while Jean held a clerical job for a publicity firm. Neither ever married. Grace, on the other hand, while still a child received a full scholarship to study piano at the Institute of Musical Art, the forerunner to the Juilliard School of Music, and thereafter a second scholarship to study at a music Academy in Fontainebleau, outside Paris. On her return to the United States, she taught piano, joined her elder sisters for a few years as the Rabinowitz trio, married, and had two children, neither of whom pursued music as a career.

The big musical careers among the six surviving Rabinowitz children belonged to Clara and George. Clara had a precocious talent that led to a solo career on both sides of the Atlantic. She was a formidable presence and the acknowledged star of the family. When Jacob died in 1915, the mantle as head

---

* George was also a pupil at City College.

of the family passed to the seventeen-year-old George. In a patriarchal family setup, it was expected of George as the eldest son that he assume a considerable degree of responsibility for his younger siblings. But in the presence of Clara, his standing was little more than titular. "Clara would come home from a concert tour and rule the roost at their home in Jackson Heights," recalls her niece, Judy Brodsky. "When she came home, back from Europe, the entire rhythm of the household would change and the sisters would cower in fear. 'Oh my God, she's home,' would go up the cry, and the rest would have to kowtow."7

It could not have been an easy situation for George, but if he was affected by his loss of face, he initially did not let it derail either his academic studies or his progress on the violin. "Public school was a cinch for me," he claimed. "I got out of there at twelve years old. I started college at sixteen."8 While in his teens, George's burgeoning musical ability meant that better teachers had to be found. After a period of study with Edgar Stowell, he became a pupil of David Mannes.

Born in 1866, Mannes was, like George, the son of poor immigrant parents. At the age of twenty-five, he was invited by Walter Damrosch to join the first-violin section of a new symphony orchestra put together for the recently built Carnegie Hall. Mannes declined the offer and opted instead for a further period of training in Berlin with de Anha and Halir, before finishing his European trip with a further six months' tutelage under the supervision of Ysaÿe in Brussels. He returned home to the concertmaster's chair in the New York Symphony and began teaching at the Third Street Music School Settlement for disadvantaged children in Manhattan, where he was director from 1910 to 1915.9 In time Mannes and his wife Clara founded their own musical school, with a particular humanitarian imprint that reflected both their characters: personal warmth and high musical standards, but without the unwanted intrusion of career pressures.

George's second teacher of note was Franz Kneisel. A year older than Mannes, he was born in Germany and, with an orchestral career in Europe well established, moved to the United States in 1885 as concertmaster of the Boston Symphony Orchestra. Kneisel is best remembered for his string quartet that proselytized chamber music throughout the country over the course of thirty-two years. For many Americans, it was their first exposure to a novel music form.10 In 1903 Kneisel left Boston and moved to New York to join the faculty of the Institute of Musical Art, then in its infancy. It was in New York that George Rabin, now in his late teens, took lessons with Kneisel, and it was through his teacher that George came to the attention of Ossip Gabrilowitsch, newly appointed conductor of the Detroit Symphony and on the lookout for fresh talent to bolster his orchestra's string sections. George signed the contract Gabrilowitsch offered. The year was 1918.

George never did take up the Detroit position. World events intervened. The First World War was devouring the youth of Europe and had entered its fourth year of slaughter. American neutrality, maintained by an isolationist Woodrow Wilson, had become increasingly difficult. German submarines were forcing America into the war.[11] The sinking of the British liner the *Lusitania*, with the loss of 128 US citizens, was the most publicized of many acts of U-boat aggression towards neutral shipping in the Atlantic. "It means that we shall lose our heads along with the rest and stop weighing right and wrong," bemoaned the reluctant President after abandoning neutrality in 1917.[12]

In 1918 the nineteen-to-forty-year-old draft came out. George, twenty years old, was called up for infantry duty. Understandably reluctant to swap the pleasures of a hard-earned first-violin stand in Detroit for the quagmire of a trench in Flanders, George searched for a way to improve his chances of survival. "I decided to join the ROTC [Reserve Officer Training Corps] to become an officer and perhaps get better treatment," he recollected. Little did he know that by that stage of the war, the average survival time for an infantry officer on the Western Front could be measured in weeks. In old age, George looked back seventy years and remembered:

> We slept for four to five months in the halls of City College. The army took over and put beds in the corridors. We used to eat at Townsend Harris High School right across the way. I was supposed to go across to the War with the 84th Division to the Argonne Forest. I was in the infantry. Then I was sent to Camp Lee in Virginia for further training. I was lucky. After being there a short while, I collapsed on the field with the flu. It developed into pneumonia, then double pneumonia. They sent me to the base hospital in the Bronx. I was down to ninety pounds. The army doctors thought I was dying, and they sent for my mother. After she came to stay with me, I passed the climax of the illness and began to recover. I was in the hospital for probably four to six weeks, and while I was there, the armistice was signed on November 11. I stayed in the hospital for another two weeks after that, and they gave me cigarettes and candy. Then I was discharged and sent home. After my discharge, I received credit from City College for my army service. I got six (or eight) credits for the term I had missed. The college was doing that for all the soldiers.[13]

What George forgot to tell his amanuensis was that he had received a bursary to attend Columbia University and study mechanical engineering. Confronted by Gabrilowitsch's contract, he had been forced to choose professions and had settled on music. There is another fact that George may have been unaware of at the time, although its global implications were enormous. The illness that had kept him from embarking for France and had brought his distraught mother to his bedside was the great influenza pandemic of 1918. George was certainly lucky to have avoided the slaughterhouse of France, but he was even more fortunate to have survived the Spanish flu, a virulent virus that killed with an efficiency that surpassed even the perverted ingenuity of mankind at war.[14]

An emaciated George returned to his mother's home at 3333 89th Street in Queens. He was in no condition to travel forthwith to Detroit and take up his contract. But there were other reasons too that led him to reconsider the move. His father had died three years earlier, leaving Sarah a young widow, unemployed, unskilled, and with a large family to support. In these parlous circumstances, she had now come close to losing her eldest son, the family's main breadwinner. To be sure, George could have wired money home from Detroit, but his narrow escape in the influenza pandemic may have left Sarah reluctant to part with her son so soon. Weighing all these factors, George backed out of his contract with Gabrilowitsch. Instead, he remained with his family in New York and opted for a first-violin seat in the National Symphony Orchestra.

Conducted by Willem Mengelberg, the famed former maestro of the Concertgebouw Orchestra of Amsterdam, the National Symphony Orchestra would merge with the New York Philharmonic in 1921, in the process giving up its name but retaining its conductor. Seven years later the New York Philharmonic merged again, this time with the New York Symphony Orchestra, founded by Walter Damrosch in 1878, and the Philharmonic, as it is known today, came into being with Arturo Toscanini at the helm. Throughout this period of orchestral flux and change, reflecting the frenetic quality to musical life in a city awash in émigré musical talent, George Rabinowitz remained a constant presence.

In 1921 the Philharmonic began a series of concerts at the Roxy Theatre. Movies would alternate with an orchestral program, which would be repeated four times each day. For this spring series of concerts, Hugo Riesenfeld was at the podium, and to his left sat George, by now securely ensconced at the fourth stand in the first-violin section. He could hardly have imagined that thirty years later he would be sitting at the same stand in the same auditorium in a similar series of concerts, watching and listening as his fifteen-year-old prodigy son blazed his way through the pyrotechnics of Paganini, signaling his arrival as the newest and greatest violin virtuoso of his generation.

One evening George was returning home from the Roxy Theatre. The train pulled into the subway station at 50th Street. George held the door open for a young woman, who thanked him and struck up a conversation, asking him about the violin he was carrying.[15] Jeanne Seidman was twenty-one years of age, the youngest of four children born to Michael Joseph Seidman (Zaidman) and Bertha Knerelman (Carrolman), Russian-Jewish émigrés. Photographs of Jeanne at that age show an attractive, slim woman with a formidable bosom. Unlike the impecunious Rabinowitz family, the Seidmans' circumstances were considerably more comfortable. But they could not boast the same impressive musical lineage.

Michael Joseph had married Bertha in Russia circa 1884, and their children, Sarah, Leo, Mark, and Jeanne, were all born before the family emigrated. Michael Joseph's youngest brother, Nathan, had been the first Zaidman to move to the United States, settling in Philadelphia. He and his Russian wife, Minnie Adelman, set up a home that became a way station for all subsequent family members leaving Russia. Nathan was an enterprising man, and his profession is variously listed as musician (violinist) and cigar dealer, the two activities not necessarily mutually exclusive. Michael Joseph, however, had been the financial driving force behind the extended family. He had bankrolled Nathan's move to America and did the same for his second brother, Aaron David.

Michael Joseph remained behind in Russia, where he worked as an overseer on the estate of a wealthy Russian while also acting as spokesman for the local Jewish community in Kishinev. The pogroms of the early 1900s, however, made life hazardous for Jews, and in 1906, he and Bertha traveled in a first-class cabin to Philadelphia to visit Nathan and Aaron David and have a good look at life in America. They liked what they saw, and the following year, on May 30, 1907, Michael Joseph and his two sons said farewell to Tsarist Russia. A month later, Bertha and the girls, eighteen-year-old Sarah and seven-year-old Jeanne, followed.[16] The 1910 census lists the family living in Philadelphia and gives Michael Joseph's occupation as a jobber of shoes. In the decade that followed, he put his business acumen to good use, and the family prospered, moving to New York where they rented an apartment at 565 West 139th Street. Their successful integration into a new society was, however, marred by tragedy. In 1918 Sarah, by now married to physician Simon Wendkos and mother to four-year-old Elkin, died from the same Spanish flu that came so close to killing George Rabinowitz.

When Jeanne first met George, she was living with her parents in their spacious and richly furnished ground-floor Manhattan apartment. "I asked if she was interested in music," recalled George, "and she said, 'yes, somewhat.' She was modest. Jeanne studied with the top teacher at the Institute of Musical Art."[17] In time, and with a famous son that propelled her into the celebrity spotlight, Jeanne would forego the modesty. Her attendance as a student at the Institute of Musical Art was embellished, and she claimed to have taught piano at the Juilliard. But a close inspection of the Juilliard's archives shows this was not the case. Jeanne had enrolled as a piano student in the 1915–16 academic year and remained until 1922–23. The year before she first met George, she received a diploma in the Regular Piano Course on June 4, 1920, and three years later, the year she married George, she was awarded a diploma in the Piano Artists' Course on June 2, 1923.

Jeanne's arrival introduced a fresh source of anxiety for the Rabinowitz family. There was a clear expectation from Sarah and her children that George's main responsibility outside the orchestra was towards his family, not to some fresh-faced, albeit talented, pianist who lived in a fancy apartment. Jeanne was immediately perceived as a threat, but George was in love, and the contest, which is what it became, pitted rivals of unequal charms. George did not, however, immediately abrogate familial responsibilities, and would moonlight for extra cash whenever opportunities presented themselves. "I had just arrived back in New York [in 1923]," he recalled, "after several weeks playing in a ship's orchestra that had traveled to South America. I bought Jeanne a big bottle of Quelque Fleurs in Rio. I asked, 'Can you lend me $5 for the marriage license?' as I was waiting for the $600 owed me by the ship."[18]

Jeanne accepted the perfume, forked out the money, and the couple married at City Hall in Manhattan before eloping. George, perennially cash-strapped, had a summer job playing violin at a resort in the Catskills, and Jeanne joined him there. Neither of their families knew of the marriage until it had taken place. The Seidmans, who were a close family, were startled by Jeanne's willfulness, but their quick acceptance of George was no doubt fuelled by a combination of factors: his good nature, his fine career prospects as a member of the famous Philharmonic, and most important of all, their obvious inability to alter circumstances.

The Rabinowitzes, on the other hand, were not so accommodating. Indeed, there is every reason to believe that the Romeo-and-Juliet intrigue surrounding the marriage and flight to the mountains of Upstate New York stemmed from the deep antipathy felt towards Jeanne by George's family. "Jeanne kept away from his family, as they did not accept her," recalled Bea

Seidman, her sister-in-law. "They were never friendly with her in all the years. George gave up his family for Jeanne."[19] Ostracized by Sarah, who wielded a powerful influence over her children, many of whom were too young to fully comprehend what had occurred, George and Jeanne returned to the city, where a new concert season was starting. The newlyweds moved into an apartment at 905 West End Avenue.

When George broke with his family, his brother Norman was still a child. He is the one surviving member of that generation, and he recalls that his mother's bitter resentment of George's behavior stemmed from a constellation of factors. First, she saw his commitment to Jeanne as a betrayal of his family, both emotionally and financially. George was the breadwinner, and there were six dependents to look out for, including the twenty-nine-year-old Clara, pursuing her fledgling career as concert soloist. Then there was the elopement and cloak-and-dagger marriage, viewed by Sarah as the ultimate deception. She never forgave him this.[20] It would take nine years and a death in the family before a rapprochement of sorts took place between them.

The year 1923 found George at his orchestral desk and Jeanne Rabinowitz starting to give private piano lessons. Across the river in Queens, Sarah Rabinowitz was compelled to take in Dr. Neulander, a dentist, and his wife as lodgers to help with the rent. The monthly rent supplied by the Neulanders was not, however, sufficient to make ends meet, so Sarah began her own business, working from home, making stylized decorative pompoms that could be attached to shoes and clothing as fashion accessories.[21] And for the first time, Clara's piano playing started to bring in much-needed money, not through concertizing, but by her good fortune in finding a pair of wealthy patrons prepared to sponsor her career. Two East Coast socialites, Mrs. Sinclair and Mrs. Lewis, were suitably impressed, not only to underwrite the costs of her tuition in France with Isidore Philipp, but also to introduce Clara to high society, a prospect that, according to Norman, alarmed their Yiddish-speaking mother because she feared her daughter would consort with Gentiles and end up marrying out of the faith. On that score, she had little to fear. For Clara the piano came first, and when, later in life and with her career in decline, she finally decided to marry, her choice settled on the good-natured, generous, musical, and Jewish Ludwig Weiller.

Of all Jacob and Sarah's nine children, only the eldest son, George, and the youngest daughter, Grace, had children in turn. On December 18, 1924, Jeanne and George's first son was born. They named him Jay after George's late father, Jacob. Very little is known of his brief life. He would have seen much of his maternal grandparents, but he had no contact with his grandmother and aunts on his father's side, where even his arrival as the first

Rabinowitz grandchild born in the New World did nothing to lessen the corrosive enmity of Sarah and her daughters. Jay died before his siblings were born, and no mention of him appears in any of the copious publicity material that would later be generated by his brother Michael's career. The only surviving relative old enough to recall meeting Jay is his uncle Norman, who remembers him as a prodigy on the piano. The legend of Jay the musical child prodigy is one that has taken root in both the Seidman and Rabinowitz families and is repeated whenever his name comes up in conversation. His aunt Bea recalls that her sister in law Jeanne "had two geniuses, Michael, and Jay, who was a pianist."22

Jay's first piano teacher was his mother. There is no record of him receiving tuition at the Institute of Musical Art. A series of photographs taken when he was probably six or seven years old deserve close scrutiny. Jay stands at a grand piano, completely at ease in front of the instrument. In one picture, a hand rests comfortably on the keyboard while with the other he holds a music score that he scrutinizes. In a second photograph, his back is to the piano and he reclines gently against the keys, his head to the side looking confidently at the camera lens, a slight smile playing across his face. There is nothing awkward about either of these two pictures, no self-conscious gaze, nor the oddities of posture associated with young children, who seldom if ever are at one with their musical instrument. Instead, the image conveyed is of a seasoned, self-assured performer undaunted by the size and technical demands posed by the instrument before him.

The fact that Jay's parents had him photographed so carefully in a series of studied poses redolent of the mature virtuoso speaks to their obvious pride in his musical abilities. It also suggests that the pictures were not simply earmarked for the family album but were taken as publicity shots with an eye on the future and any concerts that would surely have come his way, given the purported magnitude of his talent. There is no date to the pictures, but judging from Jay's height relative to the keyboard, they were probably taken a few months, perhaps weeks, before he died.

In February 1932, this cherubic, talented seven-year-old came down with a fever. He complained of a sore throat and developed a reddish rash on his face and torso. Over the next few days, his temperature rose further. Difficulties with his breathing ensued as the bacillus spread through his body. On February 24, Jay was admitted to Willard Parker Hospital in Manhattan. Scarlet fever was diagnosed. That evening his condition deteriorated. There was nothing the doctors could do other than suggest remedies to lessen the fever. George and Jeanne, like thousands of other parents of that prepenicillin era, were helpless bystanders as their child slipped into coma. At 4:55 AM on

February 25, Jay died.23 A day later he was buried in the Seidman family plot in Mount Hebron cemetery in New York.

The death of Jay devastated George and Jeanne. It came three years after the death of Jeanne's father Michael Joseph, the patriarch who had successfully transplanted his family to the New World. A glimpse of the happiness enjoyed by Jeanne when her son and father were still alive can be discerned in a 1928 family photograph. It is winter and Jeanne, Jay, Michael Joseph, and Bertha are outdoors in their coats. Young Jay, four years of age, holds his mother's hand, but it is cold and his other hand is thrust, Napoleonic-fashion, under the lapel of his jacket. As in all the few surviving photographs taken of Jay, his look is direct, alert, and confident, without trace of self-consciousness. Jeanne is smiling and patently content in the presence of her lovely child and loving parents.

With the death of Jay, the fractious Rabinowitz family came together briefly, but the schisms were too deep and intractable for any meaningful reconciliation. Bereavement briefly supplanted recriminations, papering over the years of enforced separation and lingering hurt. From now on George's relationship with his family would be characterized by sporadic contact interspersed with fresh skirmishes at slights, both imagined and real. Only Norman set himself above the fray, remaining on good terms with both sets of combatants. These internecine maneuverings among discontented relatives were, however, temporarily placed on hold. In the aftermath of Jay's sudden and untimely death, grief held sway, and the pain of George's loss was to be respected.

Adding to the sadness of those years, Bertha Seidman died a year after Jay, on July 29, 1933. Thus, in the space of four years, Jeanne had lost both parents and her first child. The spacious Seidman apartment, home to so much earlier happiness, was silent now, a quiet, lonely place, a repository of sad memories and hopes cruelly foreshortened. It was time for change and rejuvenation. In 1933, George and a pregnant Jeanne, who had been living with Bertha since the death of her husband, moved back into their own apartment at 905 West End Avenue, at 104th Street. On February 27, 1934, almost two years to the day since Jay's death, Jeanne gave birth to a daughter. They called her Bertine. Two years later, on May 2, 1936, Bertine's brother Michael was born. The children were named after their recently deceased maternal grandparents. A generation had passed, but in quick succession their link with posterity had been renewed. After the traumas of the past few years, George and Jeanne could look to the future with a renewed sense of optimism and a rekindled joy.

Memories of Jay were allowed to fade rapidly into the background. Bertine cannot recall her parents ever talking about him, grieving on the anniversary of his death, mourning his passing. There was no talk within the family of her older, precociously talented brother, no reminiscences, no memorials.[24] The only reminder of his ephemeral presence was a photograph that stood on the mantelpiece, Jay frozen in time in his period-piece sailor suit, his image silent testimony to a false dawn. To his younger siblings, Jay may have been a vague shadow that hovered unobtrusively over a distant family history, but to his parents he retained a more immediate, enduring intimacy. His short, sweet life, so suddenly and prematurely ended, could never be forgotten. In particular, it sensitized Jeanne to the fragility and impermanence of existence and profoundly influenced how she saw her role as mother and protector of her children.

CHAPTER 2
WILLIE SPIELBERG'S
LITTLE HALF-SIZE VIOLIN

*T*he Rabinowitz household was a happy, lively place after the arrival of Bertine and Michael. The family occupied one of those "magnificent prewar apartment with twenty-foot living rooms and twenty-foot dining rooms," recalls Bertine:

> We had lots of friends in the building. Everyone was our uncle and aunt, everybody was very friendly to us and would visit our apartment. It was a very lovely childhood, always full of music, which of course I did not appreciate until later on. But with my father in the orchestra and my mother teaching piano, there was always music in the house.[1]

The children's world was indeed awash in music, for contact had been resumed with George's relatives. His eldest sister, Clara, was performing widely as a piano soloist; Rose, Jean, and Grace continued their summer performances and occasional radio broadcasts as the Rabinowitz trio; while youngest brother Norman supplemented his salary as an accountant by moonlighting on the violin.

As if to symbolize the fresh start their family was making after the recent spate of personal losses, George and Jeanne decided to change the family surname. Rabinowitz was abbreviated to Rabin.* To confuse matters, Norman —

---

* George's shortened surname appears in the New York Philharmonic's program notes for the first time in 1939.

acting on the advice of his agent, who thought an anglicized cognomen would be easier to sell to impresarios — abandoned Rabinowitz for Robbins.[2] Clara, on the other hand, went in the opposite direction as it were, stressing her European origins (her programs mention she was born in Bucharest), and altered the spelling of Rabinowitz to Rabinowitch. Whether Sarah approved of these changes made by her children is not known, although they are unlikely to have surprised her, given the considerable degree of phonemic flexibility adopted by immigrant families in general as they created modern names to match their newly minted identities.

Photographs of the Rabins from the late 1930s show two contented children, Bertine with her dark, straight hair and quiet smile, Michael with a mass of blond curls and a wild impish grin. The siblings spent a lot of time together when young, although Bertine recalls: "We fought a lot when we were little. Not hostile fighting though. But as soon as Michael got strong enough, the fighting stopped."[3]

The neighborhood on the Upper West Side of Manhattan was predominantly Jewish, artistic, intellectual, and safe. When the time came for Bertine's education to begin, she simply had to walk unchaperoned three blocks east to the corner of 104th Street and Amsterdam Avenue to the local kindergarten. "An archaic structure, with toilets in the basement," is how she remembers it. Two years later, Michael joined her on the walk. School was fun for both, and they remained pupils at PS [Public School] 54 until the fifth and third grades respectively. Bertine retains strong memories of this urban neighborhood idyll.

> On the way to school, we passed the homes of other members of the New York Philharmonic, who were friends of my parents. We called them our aunts and uncles. We would always stop in their houses if we had time on the way back from lunch. They would give us some pennies, and we would go to the candy store and take the candy to school. It was a very normal, happy childhood. I remember playing marbles outside with neighborhood friends.[4]

Michael's musical talent manifested early. Tales of the one-year-old beating perfect time with his dinner spoon are probably apocryphal, put out as quaint snippets of publicity by his management when his career first began to take off. But his perfect pitch was a fact, and as a three-year-old, he would amuse and amaze his family by correctly calling out the notes that corresponded to the sounds of car horns and other city noises. Bertine began piano lessons with her mother at six years of age, and two years later, Michael followed her. It was not an easy instrumental baptism for either. Jeanne was a fierce, demanding teacher who completely intimidated her children, not averse to screaming and pinching to get across her point. Her fiery temperament may account for the fact that she had few private pupils. A concert program from her studio dating from 1943 provides evidence of this. Apart from her two children, Jeanne had only two, or possibly three, other students: Myrel Sachson, Hortense Pincus, and one Gloria Strassner, the latter appearing under the title "Guest Artist," suggesting Ms. Strassner had a different teacher.

By then Michael had been learning for approximately one year, and the program is the only known extant document that gives a clue as to his ability on the piano. It also reveals a slightly pretentious quality to the afternoon's proceedings. Two versions of the program exist, and in the second, the order of some of the pieces has been changed, with the following apology: "Due to an unfortunate error by the printer — the third group will precede the second." However, there was no printer. The programs had been handwritten by Jeanne with spelling mistakes roughly corrected. The concert is divided into two parts. In part 1, Michael is the first performer, playing two minuets (in G minor and G major) by Bach, followed by Sonata Opus 36, No. 1, by Clementi. Bertine follows Myrel Sachson with two inventions (in A minor and A major) by Bach and Mozart's Sonata in C Major. Following a break, Michael is back with three obscure pieces by Burgmüller: "Grace," "La Styrienne" and "The Chatterbox." The other students worked their way through a miscellany of pieces for the most part obscure.

In a 1951 interview with Harold Schonberg of the *New York Times,* George mentioned that Michael began piano lessons "at around seven years of age," and "very good, too" was his assessment of his son's playing.[5] George may have been off by a year when it came to dates, but his appraisal of Michael's abilities was clearly accurate. For as Jeanne's program makes clear, within a year Michael had progressed to playing Bach and Clementi in public, even if the audience comprised a small group of parents gathered in the Rabins' apartment on West End Avenue. There is, however, nothing to suggest that either of the Rabin children had Jay's extraordinary pianistic abilities. But they were undoubtedly talented young performers, the products of a richly endowed musical gene pool and a home environment that encouraged, indeed expected, the expression of this talent.

The Rabin home was not just a hub of musical activity. It was also a reflection of Jeanne's formidable energy and her gregarious nature. "She could do everything," recollects Bertine:

> She was a wonderful pianist. Everything she did she did well. She was a fabulous cook. She was a wonderful entertainer. People loved her. She had a great personality. She could enchant anybody

she wanted to enchant. She did incredibly wonderful things to help people, musicians. She would feed people, house people, make contacts for them. She must have lived thirty-six hours a day. Tremendous.[6]

Bea Seidman remembered that "Jeanne was a very overpowering person. She was a brilliant person, a wonderful conversationalist, and she had a million friends. I have never, never ever in my life met a woman like her, except perhaps her mother, Bertha."[7]

Sybil Sklar, Jeanne's niece, confirms this impression of an indomitable woman, a force of nature with endless energy who could spend the day teaching music and attending to multiple tasks, only to return home and at short notice whip up a fabulous dinner party for twenty people without betraying the least signs of exhaustion or irritability. She thrived on a frenetic lifestyle that embraced musical activity at its core.[8] Sybil's daughter Pamela remembers her great-aunt in similar vein.

Jeanne could be very loving. And enthusiastic. She loved Felix, our cat, but her voice was big and deep, and whenever she came over to our place and called out to Felix, "Here pussycat, oh pussycat," he would do a complete 180-degree turn and run and hide in the fireplace. Later he would come out with ashes all over. But the loudness really was tempered with kindness. Still, I think it must have been tough being her child unless you had the exact goals she had.[9]

A typical evening at the Rabin apartment would involve a sumptuous supper cooked by Jeanne, usually with a number of musicians present, some of whom would have been colleagues of George's. The meal would often be followed by impromptu chamber music. Bertine and Michael were privy to this social whirlwind, and many were the nights that they fell asleep to the sounds of a Mozart quartet or a Beethoven sonata.

George was the very antithesis of Jeanne. Quietly spoken and unobtrusive, he was a mild-mannered, passive man who adored his wife and appeared content to let her set the pace of their lives. "Jeanne and George were very different from most other couples that I had ever seen," recollects Pamela Sklar. "Mrs. Loud and Mr. Soft. She would yell '*George!*' And he would go, 'Yes dear.' But he didn't sound as though he was cowed unless he had learned to react like this."[10]

Bertine remembers him as the most wonderful, gentle father, the buffer between her and Michael on the one hand and the impassioned demands of Jeanne on the other, demands that at times were excessive and overwhelming. For there was another side to Jeanne that counterbalanced the vivacious, generous hostess. The force of her character demanded obedience and gratitude. She was unable to brook dissent, and displayed a ruthlessness when it came to enforcing her will. She was certainly hard on herself, given the pace at which she led her life, but those same demands were foisted on her children — the relentless pursuit of excellence, the drive for perfection, the expectation of long, exhausting hours dedicated to practicing music. That she was devoted to her children and loved them was not in question, although the manner in which she controlled Bertine and Michael at times must have left them ambivalent and confused in their attitudes toward her. When the children were young, this was less of a problem, and the fact that Bertine can look back over the early years of her childhood with such fondness speaks to the happy home environment that prevailed. But as the children grew older and as Michael's musical talent began to flower, it was inevitable that Jeanne's rigidity and unshakeable sense of what was right for her children — and in particular, her son — would lead to conflict.

The years of strife and filial defiance were still a long way off. First, George and Jeanne would discover that they had, for the second time, produced a child of the most remarkable musical gifts. As with all wunderkinder, his talent would choose to announce itself, without prompting or coercion, in the most natural yet sublime fashion. Michael's parents knew he was musical. There was his perfect pitch and the episode at three years of age when he surprised Jeanne by turning pages for her, without mistake, as she accompanied George in the Cesar Franck Sonata. But perfect pitch, although impressive in one so young, did not necessarily herald virtuosity, and while Michael at seven years of age played the piano well, there had been nothing in his year of lessons with Jeanne to make her believe providence had delivered another miracle.

And then, one summer's day, the Rabins climbed into their Plymouth and drove up to the Peekskills to visit some good friends, the Spielbergs. Little could they have known that this trip into the country, one they had made countless times before, would profoundly change all their lives, taking them on that rare and wonderful, albeit hazardous, journey reserved only for a select handful in any one generation. "The Spielbergs were very good friends of my parents and they had a beautiful home," recalls Bertine:

> Willie Spielberg was a doctor. His wife was called Bubbles and I think she had some kind of yappy dog. Their home was surrounded by a lot of land, and what impressed me the most, and

> Michael too, was that they bred white turkeys. On this visit, Michael was rummaging in a cupboard, exploring the way kids do, and he found this half-size violin, a child's violin. When the time came to leave, he did not want to let it go. He loved it, evidently. And Willie let him keep it. When we got back to New York, my Dad patched the instrument up, put on new strings and a bridge, and started giving Michael a few lessons. That's how the whole business began.[11]

Michael was seven years old when he laid claim to Willie Spielberg's half-size violin. His piano lessons with Jeanne did not immediately cease, but his preference for the violin was immediately apparent. He was fortunate in having a violinist father to guide his first steps, and George was the most gentle and nurturing teacher, but Jeanne was not going to allow one year's progress on the piano to be peremptorily discarded because of her son's sudden infatuation with another instrument. So by Labor Day of 1943, the traditional end of summer and the start of the new academic year, Michael was pursuing both piano and violin under the joint tutelage of his parents.

Initially, there was little change to the usual rhythms of his childhood: the short walk each day with Bertine to the school on Amsterdam Avenue, his mornings devoted to the third-grade curriculum, the walk home for lunch, time set aside for practicing the piano often under the gimlet eye of his mother, and then playtime with other neighborhood children. The one new addition, when George was not busy with rehearsals or concerts with the Philharmonic, was the evening violin lesson. But by early 1944, the routines established over the preceding months were starting to unravel. A newfound excitement, an anticipatory buzz, now permeated the Rabin apartment, and it all emanated from those startling sounds Michael was producing on Willie Spielberg's patched-up little fiddle. To George's amazement, he soon realized Michael's ability had outstripped whatever pedagogic wisdom he had to offer. In the space of little more than a few months, pupil had transcended master, a child had eclipsed his father.

A new teacher was needed. George, by virtue of his position in the New York Philharmonic, would have been familiar with a plethora of options presented by the culturally rich environment of mid-century Manhattan. Faced with a wide choice, he did not equivocate and, with Michael in tow, paid a call on Ivan Galamian, who had that year settled with his wife, Judith, into an apartment on West 73rd Street.

By 1944, the forty-one-year-old Galamian had been in the United States for seven years, having moved from Paris and the gathering threat of a second major European conflagration. George's choice was at first glance a wise one, for Galamian came with a proven pedigree, not just as a great teacher, but as one who had had considerable experience developing the potentially fragile talents of child prodigies. When Galamian first heard Michael play, he was sufficiently impressed to immediately pass him over to the Manchurian émigré, Yura Osmolovsky, a senior student who also doubled as his assistant. During these early years, Osmolovsky had a room in Galamian's apartment and would have given Galamian daily feedback on the progress of his students.

Fredell Lack, later to become a professor of violin at the University of Houston's School of Music, was dating Osmolovsky at the time and recalls her boyfriend telling her, "I have this fantastic kid. You wait, great things will be heard of him."[12] The process of utilizing a practice coach was customary for Galamian, and the senior student's task was to assist newcomers in their work routine, instilling both the principles and content of what constituted useful practice. In the years to come, as Michael attained a similar elevated status, he too would be asked to mentor some of Galamian's younger, more promising students such as Paul Rosenthal, who remembers with awe how Michael, six years his senior and by then world-renowned, assisted him with the greatest patience, good humor, and disarming absence of hubris.[13]

Michael's meeting with Galamian was to prove one of the pivotal events in his life. The two would develop an intense, loving, at times complicated relationship that persisted until Michael's death. Aside from Jeanne, no one individual exerted such a profound and enduring influence on Michael. Galamian had taught a number of precocious talents before Michael's arrival, and he would, during the subsequent four decades, guide many other remarkable careers. But among the stellar roster of violin virtuosos that emerged with the Galamian imprint, Itzhak Perlman, Pinchas Zukerman, and Kyung-Wha Chung among others, none would ever be held in such loving esteem by their formidable teacher.

Ivan Galamian was born in 1903 in Tabriz, Iran, to Armenian parents. When he was two years old, his family settled in Moscow, in an affluent neighborhood. Despite the turmoil of a Russia in revolution, the advent of World War I, and the influenza pandemic that had so nearly killed one George Rabinowitz awaiting his embarkation orders a world away, Galamian's violin studies with Professor Konstantin Mostras at the Moscow Philharmonia School proceded with surprisingly little interruption, and on graduating in 1919, he obtained a coveted position in the Bolshoi Theatre Orchestra. However, as the Bolsheviks solidified their grip on Russia and imposed their doctrine, the Galamians were stripped of their wealth, and Ivan was, for a brief period, thrown into prison, presumably for the bourgeois sin of once having had wealthy parents. His release from jail owed everything to his position in a prestigious orchestra, but the shock of how his family had been treated and the uncertain future that awaited Russians of his generation were the impetus for his flight to Germany, en route to Paris. On arriving in Paris, Galamian spent two years studying with Lucien Capet before making his well-received European concert debut on December 24, 1924.[14]

There was another reason that the year 1924 was important for Galamian. The Conservatoire Russe de Paris came into being, with Serge Rachmaninoff as Honorary President. The Conservatoire boasted an impressive faculty and was considered a magnet for the sizeable and accomplished armada of exiled Russian musical talent dispersed by the revolution. Galamian, who was already doing some teaching as an assistant to Capet, was offered a position as professor of violin and promptly accepted. For the next two years, Jean Galamian, as he was now known, pursued a dual career, as teacher and as soloist. Concerts were played in France, Germany, and Holland to excellent reviews. But by 1926 it was clear that teaching was his true métier, one that could not flourish alongside the peripatetic existence of soloist.

Two notable violin prodigies passed through Galamian's hands while he taught in Paris. The first was Paul Makanowitzky, the son of an expatriate Ukrainian violinist. The second was Roland Gundry, of Franco-American descent, who arrived at Galamian's studio approximately a decade after the four-year-old Paul first appeared. In 1937 Galamian accompanied Gundry to the United States, where the fifteen-year-old made his Town Hall debut in New York City. By then, Galamian was attracting an increasing number of American students. The year of Gundry's Town Hall debut marked the point at which Galamian left Paris for the last time and put down roots in the New World, vowing "to become the greatest violin teacher in America."[15] Seven years later, Michael Rabin entered his life.

On settling permanently in the United States, Galamian opened his studio on West 54th Street in Manhattan and also began teaching at the Henry Street Settlement Music School. In 1941 Galamian married Judith Johnson, who was instrumental in helping him start a summer music camp at Elizabethtown, in Upstate New York.[16] The choice of venue had much to do with Galamian's close friendship with the great Russian cellist, Gregor Piatigorsky, who lived nearby. The music camp was named Meadowmount, and it was modeled after a famous school for violin students founded by Piotr Stolyarski in Odessa in 1911.

Meadowmount became Galamian's summer retreat, a place where his New York students could escape to from the sticky, oppressive metropolis and continue their tuition amid bucolic surroundings. It was to Meadowmount that Galamian invited Michael in the summer of 1944. There the boy continued his meticulous practice regime first outlined a few months back in New York. It began with a carefully crafted scale system in broken thirds, fourths, fifths, and sixths; scales in one position; scales on one string; scales in three and four octaves; scales of varied lengths and different groupings of notes; arpeggios in one position; arpeggios over three and four octaves — the whole intricate web of notes divided in endless rhythmic variations and complex bowings, a unique approach to learning the violin that left no aspect of the instrument untouched. It was an exhaustingly comprehensive and highly personalized method of laying down technique that rivaled the efforts of older celebrated pedagogues such as Leopold Auer and Carl Flesch. It is certain that Michael took to his tuition with gusto and weathered the long hours of practice demanded of him.

The Rabin family had rented a house known as "The Lilacs," a third of a mile from the main buildings at Meadowmount. Michael stayed with them and not in the school dormitory where other students resided over the summer. He would spend much of the day at home practicing. When he needed to meet his tutor, Jeanne would drive him into Meadowmount. A brief period of relaxation followed in the afternoon before the practicing started up again. This unyielding regime, Michael's capacity for hard work that belied his young age, and a prodigious natural ability on the instrument coalesced to produce astounding progress. Such was the rapidity of his development that by September 1944, Galamian had stepped in and personally taken charge of the boy wonder.

Michael's advances were not lost on his parents either, and as summer drew to a close and the family made their way back home, Jeanne and George decided that conventional schooling was likely to prove a hindrance to their son's further musical development. It was a decision with far-reaching consequences. At Meadowmount, the first steps were put into place separating Michael from his peers. He was, of course, still very young, and a high degree of parental involvement was understandable at that stage. But this segregation of domicile at Meadowmount would persist into his teenage years and owed much to Jeanne's reluctance to relinquish control. Now a second layer of separation was added, a conscious distancing of their talented son from the rank and file of the public schools. The short walk with Bertine to Amsterdam Avenue, that pleasant, carefree stroll among doting aunts and uncles, the trip to the candy store, and the games of marbles on the neighborhood sidewalks had come to an end. With it, a chapter in Michael's childhood closed.

He did not resist the changes that were introduced, for he was a compliant and respectful child, gentle, unassuming and loving. Great events would soon engulf him and, by extension, his family, opening up unimaginable opportunities to travel, to rub shoulders with the famous, and to earn large amounts of money. But there was a downside to all these changes, present and pending. The closing of this particular chapter in Michael's life was unwittingly premature, the curtailment of a carefree childhood overhasty, and in the process, an important developmental trajectory was truncated.

In the fall of 1944, Michael was removed from conventional schooling and sent to the Professional Children's School at 132 West 60th Street. "We both went," recalls Bertine:

> I think they sent me to keep him company, so that we could travel together, because the school was a distance from our house. We used to take the trolley car down. We knew the driver — we always had the same driver. The school had abbreviated hours. They had children who were professionals, in show business, and they may have offered correspondence courses, if a child was in a company that was on the road, so he or she could continue with schoolwork.[17]

Records from the Professional Children's School for the 1944–45 academic year reveal that Michael's performance in the fourth grade was slightly better than the class average. His spelling was rated an A+ (97 to 100), while for reading, geography, and French he received an A- (90 to 94). Writing, English, and deportment were graded B+ (85 to 90). Only in science did his B+ rating fall below the class average of A-. The report also reveals that Michael was in good health and punctual, missing just four days of school and coming late once. Promotion to grade 5 followed, and for the 1945–46 year, the same set of subjects was taken, with Michael continuing to excel in spelling and history while remaining below average in science.[18] Promotion to the sixth grade was recommended, but Michael, who was ten years old by now, did not return. For the 1946–47 academic year, which coincided with Galamian joining the Juilliard faculty, Bertine took the downtown streetcar alone. So rapid had been Michael's progress on the violin that his parents considered further school attendance, even at so specialized an institution as the Professional Children's School, an obstacle to be bypassed. From now on Michael would be home tutored, the greater part of his day devoted to mastering his instrument.

Events for Michael had moved with a dizzying rapidity over the past couple of years. By the time he turned ten years old, a pattern of exhausting hard work coupled with minimal, tightly regulated peer contact had been established. This would remain in force for much of the next decade.

"Practice, practice, practice" had been the Stolyarski credo. Galamian passionately subscribed to it. Jeanne enforced it. There is a story from this period in Michael's life, often repeated, that gives some limited insight into the way he practiced. The legend goes that as a child Michael asked for a bowl and six marbles. Once he had successfully mastered a particular technical or musical challenge, he would place one of the marbles in the bowl. Only after all six marbles were in the bowl, denoting six consecutive and perfect renditions, would he move on to the next section.[19]

If indeed true, this speaks to a remarkable discipline in one so young. There is, however, reason to believe that this anecdote, rather than exaggerating the compulsive ritual of perfect repetition, may underreport what was required of him. Bertine retains vivid memories of this period. "Michael had his own bedroom, so he practiced there," she recalls:

> I practiced in the living room, and I would sneak in a book and practice by heart while reading. My mother would go out shopping, and she would say, "Don't stop practicing till I come back," and stuff like that. My father would be the good guy. He would come in and say, "Okay, you can stop." But by then, my parents had largely started concentrating on Michael, so I was more or less let off the hook. I was still practicing and going to lessons, but the concentration was on Michael. He was by now being tutored at home, not seeing friends and not being allowed out to play.

Bertine considers herself fortunate to have escaped the demands placed on her younger brother.

> Unlike Michael, I had friends, and they would come to our apartment and hear Michael practicing. Sometimes my mother would be yelling at Michael, and I remember being embarrassed because my friends were there and my mother was screaming at Michael, or something like that. But I also remember all my friends being just amazed by Michael practicing like that.

The screaming and verbal harangues were not the only pressures Michael had to endure from his mother. "These days it would probably be called child abuse," reflected Bertine:

> He probably got hit if he played a note out of tune sometimes. Or she would demand that he play a passage 100 times. Extraordinary things like that. There was nothing I could do about it. Maybe I

feel guilty because I was happy that it wasn't me going through that.[20]

Troubling as these recollections are, there were also many happy times for both children. And Jeanne had another side to her that was warm and loving. "Outside of music she was very tender" is how Bertine remembers her mother. During these early years, there were no indications that Michael was unhappy. Just the contrary. "He enjoyed playing the violin," recalls Bertine:

> In the beginning, I do not remember him complaining about the hard work. There was an acceptance that this was the way it had to be. And then everybody outside the home told him how wonderful he was. He knew that he was doing something very special. He knew even then that he was a very special person. There were rewards for him.[21]

And the fun times that Bertine and Michael shared as children a few years earlier did not suddenly evaporate as his talent revealed itself. Certainly these moments were curtailed, but when Bertine and Michael were left to their own devices, the natural boisterousness of childhood reasserted itself. The brief interludes of fun are fondly recalled by Bertine:

> We would spend evenings alone when we were little kids. I guess my father went to the Philharmonic, and my mother would go with him, and we'd be alone and we were little. Of course, we used to do really bad things. The best thing was we would fill paper bags with water and drop them out of the window with some people walking by. We were on the fifth floor. We would drop them and duck in. Other times, we would go through all the drawers to see what was good. We were really friends.[22]

For Michael, these periods of play were too brief. He was at a crucial stage in his personality development. The period from the sixth year until puberty has been termed one of "industry versus inferiority," a time when children must learn the skills valued by society.[23] These include not only reading, writing, and arithmetic, but also physical skills and the ability to get along with other people. These basic social skills are developed through exposure to peers in school and the neighborhood. The critical watershed period in personal development, if successfully mastered, gives children a sense of social competence. If not, feelings of inferiority can arise, manifesting as awkward and socially diffident behaviors. The industry-versus-inferiority period is the prelude to adolescence, another of life's developmental stages. Should a child have difficulty traversing these years, he or she arrives at adolescence ill-prepared for the next set of challenges. This cycle of maturation, present from birth and destined to continue through to old age, may be derailed at any point, for successfully moving on from one stage to the next is dependent on developing the age-appropriate intellectual and social skills. The analogy with respect to technical accomplishment on the violin is self-evident. However, success in one area at the expense of another, that disconnect between the cognitive and social, can leave a child developmentally astray.

Understanding these basic principles is essential if we are to appreciate the life and career of Michael Rabin. By 1946, the boy had made some astonishing gains. His musical development and technical accomplishments with respect to the mechanics of violin playing were spectacular, and if these were not matched by other basic educational skills, the report cards from the Professional Children's School nevertheless provides clear proof that Michael was an intelligent child functioning above grade level. His extraordinary progress on the violin was built on a disciplined process of mastering a particular challenge, placing the marble in the bowl and repeating the exercise six times before moving on. On a technical level, this approach had proved imminently successful. However, the long hours devoted to practice, the withdrawal from regular school followed by the cessation of all school attendance, left the boy without friends. Social development was lagging behind its intellectual twin. Cut off from peers, there was simply no place for Michael to learn how to play with children his own age, and it had begun to show. On those brief occasions when he was allowed down on the street to mingle with the neighborhood kids, he appeared diffident and awkward in his interactions and hopeless when it came to throwing and catching a ball.24 Apart from his contact with Bertine and the occasional opportunity for high jinks and sporadic pranks, there had been no time to develop friendships. Most of his energy and a great portion of his waking hours were devoted to his violin.

The summer months did not bring a letup in this schedule. "When the kids would go out and play baseball, my parents wouldn't let him go because he might hurt his hands," recalls Bertine. "Mr. Galamian said the same thing."25 If interaction with children in general was very limited, mixing with those his own age was virtually nonexistent. Michael's precocious talent had catapulted him into a group of older students who were chronologically, but not technically, his superiors. There were chamber-music sessions at Meadowmount that Michael occasionally took part in and that fostered contact with other children, but these meetings were always circumscribed and never involved play outside of music. Jeanne, ever-present, hypervigilant, supervised everything.

In the same vein, parental pride ensured that Michael's talent was paraded before a constant stream of famous musicians. George knew many eminent conductors and soloists, some of whom were counted as family friends. While undoubtedly helpful in securing Michael's reputation and opening doors when it came to future concerts, a downside to this activity was that it locked Michael ever further into an adult world, where carefree play and the rough and tumble of boyhood had no place. "He played for all the musicians at the time," Bertine recollects:

> When he was very young, they all marveled at his talent. I remember in the summer we would visit the conductor of the Philharmonic, Artur Rodzinski, and his wife and little boy. It was 1945 and Rodzinski had a home in Lake Placid close to Meadowmount. Michael would always play for him. I would also play the piano for him. He was always playing for the very finest musicians.26

It was in the summer of 1945 or 1946 that George and Jeanne had Michael photographed professionally at Carl's Studio in Elizabethtown. The resemblances between these photographs and those of Jay taken more than a decade earlier are striking, despite the dictates of fashion that replaced Jay's period-piece sailor's outfit with Michael's more informal open-neck attire. There is the familial facial likeness, but what is most uncanny about the photographs is how confident and natural the two boys appear with their respective instruments. In Michael's case, there are a series of images showing him holding the violin, the instrument either at rest under his arm or else tucked under his chin and ready to play. His posture is immaculate, the violin a comfortable fit, his left hand beautifully poised, both in first position and the more demanding high E-string position. We do not see the bow grip, but that hardly detracts from the nonchalant ease he displays holding both instrument and bow.

As with Jay, the photographs were taken not just to capture a moment in time but also with a very definite eye on the years ahead. And to Jeanne and George, Michael's future must have beckoned brightly as their son closed out the first decade of his eventful life. They had secured the most famous teacher in America for him, a renowned conductor among others had been witness to his precocious ability, and news was afoot in influential musical circles that a new wunderkind had appeared, one whose gifts were expected to rival the best of his and earlier generations. Moreover, his temperament was gentle, undemanding, kind. Everyone who met Michael commented on this. He was a sweet boy who played the violin like an angel.

CHAPTER 3
WUNDERKINDER NEVER CEASE

The start of the 1946–47 academic year marked the point at which Galamian joined the musical faculty at Juilliard. A year later his star pupil, eleven-year-old Michael Rabin, followed him with a scholarship to cover the expenses of his tuition that included not only violin lessons but also musical theory classes and enrollment in the Juilliard Preparatory Division's orchestra. He was practicing his violin six to eight hours a day, although fellow Galamian student Chaim Taub, who would later become concertmaster of the Israel Philharmonic Orchestra, claimed this figure was a considerable underestimate.[1]

The indispensable regime of scales and arpeggios devised by Galamian had by now been thoroughly mastered, establishing the bedrock of what would soon be regarded with awe by violinists both professional and amateur as the famous Rabin technique. Prescribed ritual, however, demanded that these exercises be constantly revisited, and as such, the marathon practice sessions invariably began with scales and arpeggios in a particular key signature. The key of A major was a favorite of Galamian, and it was not unknown for a student to devote his or her eight weeks at Meadowmount to it, going over the notes with different bowings while working on sound and production coordination. Scales would be followed by a selection of etudes, and the bowing exercises introduced into the scales would be carried over into the etudes as well. There was a set method to the studies chosen by Galamian, with the pieces escalating in technical difficulties as the student progressed. Beginning with the Dont Etudes Op. 37, students would move on successively through Kreutzer, Fiorillo, Rode, and Gavinies to the Dont Op. 35, as a prelude to the Wieniawski caprices and, ultimately, the caprices of Paganini.[2]

Central to the Galamian approach were the Op. 35 and Op. 37 etudes of Jacob Dont. In part, Galamian's attachment to these series of technical exercises may be traced to his own lineage as a teacher. Galamian had studied with Mostras in Moscow, who had been a pupil of Leopold Auer, who in turn had been a student of Dont. Given the rapidity of Michael's progress, he was soon introduced to the etudes, and his extraordinary ability to play these technically challenging pieces gave rise to a Meadowmount legend. Whether the exact details of the following anecdote are true or not hardly matters, for it is the gist of the story that illustrates the level of accomplishment attained by Michael at this early age. The story goes that Galamian set his Meadowmount students the task of perfecting Dont's Etude No. 7, from the Op. 35 set. By way of incentive, a token dollar was offered as a reward to the student who could play every note of the daunting study in tune. Despite an impressive array of talent at his summer camp, Galamian had to part with one dollar only. It went to Michael.[3]

The year 1947 also marks Michael's first public concert. The concert was initially scheduled for the evening of April 9 in Providence, Rhode Island, and was part of a spring music festival presented by the Sisterhood and Brotherhood of Temple Beth-El. The guest artist was advertised as Master Michael Rabin, "A Boy and his Violin," and the invitation ran: "In accordance with our aims to foster cultural activities in the Jewish Community, the Sisterhood and Brotherhood of Temple Beth-El cordially invite you to attend a music festival to be held on Wednesday evening, April 9th, in the Main Temple." Special mention was made of Michael's youth: "Because of the age of our artist this will interest young people with musical aspirations and we are extending this invitation to your children as well."[4]

Michael, however, took ill the week of the concert, and the event was postponed until April 23. Jeanne accompanied her son in a program that included Handel's Sonata in A Major, No. 1, and the Concerto in D Minor, Op. 22, by Wieniawski. After intermission, Michael returned with Paganini Caprices 19, 13 and 5, "Caprice Basque," Op. 24, by Sarasate, "Melody" by Gluck (arranged by Kreisler) and the *Polonaise Brillante,* Op. 4, by Wieniawski. Rembert Wurlitzer in New York loaned Michael an Amati violin for the concert. The day before he stepped out onto the stage for the first time, Michael received good wishes and advice from his father, somewhat formally expressed via telegram from Knoxville, Tennessee, where the New York Philharmonic was on tour. "Hope you have a most successful concert. Make sure you have everything. Love, George Rabin."[5]

The repertoire chosen was astonishing. Laden with pyrotechnic show-stoppers, it illustrated not only the degree but also the pace of Michael's progress to date. He had been playing the violin for a little over three years and yet had arrived at a point where he could, with confidence, tackle a program that would challenge any seasoned virtuoso. The content of the concert was undoubtedly decided by Galamian, who in settling on Sarasate, Wieniawski, and Paganini, was announcing, in unequivocal fashion, the official arrival of his latest wunderkind.

Michael's debut received a glowing review in the local paper:

> This was a program which had to be heard and seen to be believed. Very rarely is it possible to acclaim a genius without reservation and predictions are not in our line. This time it seems safe to state that this was a genius in action and it seems safe to predict that Master Rabin is due for great prominence in the near future. This lad approached the program with boldness, sheer technique and a mature tone. He had fire and brilliance and warmth. He had speed and clarity and almost perfect control over the difficult harmonics. And he has been studying violin only three years. Since an event of this kind inevitably suggests parallels, Michael Rabin seems to compare with Menuhin at the same age (or even with Menuhin today), and in matter of tone there seems resemblance to the style of Elman. Some of this may have been due to the violin which was a genuine Amati he loaned for this recital.[6]

In choosing Providence, Rhode Island, for Michael's debut, Galamian and Michael's parents had settled on a town and a venue quietly removed from the glare of New York publicity. The choice of Providence probably had nothing to do with semantics but was nevertheless rich in symbolic meaning, for the word carries many definitions, all of which were applicable to that memorable spring evening: "foresight, anticipation of and preparation for the future, prudent management, the foreknowing and protective care and government of a spiritual power, a particular act of divine intervention, an act of God."[7]

In the immediate aftermath of Michael's success, Galamian, George, and Jeanne did indeed move with prudence. On May 10, Michael and other select Galamian pupils gave a concert at Town Hall in New York City. He performed Paganini Caprices 22, 16, 9, and 5. Later that same year, Michael traveled to Allentown, Pennsylvania, where on October 17, he played the Sonata in E Minor by Veracini, the Partita No. 1 in B Minor for unaccompanied violin by

Bach, Lalo's *Symphonie espagnole* in an arrangement for violin and piano, the Introduction and Rondo Capriccioso by Saint-Saëns, and Caprices 11, 17, and 24 by Paganini.

Within a fortnight, son and mother were in Montreal, where they repeated the Allentown program with the addition of Paganini's Fifth Caprice. The reviews were ecstatic:

> Young he is, 11 years old in fact. It seems that wunderkinder never cease where the violin is concerned. And this youngster is a true one. Rabin's was an astonishing performance. To hear one who is little more than a child attempt such things as movements from one of Bach's unaccompanied sonatas, Lalo's Symphonie espagnole and a quartet of Paganini Caprices is alone cause for wide-eyed wonder. To hear him execute them musically, sensitively, accurately, and with masculine strength is something else again....
>
> He plays cleanly, accurately, with authority and what is best of all, with a beautiful sense of musical values.... He knows, this little boy, how to phrase long melodies so that they rise and fall as the composer intended they should. His sense of form is perfect, his instinctive feeling for larger patterns, astounding. From the Sarabande and Bourrée of Bach's Partita in B Minor he was able to draw an astonishing amount of the grandeur and profundity inherent in them....
>
> But it was with the Paganini Caprices that he awakened most of the audience to a sense of what he is worth. Rabin never faltered throughout these grueling tests. He is a sturdy, modest boy with a cherubic, sensitive face. He executed each caprice with a minimum of fuss and a maximum of energy, with absolute accuracy and a truly magnificent sense of phrasing. He received a thunderous ovation from the audience.[8]

Prior to his Montreal performance, Michael again received the good wishes of his father and sister via telegram. These early, brief concert forays to nearby cities hinted at how Michael and his sister Bertine would come to spend in large measure the remaining years of their childhood—Michael on tour with Jeanne, George at home with Bertine, following events from a distance while staying in touch via telegram, postcard, and letter. "It was sort of like the family project," recalls Bertine. "My mother would leave my father and travel around with Michael for four or five months at a time. And I lived with my father."[9] It was not, however, until 1950 that this pattern of parental and sibling separation took hold in a major way. For the remainder of the 1940s, George and Jeanne in consort with Galamian moved cautiously as they introduced Michael to the public — he closed out the calendar year with a return visit to Providence and a performance of the first movement of Lalo's *Symphonie espagnole* at the Juilliard Christmas concert.

By now Jeanne had taken to shaping Michael's life and molding the public's perception of her wonderchild. She was not only mother and accompanist to her son but also his first publicity manager, a self-assumed role dedicated to creating a persona for Michael from a heady mix of fact, hyperbole, and invention. "As soon as Michael was able to speak," Jeanne reported in a 1947 interview with the *Providence Sunday Journal:*

> he displayed an amazing memory. He was given a game which consisted of fifty-six animals, each of which was numbered, and he could name the animals and numbers in any order. As he grew older and learned to read, he showed a marked preference for biographies and knows from memory the dates of all famous musicians and composers, in addition to all the Presidents of the United States. His musical studies began when he was six years old. I gave him piano lessons…. He made remarkable progress [and] had great natural facility, which surmounted all technical difficulties. He gave every evidence of developing into a fine concert pianist.

"Many hours of intensive practice daily make it necessary for Michael to have a private tutor for his educational studies," Jeanne further divulged. And as the interviewer noted:

> Here, as in his music, [Michael's] remarkable memory has been a great aid. At 11 he is completing grade school work. In spite of all these exacting and important obligations, he is a normal, active boy. He is full of energy, friendly and has a sense of humor. Swimming, skating and bicycling interest him. He likes to play chess, has a stamp collection and loves to use a typewriter. He has great interest in mechanical things….
>
> Besides 12 standard concertos, he has memorized the 24 Paganini caprices, four Bach Sonatas for the violin alone and many other works. His ambition is to own a Strad. "He loves to play in public," reported Jeanne, "the larger the audience the better. In spite of all the praise after each performance, he's never satisfied and always strives for greater perfection."[10]

Jeanne can be forgiven the hyperbole. What feelings did she experience sitting on stage before spellbound audiences as her eleven-year-old son propelled himself through some of the most demanding music ever written for the violin? Joy, love, astonishment, and pride would certainly not have been out of place. After the pain of losing one son, his precocious abilities as a pianist cruelly ended by scarlet fever, what surge of emotion did she feel confronted by a second son whose talent was even greater and offered the limitless possibilities of a future bright with hope? When Jeanne spoke of Michael's facility on the piano that "surmounted all technical difficulties," was she not thinking, albeit subconsciously, of Jay? The despair that must have engulfed her and George in the early 1930s as they reeled from a rapid succession of painful losses had now given way to scarcely imaginable triumph and the glimmers of fame. For Jeanne, who had her aspirations as a pianist, the adulation of audiences in Providence, Montreal, and Allentown must have been gratifying too, even if the joy was largely vicarious, channeled as it was through the genius of her son. And yet, it must also be recognized that by mixing her accurate account of Michael's musical talent and his fealty to a Herculean work ethic with an amplified view of his other abilities, she was setting the bar uncomfortably high.

The Rabins were not wealthy, which meant that Michael was dependent on the largesse of benefactors when it came to choosing a violin for his performances. Rembert Wurlitzer of New York had loaned him an Amati for his first concerts, but even at this young age, it was obvious that Michael's style of playing, with its big, voluptuous sound, was not suited to the more restrained tonal characteristics of Amati instruments. Although Jeanne had told reporters that her son dreamed of owning a Stradivarius violin, by the time Michael had returned to Montreal on January 11, 1948, for a concert in Plateau Hall, Wurlitzer had, at the instigation of Galamian, exchanged the Amati for a 1703 Joseph Guarnerius.

Michael offered his audience a new program that began with the Sonata in D Major by Vivaldi (arranged by Respighi), the Partita No. 2 in D Minor for unaccompanied violin by Bach (including the chaconne), the Concerto No. 5 in A Minor by Vieuxtemps, the "Nigun" from the *Baal Shem Suite* by Bloch, the Introduction and Tarantella by Sarasate, and Paganini Caprices 9, 16, 13, and 5. If anything, the reviews were even more laudatory. "When Michael Rabin played at the YMHA series with his mother last season," said one critic, "he was merely just a very talented child. This year he is a first-rate artist, and if he continues to progress at this rate, he promises to become one of the greatest artists of our time."[11] Among the paeans of praise showered on Michael after his recital was a note from a woman who had seen, heard, and known all the great violin virtuosos of the past half century. Madame Eugene

Ysaÿe, widowed since the passing of her famous husband in 1931, had been in the audience and felt moved to write a personal note of congratulation.

On March 10, Michael gave his first solo New York recital open to the public. The occasion was the Brooklyn Orchestral Association Benefit Concert, where as a prelude to his regular fare of Paganini and Sarasate, he performed the "Variations on a Theme by Corelli," arranged by a man who would soon prove enormously influential to his career, Zino Francescatti. Three weeks after he turned twelve, he made his third visit to the Temple Beth-El hall on Rhode Island for a recital that included the slow movement from Tchaikowsky's D Major Violin Concerto, "Tambourin Chinois" by Kreisler, and the "Serenade of Jewish Folk Songs" by Schalit, among other more familiar Rabin concert pieces. The habitual summer of music making at Meadowmount now included his first recital at the Social Center in Elizabethtown — a benefit concert in front of an audience made up mostly of Galamian students, teaching assistants, and a smattering of the general public.

By summer's end, Michael had played nine recitals in little over a year. All had been accompanied by his mother. The venues had been modest, although care had been taken to have the local music critics in attendance. If the pace of his entree to public performing was gentle, there was also something protective about the choice of pieces played. The weighty musical masterpieces of Beethoven and Brahms were not yet on the agenda, an important distinction to bear in mind when comparisons were made between the respective merits of Michael and the other great American violin wunderkind of the twentieth century, Yehudi Menuhin. For Menuhin had, at the age of eleven, already performed the Beethoven Violin Concerto with the New York Philharmonic at Carnegie Hall.[12]

But if Galamian was wisely keeping his precious charge away from challenges that demanded substantial musical intellect in addition to solid technical accomplishment, he was allowing Michael unbridled freedom to dazzle audiences with the great nineteenth-century composer-violinist repertoire, an oeuvre that was unsurpassed for its sheer virtuosity. And yet it would be inaccurate to conclude that these early concerts were simply examples of precocious technical aptitude, a tour de force without musical depth. For interspersed among all the brilliance of Wieniawski, Vieuxtemps, and Paganini were the Bach unaccompanied masterpieces, music of the highest order that demanded far more than the mere mechanics of playing the violin. There is every indication that here, too, Michael was up to the task — without exception, the concert reviewers had commented on his ability to hold the musical line and interpret with distinction the complexities of Bach's polyphonic invention.

Michael had yet to make his concerto debut with an orchestra. He had already performed a number of violin and piano transcriptions of virtuoso concertos in recital, but for Michael's orchestral debut, Galamian reverted to caution and chose a more modest work, Mozart's Third Concerto in G Major. While no less an authority than Jascha Heifetz considered the Mozart concertos among the most difficult in the violin repertoire, Mozart's G major work did not pose the same musical and technical challenges as his later D and A major works.13

The venue was once again Rhode Island. Not only were the concerto, venue, and orchestra carefully handpicked to ease Michael into an unfamiliar role, but his calendar was kept clear of engagements in the months leading up to three performances scheduled for December 1, 3, and 5. Francis Madeira conducted the Rhode Island Symphony Orchestra. "With best wishes and warmest admiration for a great violinist" were his sentiments inscribed in Michael's program.14 The critics shared his enthusiasm. A reviewer from the *Pawtucket Times* reported:

> Twelve-year-old Michael Rabin of New York City appeared as violinist, leaving no room for doubt that he merits the high acclaim of music critics who have hailed him a prodigy. His flawless technique, maturity of interpretation and purity of tone are ingredients which make his playing a delightful treat. He has a manner as modest as his skill is great, and after a variety of exacting numbers he was given an enthusiastic applause. The violin he plays is a Joseph Guarnerius, made in Italy in 1703. The youth's Mozart Concerto No. 3 in G Major was something to remember.15

The last comment was even more noteworthy given the four encores Michael had rattled off. The dazzle of Paganini Caprices 11, 13, 5, and 4 had not obscured the merits of his concerto interpretation.

Publicity for the concerts took different forms. The *Woonsocket Call,* in all seriousness, showed a picture of Michael playing the violin while having his brow wiped by his mother. "So vigorously does he register his emotions," ran the caption, "his mother comes to his assistance wiping off perspiration."16 Fliers for the event not surprisingly emphasized Michael's youth: "Twelve-year-old wonder violinist widely acclaimed as a successor to the former boy prodigy, Yehudi Menuhin."17

The comparisons with Menuhin were becoming increasingly frequent and inevitable given the boys' many similarities in background and circumstance — immigrant Jewish families, first-generation Americans, native New Yorkers, wunderkinder, musical siblings, and concert careers as children.

There were, however, notable differences too. For if Michael as a child lacked the boy Menuhin's maturity as an interpreter of great music, there is evidence his phenomenal technique was more solidly entrenched. Menuhin's virtuosity as a child was legendary, and yet, after bowling over Ysaÿe with the first movement of Lalo's *Symphonie espagnole,* the prodigy floundered when the Belgian maestro asked him to play a four-octave A major arpeggio.[18] Such a request would hardly have troubled the boy Rabin, thanks to the rigors of the Galamian method. In midlife, as Menuhin's technical facility waned, he would come to rue a proficiency that owed much to intuition. For Michael, who in time would also face his own set of difficulties, maintaining technical excellence was seldom a problem.

There is, however, a revealing anecdote from that period that illustrates that even in Michael's case, where countless boyhood hours had been devoted to surmounting myriad technical difficulties, there was an intuitive element to his mastery as well. He too had some inbuilt, preordained, hardwired ability, or what Dimitri Mitropoulos would refer to as a God-given blessing, that in essence lay at the core of his extraordinary technical facility. The violinist Charles Libove, ten years Michael's senior and a Galamian pupil, recalled that at Meadowmount, some of the students would impishly interrogate Michael about how he did certain things on the violin — asking questions that made Michael stop and think about actions that he had taken for granted. And in trying to work out the how and why of a particular technical challenge, he would become flustered and his playing would falter. Galamian, initially unaware of how a few older students were derailing his star pupil, was bewildered by Michael's sudden failings. When the reasons became clear, Galamian quickly forbade such behavior. Questioning Michael was strictly off-limits.[19]

IN 1949 WHEN Michael turned thirteen, he celebrated his bar mitzvah. The invitation sent to family and friends was in rhyme and made indirect reference to Michael's burgeoning concert career.

> The years have flown
> the child has grown
> On the very threshold of manhood now
> He stands ready to take his bow
>
> So come, dear friends, join us, have fun
> Congratulate us upon the bar mitzvah of our son
> This joyous occasion let us celebrate
> Do come in time and stay real late

> The place 905 West End Avenue, Michael Rabin your host
> The time 4:30 PM when we'll drink his toast
> Supper will follow, your hunger to abate
> Sunday May 29th is a red letter date.[20]

The invitation bore the stamp of Jeanne, and it was her culinary skills and vibrant personality that guests would most remember, not the shy demeanor of her virtuoso son. If Michael's bar mitzvah party was an opportunity for Jeanne to shine as hostess, Michael was back in the spotlight later that year when he entered and won the Edgar Stillman-Kelley Jr. Scholarship of the National Federation of Music Clubs, beating out thirty-one competitors from eleven Northeastern states who were all under seventeen years of age. The terms of the award guaranteed that Michael would receive $250 each year for a total of $750 over three years, providing his rate of progress warranted the annual renewal.[21] Michael received the news while in Westport with Galamian and wrote to express his thanks:

> I want to thank the junior division of the Federation for bestowing upon me such an honor. I want to tell you how much I appreciate the scholarship and realize that I must work harder than ever before to make you all really proud of me. I should like to take the opportunity to make a correction in the spelling of my dear teacher's name. He is Ivan Galamian, not Salamian, as appeared in previous publicity. Also, I have in my repertoire at least 20 concerti and I know all six of the Bach Sonatas. Of course, one never finishes learning them. I am always reviewing them to improve my performance. I'm enclosing a picture of myself for the cover of the magazine and I should love to have a copy of it when it is published. With many thanks.[22]

The Stillman-Kelley Scholarship was the only open competition Michael would ever enter.* While some great violinists had launched careers this way, David Oistrakh's 1937 triumph at the Ysaÿe Competition in Brussels† or Ginette Neveu's 1935 success at the Wieniawski Concours in Warsaw being two notable examples, the scholarship Michael won was not in the same league. This one foray aside, Michael, like other child prodigies such as

---

* Michael had entered an internal Juilliard competition when he was thirteen years old. He played the Prokofiev Second Violin Concerto. The winner of the competition was Joyce Flissler, many years older than Michael.

† Later named the Queen Elizabeth Competition.

Heifetz, Menuhin, and Milstein, would be spared the cutthroat cycle of music competitions where talented young musicians jousted for their futures. His win was nevertheless significant because it provided further critical affirmation of his talent, brought in some welcome financial help, boosted his publicity dossier, and expanded his local reputation well beyond the confines of New York and Rhode Island. But what was also notable about this episode in Michael's life went beyond the significance of his winning and touched on the way that his success had been achieved. For the content of Michael's public thank-you letter to the committee was heavily influenced by his mother. "I realize that I must work harder than ever before…. I am always reviewing them [Bach] to improve my performance."[23] This admission came from a boy already practicing eight hours a day.

Michael gave two further recitals before the year's end, with his mother at the piano. It was in these concerts that he played for the first time in public the Wieniawski Concerto in F-sharp Minor, a work that would soon become one of his signature pieces. Michael, no doubt reflecting the preferences of Galamian, was one of the last violin virtuosos who regularly included concertos with piano arrangements in his recitals. Soon concert programming would undergo considerable revision, ending this practice, but Michael's career was in some aspects a throwback to earlier generations of violinists who, pro forma, incorporated these major works into their programs. Michael's first Wieniawski F-sharp Minor performance was presented by the Schubert Club of Stamford, Connecticut on November 9, 1949, and he repeated it six days later at the Plaza Hotel in New York, where he shared the evening with Martha Lipton, a soprano from the Metropolitan Opera Company.

The year 1949 had passed with distinction and Michael was on the cusp of a great career. Rave reviews, public adulation, rare violins on loan from Wurlitzer, endorsements from a roster of celebrated musicians, a technique that had no limitations, a seemingly rock-solid stage temperament, a flawless memory, the master hand of Galamian at the helm to guide him, and devoted parents carefully chaperoning his introduction to his audience — the omens were indeed fortuitous. Amid the fervor of those months, it was away from the glare of public exposure that an event had taken place quietly, concealed from the media, that would prove most influential to Michael's career. He met Zino Francescatti.

There are two versions of the exact circumstances of the meeting and what subsequently transpired. Elizabeth Green, in her book on Galamian, *Miraculous Teacher,* claims that Francescatti first met Michael at Meadowmount when the twelve-year-old played a Sunday recital that included twelve Paganini caprices. The following Sunday, Michael played the remaining twelve. Francescatti had himself just recorded all twenty-four caprices for Columbia. He was so impressed by Michael's performance that within a week he had arranged for Michael to record some of them too, with Columbia. "He's a twelve year old boy," Green quotes Francescatti telling the company. "You should have him make a record now so that when he is twenty he can realize he played like this when he was twelve."[24] According to Green, Michael recorded eleven caprices for Columbia that year, but their release was held back for two years to allow both artists a clear field. When they finally came out, Michael was fourteen, and the liner notes did not mention the lag time between recording and release, leading to the erroneous impression that Michael's recording debut was at fourteen. The management at Columbia made no effort to put the facts straight, assuming that a couple of years here and there were hardly likely to sway the listening public's opinion in the face of such remarkable playing.

An alternative account of events was provided by Galamian's pupil Fredell Lack, who lived next door to Galamian at 160 West 73rd Street. She recalls being present in Galamian's apartment when the thirteen-year-old Michael played all twenty-four caprices for Francescatti. The French virtuoso was overwhelmed by what he saw and heard. After effusively complementing boy and teacher, he spontaneously reached for the telephone and, in front of everyone present, called Columbia Records to arrange an audition.[25] Fredell Lack's account does not dispute the influence of Francescatti in facilitating the first Paganini recordings, but it challenges Green's account of where the two virtuosi, fledgling and master, first met. Francescatti subsequently befriended Rabin, and a series of letters written by the boy to his esteemed elder colleague tends to support Lack's version of events.* For in 1951, Michael wrote to Francescatti and, at Galamian's request, invited him to visit Meadowmount for the first time.

Francescatti, at the peak of his powers, was clearly struck by Michael and used his influence to help him in many ways. Not only did he facilitate Michael's first commercial recordings, but he also introduced the boy to the firm of Judson, O'Neill and Judd Inc., a division of Columbia Artists Management Inc. where Arthur Judson became Michael's first concert manager. In addition, it would not be long before Francescatti's good offices catapulted Michael to national prominence by securing an engagement with Donald Voorhees on the *Telephone Hour*.

---

* A 1999 Sony re-release of the eleven caprices gives their recording dates as May 19 and 25, 1950.

CHAPTER 4
CARNEGIE HALL

*A*way from the concert platform, life at home continued with its own established, carefully modulated cycles. A hierarchy of tasks had been established for Michael, with the violin dominating everything. There was schoolwork to complete with the tutor, and Michael took this seriously enough, but math and science were now considered more as an obligation than a necessity. Bertine, who had left the Professional Children's School for Hunter High School in 1948, remained close to her brother. They shared an obvious interest in music, and both children adored the family pet cats, Peterkin and Kiki. But the two siblings were by now leading very different lives. During his second trip to Montreal in January 1948, Michael penned a postcard to his sister, and a second card followed from Rhode Island later that year. As his agenda filled and he began spending a large part of the year on the road, the cards gave way to letters, and the travelogue content was slowly replaced by more personal observations and feelings.

Bertine's memories of the late 1940s and early 1950s give added insights into Michael's family life. "It was during the summer," she recalls, "that our lives were for the most part 'normal'. We would go to Meadowmount and rent a house nearby. We'd go swimming, go to fairs, and do things like that, but it was always with kids from the music circle."[1] When Michael was twelve he was given a camera, and for the next five years he took it everywhere, be it to the apartments of family friends, Meadowmount, or on tour. In the process he compiled a pictorial record of his life, a period of intense musical activity, as his career took flight and his path began intersecting with the lives of the great and famous in music and show business.

The photos may be divided into two broad groupings. The first contains images of acquaintances in Westport during the summer months, unidentified children with their parents, people whom Michael would have met briefly and to whom he formed no lasting attachment. Embedded among the many faces captured are youngsters who are recognizable and who went on to establish major musical careers, including family friend Erick Friedman. But for the most part, these pictures without labels are a miscellany of forgotten faces and fleeting associations. There is no picture of a best friend or a first girlfriend. Rather, the images mostly convey a sense of summer relaxation, the children in bathing suits as they frolic and pose against a backdrop of lakes and woodlands. Whether Michael was able to enter as completely into the spirit of gay summer abandon is questionable. His parents backed off a little from their control when in the country, but the rigid work ethic was never entirely suspended.

The second set of pictures, however, is more informative. Square black-and-white prints with scalloped borders show Galamian at Meadowmount; Galamian and Michael joined by the cellist Leonard Rose, a family friend; Galamian with a succession of celebrated guests, including Szigeti, Piatigorsky, and Francescatti, the latter photographed in 1953. Away from Westport, there are pictures of Dimitri Mitropoulos, Josef Gingold, George Szell, Claudio Arrau, and Artur Balsam, among others. Artur Rodzinski is photographed alone, with his glamorous wife, and with his young son, and on some of these photos, *on verso,* Michael has written "Uncle Arthur." Jeanne pops up in a few of the images, George less often, Bertine very rarely. These are, with few exceptions, photographs of famous musicians relaxing, with wives and colleagues, laughing, drinking, smoking, joking around, chatting, eating, all happy to be filmed by a boy whose divine talent had allowed him access to their rarefied world.*

The start of a new decade marked the point at which Michael's career really took off, the period in which his regional reputation as a wunderkind rapidly expanded to national and international prominence. Up until 1950, there were numerous indications that Galamian had been proceeding cautiously in exposing Michael to the pressures and demands of public adulation. But from 1950 on, the floodgates opened. It was a momentum that could have been checked, but it was not. An early catalyst was a National Orchestra Association event entitled "Great Oaks from Little Acorns Grow,"

---

* The photographs are complemented by the entries in Michael's autograph book. "To the great little Michael, looking forward to the day of our collaboration," wrote Dimitri Mitropoulos in 1948. "With all good wishes for great success," jotted Jascha Heifetz in 1950. "To the greatest violin talent I have ever heard," enthused Alfred Wallenstein in 1950. "Thank you for playing so wonderfully," inscribed Nathan Milstein in 1948, among entries from many other musicians.

which brought together 146 youths in a series of different musical performances.[2] Four music schools from New York City participated in the event, including the Music School Settlement, where George Rabinowitz had taken his first violin lessons.

Michael was the soloist for the afternoon. Soon after 2:30 PM on Saturday, February 11, he stepped out onto the stage at Carnegie Hall for the first time and proceeded to give a superb rendition of the Vieuxtemps Fifth Concerto in A Minor with Leon Barzin conducting. "Young Mr. Rabin has great and rare gifts," noted a critic from the *New York Herald Tribune*:

> He has a sure bow arm, tremendous mechanical facility and a big tone, full and resounding, but in no sense overweighty. A musician still in his teens, Mr. Rabin saw to it that the Vieuxtemps never bogged down in slush: He played it grandly, for the cleanness of its line and the brashness of its fireworks.[3]

The review in the *New York Times* was shorter but no less positive, and concluded: "The boy will be worth watching."[4]

Fresh from his triumph with the Vieuxtemps at Carnegie Hall, Michael headed up to Derby, Connecticut, for a concert under the auspices of the local women's club. He played the Wieniawski Concerto in F Minor, accompanied by his mother. The event was a prelude to a far more exciting and challenging adventure. On April 4, 1950, Michael, with Jeanne at the helm, departed for his first international tour, a ten-day visit to Cuba that included a performance with an orchestra in Havana and a recital in Matanzas. The tour had been organized by "Uncle Arthur" Rodzinski, who had taken up the baton in Havana after leaving his position as musical director of the New York Philharmonic in 1947.

Michael arrived in Havana to great fanfare, one newspaper running his photograph with the caption "Un genio de 13 anos" (a thirteen-year-old genius).[5] In his first concert on April 9, he played the Wieniawski Concerto in F Minor, and success was reported in the *New York Times* the following day: "Michael Rabin of New York wins acclaim in Havana. Artur Rodzinski directing the Havana Philharmonic said of [him], 'He is marvelous, fantastic. He has a tremendous future!'"[6] The local critics were in agreement. Said a reporter from the *Havana Post:* "Rabin has the most astonishing technique, natural feeling and incredibly deep understanding of music coupled with the most beautiful tone."[7]

Once again Rembert Wurlitzer had come to Michael's aid with the loan of a rare violin. Gone was the Joseph Guarnerius, replaced by a del Gesù. The progression in the quality of borrowed instruments mirrored Michael's growing stature as an artist — the initial Amati giving way to a Joseph Guarnerius, which in turn lasted but a few months before seceding to a del Gesù (1734), valued at $30,000.

The Cuban critics also took note of Jeanne Rabin's powerful presence, one writing:

> Michael Rabin seems to be continuously under the spell of his parents. The first factor in the artistic evolution of this young boy must be his mother, Jeanne Rabin, who always accompanies him on the piano. She must be the flint upon which he tries his steel. She is his teacher, adviser, critic, friend. He probably needs security from the eternal grind of material wants, and his parents see to it that he gets it.[8]

Michael loved his time in Cuba. Later in life, he recalled with great fondness his impressions of prerevolutionary Cuba, the vibrancy of the society and the lush, beautiful vegetation.[9] A postcard written to Bertine, dated April 8, has a picture of the Havana Race Track with a caption that encapsulates the hedonism associated with the island in the 1950s:

> Havana, luxuriant with tropical foliage, brilliant flowers, gloriously warm, offers every opportunity for pleasant recreation: ocean bathing, swimming, sailing, golfing, tennis playing, polo tournaments, motor-boating, deep sea fishing, motoring and races of international importance.

Below this, Michael added in his neatly flowing cursive, reflecting the perspective of a thirteen-year-old boy with a passion for motor cars:

> Having a very good and interesting time here. Sorry you couldn't be here too. Everything is very exciting here — the bus drivers go very fast blowing their horns and missing cars and people by inches! Unfortunately haven't seen any real race horses yet, but if I do, I [will] try to photograph any for you. How are the cats?
>   Love, Michael.[10]

Michael did not get around to photographing horses, but he did capture the Rodzinskis on his Kodak, the elderly, graying conductor, his young blond wife, and their son Rikki, no more than five or six years old. There is one touching photograph, probably taken by Jeanne, in which Michael is flanked by the

Rodzinskis, father and son, the conductor with his arm affectionately thrown around Michael's shoulder, while Michael, smiling happily, holds young Rikki's arm. In the background, we glimpse the Spanish-style architecture of the Rodzinski home, the verdant flora, and the richness of the grass underfoot.

Michael was no doubt sorry to leave Cuba after such a short stay, for the indolence of the life in the Caribbean — the afternoon siesta and the more leisurely flow to the pace of daily routines — must have been a refreshing antidote to his driven mother. But the Rabins could not delay their departure beyond April 13. Michael's appointment book was filling up, and he was due onstage at Carnegie Hall in four days' time.

It was on his trip to Cuba that Michael flew in an airplane for the first time. He was instantaneously taken by the experience and began keeping a flight log. Over the course of his career, he would obsessively document every air trip he took in a black, lined notebook that never left his side. It is a remarkable document, a testament to the itinerant life of a virtuoso: the vast lists of countries, cities, and towns visited; the enormous distances covered and time zones crossed; the endless hours spent in the air — in short, the sum total of his working life, and an indication of the relentless manner in which he pushed himself from concert hall to concert hall across five continents during two decades in front of the public.

There are eighty-one pages to the book, alternately filled with facts in Michael's beautifully legible writing. The flight log begins with a title in uppercase letters: "Abbreviations and Explanations." This single page, which is a legend, lists twenty-six airline companies that Michael flew on and provides two- or three-letter abbreviations for each. Thereafter the book is given over to recording each flight, with the pages divided into eight columns: the New York airport he departed from, the airline used, departure and arrival cities, the number of air miles traveled, the duration of the flight, the type of aircraft used, the date of the flight, and finally, the summation of miles traveled. When Michael returned from his first flight to Havana, he noted that the outward trip had taken four hours and forty-seven minutes to cover the 1,302 air miles, whereas the return trip had taken five hours and three minutes for a slightly longer route of 1,346 miles. Over the course of a career that would make him the most traveled virtuoso of his generation, Michael would never miss an entry.

The book is also revealing for what it tells the reader about Michael: the obsessive, meticulous nature of the entries; the compulsive way in which the numbers are added up; the unwavering desire to record in the greatest detail the raw nuts and bolts of his traveling life — the precision of his entries a godsend to any biographer and a sign of how he ordered his life. The similarities between the conscientious and fastidious journal entries and the well-drilled, exacting daily practice sessions are evident.

The day Michael performed with the Havana Symphony Orchestra, another event with far wider repercussions was unfolding back home. On April 9, Ayer Radio News, broadcasting from 30 Rockefeller Plaza, announced the following on their news clip: "Michael Rabin is the youngest soloist ever to be featured on the *Telephone Hour*. He will make his radio debut on the program on August 7, 1950."[11] Zino Francescatti had generously opened a door, and Michael's talent would soon be revealed to the nation. It is hard to exaggerate the importance of this event. Michael was joining an elite of violin virtuosos who had received this most sought-after of invitations. Heifetz, Menuhin, Kreisler, Stern, Morini, Ricci, and of course Francescatti himself had been featured, and now it was Michael's turn as a child wonder to be heard by millions of Americans in their living rooms.

Whatever excitement Michael felt at this pending milestone had to be put on hold, however. There were more pressing matters at hand. Four days after his return from Havana, Michael was back on stage at Carnegie Hall with the same Wieniawski concerto that had so impressed Uncle Arthur and the Cubans. Appearing as part of Leon Barzin's Annual Merit Award Program, run in conjunction with the National Orchestral Association, it was clear that Michael's speedy return to such august surroundings owed much to the stunning impression he had created on this very stage two months earlier with the Vieuxtemps concerto. If anything, his Wieniawski was an even greater triumph. "Boy Violinist Is Phenomenal," ran the headlines.[12]

George Rabin was very proud of his son. As a professional violinist and father to the prodigy, he was perfectly positioned to fully appreciate his son's singular gifts. In his youth, George would have traveled a similar violinistic route, albeit with a different repertoire and at a slower pace. But fine player that he was, there were parts of the violin repertoire that were technically beyond him, the very parts his teenage son would nonchalantly toss off to such critical acclaim. It is therefore likely that at times George, with his professional insights, must have been awed by his son's prodigious abilities.

There is every indication he reacted to this with pride, love, and a father's desire to nurture, using his position as a member of the New York Philharmonic to bring his son to the attention of a series of famed conductors and violinists. It was George who had introduced Michael to Rodzinski. Now he did the same with Dimitri Mitropoulos, who had taken over the reins at the Philharmonic from Bruno Walter, Rodzinzki's successor. Mitropoulos's assessment of Michael's playing has been often quoted and was music to the ears of Judson's team, who quickly incorporated it into their publicity material: "Michael Rabin is really the genius violinist of tomorrow, already equipped with all that is necessary to be a great artist and give great thrills to the music world. He is a blessed boy and already completely devoted to his mission."13

After Mitropoulos, Rabin Senior garnered George Szell. The Cleveland maestro, not to be outdone, weighed in with his powerful endorsement: "To whom it may concern: Michael Rabin is the greatest violin talent that has come to my attention during the past two or three decades."14 Coming from a man feared for his exacting standards, parsimony with praise, and familiarity with all the great violin soloists of the twentieth century, these were remarkable words indeed.

Thereafter, George with Michael in tow paid a visit to Boston's Serge Koussevitzky, in residence at Tanglewood. The upshot of this meeting was reported on an Ayer news clip: "Michael played for a long, long time with the Maestro giving his close attention. Then they really talked! Now Michael is playing string quartets with such masters as cellist Gregor Piatigorsky. And you will probably hear Michael as guest soloist with Koussevitzky and the Boston Symphony before long."15

Not all the introductions went so smoothly, however. Michael's meeting with Mischa Elman produced an unfortunate gaffe, as related by Hy Gardner on his celebrity radio show:

> Recently, Michael made his debut in Havana and was hailed as a genius. His father, a member of the New York Philharmonic Orchestra, arranged one afternoon for the lad to display his wares for Mischa Elman. The latter listened attentively, then wrapped his arms around him. "You have great hands, a fine feeling for music and a great future," he said. "Just how great you become is up to yourself. You must practice many hours a day, every day. You must remember that while you were born with such a great gift, it must be developed. Like men digging for oil, you cannot stop until you strike oil. Tell me," he said with a smile, "what is your greatest ambition?" The prodigy looked up at Mr. Elman and said, "To play like Jascha Heifetz."16

Elman, long the butt of a famous Godowsky put-down vis-à-vis Jascha Heifetz, was furious. His longtime accompanist Josef Seiger remembers that for months afterwards, Michael's name could not be mentioned in Elman's presence. And then the older man relented, and before too long, he too joined Michael's growing legion of admirers. In time Elman began inviting

him to his apartment for chamber music evenings, where Michael would join
Seiger and Lillian Fuchs, among others, occasionally switching between
violin and viola with equal ease.[17]

The list of musicians impressed by Michael's talent was stellar, but these
meetings with older colleagues, be they conductors or violinists, were brief,
and geared toward the boy playing to impress and in turn receiving the acco-
lades that carried musical weight. Michael's tender age precluded these interactions progressing further into friendship — unlike the young Menuhin,
whose relationship with an older Enesco transcended such a divide.

There was, however, one musician apart from Galamian who came close
to befriending Michael. Zino Francescatti's influence went beyond procuring
agent, broadcasts, and recordings, and by mid-year the two violinists had
started corresponding. Michael was the more prolific writer, and from his letters we can discern the prodding parental hand of Jeanne. "Dear Mr.
Francescatti," he wrote on June 5, 1950:

> Many thanks for the beautiful picture and wonderful autograph.
> It was very sweet of you and I certainly do appreciate it very much.
> It was such a great pleasure to spend the evening with you and
> Mme. Francescatti and meet your charming mother. I am looking
> forward to seeing you again and hope you stay in the best of
> health during the summer. My love and best regards to all of you
> in which my parents join me.
>   Sincerely,
>   Michael Rabin[18]

Less than two months later, on the eve of his *Telephone Hour* performance,
Michael wrote again: "How are you and Mrs. Francescatti and your mother?
I do hope you are all having a wonderful summer and a good rest." Once
again, the maternal influence in the letter was apparent, for how could a child
whose waking hours were defined by at least eight hours of practice every day
conceive of a good rest? The very notion was an abstraction, as his next sentence makes clear: "It has been very cool here, which is good for practicing.
I have been reviewing the Tchaikowsky and Mendelssohn concertos, and
next week, thanks to you, I am going to New York to play on 'The Telephone
Hour' on August 7 — I hope you can get the station and find time to listen
as I should love your criticism." Jeanne was not, however, the only one
looking over Michael's shoulder as he penned this note, for it also bears the
imprimatur of Galamian, always anxious to enhance the growing reputation
of his summer school.

Mr. Galamian and I are hoping that you will be able to come to Meadowmount (Westport) and see the wonderful school he has. We have a house about ⅓ of a mile from his place. We all would be so thrilled to see you. We have enough room for you to stay here if you care to....

Love,

Michael Rabin

"Mike"[19]

On August 7, 1950, Michael made his much-heralded appearance on the *Telephone Hour's* tenth anniversary program, but not before special permission had been obtained from the local musicians' union because of the soloist's young age.[20] He was accompanied by Donald Voorhees and the Bell Telephone Orchestra. "Michael borrowed a Guarnerius violin and played the Paganini Caprice No. 17 and the finale of the E Minor Violin Concerto by Mendelssohn, that standard testing piece of all violinists," noted *Newsweek:*

> When his trial by air was over, Michael was tired. Nevertheless, by 7:30 the next morning he was out on the streets of New York with his shiny new bicycle, his current pride and joy. But like all good violinists, Michael is also a good table tennis player and is hoping someday to take on Jascha Heifetz, dean of ping-pong peddling fiddlers.[21]

Michael did not have to wait long before meeting his idol, which took place on October 30. "Four o'clock today is H-hour for 14-year-old Michael Rabin, colorful young violinist," wrote a columnist for the *New York World Telegram and Sun:*

> He will be photographed with Jascha Heifetz. The brilliant Mr. Heifetz is his idol and the extremely reticent Mr. H. has made the comment that with hard work the teenager has possibilities for the future, words that have Michael working harder than ever at his practice sessions. Today's picture taking will be long remembered.[22]

The photograph that was released shows Heifetz playing, Voorhees conducting, and in the bottom right hand corner, in profile, the face of young Michael, looking up at Heifetz, who towers physically and metaphorically above him. It was at this meeting that Heifetz — reserved, austere, a world removed from the effusive bear-hug embrace of Mischa Elman — autographed Michael's score of the Bach sonatas and partitas. There were no encouraging remarks, no warm regards expressed — just the bare signature, "Heifetz."

As Michael's career surged, his management set about molding his image:

> All-American boy is a tag that fits him neatly. Like any other 14-year-old, he's pining to be 18 so he can get his driver's license. And in lieu of a car to drive right now, he has a bike that after his violin is his most prized possession. He polishes it within an inch of its life and has it fitted with every gadget, reflectors, headlights and all. "You'd think it was a Cadillac," exclaimed his mother.... He's studying second-year high school subjects and still finds time for things like swimming, ping-pong and stamp collecting. If you want to see him really beam, though, ask him about the Guarnerius del Gesu, an exquisite violin valued at $35,000, loaned him for his concerts. This he does not take casually either. Quite a fellow, Mike.[23]

The image Judson, O'Neill and Judd wanted to convey therefore had three central tenets. First, the boy had extraordinary musical gifts and consorted with the great musicians of the day; second, the boy came from a talented but down-to-earth, uncomplicated family — parents, two kids, and pets; and third, that Mike was really just like any other kid his age, sharing the same passions and interests. Like all personas, it contained a mixture of facts and myths. In time, some would endure. Others would be cruelly exposed.

The day after Michael's *Telephone Hour* performance, Zino Francescatti wrote to congratulate him:

> My dear Mike,
>   ...Last night we heard your great playing on the telephone hour. It came wonderfully and everything was clean and perfect — the 17th caprice with the chromatics and octaves was outstanding and the Mendelssohn in a good tempo.... You did very well.... Your parents and Mr. Galamian can be proud of you, but please — keep always your simplicity, have a great musical humility — and never be satisfied with even the best. Perfection in everything must be our goal.
>   My mother and my wife send to you their most hearty congratulations for last evening. With our best affectionate thoughts.
>   Your friend,
>   Zino Francescatti.[24]

In Michael's quick reply to Francescatti's letter can be discerned not only his gratitude but also his growing hero-worship of the older man:

> Dear Mr. Francescatti,
>
> Thank you very much for your very sweet letter and wonderful advice. I was thrilled to hear from you.
>
> It made me very happy to know that you thought I played well on the "Telephone Hour." Coming from you it certainly is flattering! Once more I want to thank you for helping me get on the Telephone Hour. It really was a joy to play, especially since Mr. Voorhees and Mr. Magill are such wonderful people to be associated with. They were so kind and considerate. They both hold you in very high regard and they told me what a wonderful person and what a marvelous artist you are, and believe me, I certainly agree with them.
>
> Besides working and practicing on many things, I am now studying "Tzigane." I have your recording of it in the city, and it is so fantastic that it inspired me to buy the music and try and learn it. I think it is thrilling music. When I can play it a little bit it would be wonderful if you could give me some pointers on it, as I feel nobody plays it as you do.
>
> It really would be a great joy for all of us if you could come to Meadowmount. We are all waiting very impatiently to see you. Please try to come....
>
> With much love and respect,
> Mike.[25]

In a year crowded with achievement and notable firsts, Michael still had one major hurdle to negotiate: his Carnegie Hall debut recital. The week before this auspicious event, on a visit to Buffalo, he had tried out yet another borrowed violin — this time a del Gesù that belonged to Leopold Godowsky Jr. and had once been played by Paganini. Michael loved the instrument and was allowed to keep it for his pending recital. He had stood on the Carnegie stage twice in the past year, on both occasions with a youth orchestra behind him. Now the orchestra would be dispensed with and he would face the tiers alone, apart from piano, asking to be judged for his ability, not his age.

It was his greatest musical challenge, a career-defining moment more auspicious than any to date. He would need to be at the top of his form, and the same would be asked of his accompanist. Thus far Jeanne Rabin had performed admirably in backwaters such as Providence, Allentown, and Matanzas, but Carnegie Hall was too big a stage for her. The program chosen for Michael for this concert was not daunting from a pianistic perspective, and Jeanne had played the repertoire before, but public perception needed to be factored in now. Heifetz had Brooks Smith and Emanuel Bay; Stern had Alexander Zakin; Oistrakh had Vladimir Yampolski and Sviatoslav Richter. Michael could no longer have his mother. Whether Jeanne herself recognized this is not known, nor is whether she resented having to stand down for the big occasion. But gone she was. When Michael played his recital on November 24, Leopold Mittman was at the piano.

The Carnegie Hall program contained repertoire that Michael had, for the most part, played many times before: the Sonata in A Major by Tartini (arranged by Kreisler), the Partita in D Minor, No. 2, by Bach (including the chaconne), and the Concerto in F-Sharp Minor by Wieniawski came before intermission, to be followed by the Recitative and Scherzo Caprice for solo violin by Kreisler, four Paganini caprices (13,16, 21, and 5, the latter by now a Rabin warhorse), "Song Without Words" by Mendelssohn, and Bartòk's *Rumanian Folk Dances*. The recital was eagerly awaited by the musical public and the violin cognoscenti. "[They] opened up the top two balconies of Carnegie Hall last night for the recital of Michael Rabin. Ordinarily that might seem like too many seats for the debut of a 14-year-old violinist, but this was something special," noted the *Times.*[26]

The critic and composer Arthur Berger, writing in the *New York Herald Tribune,* echoed this assessment of the occasion:

> The violinists were out in large numbers last night* to give their official stamp of approval to the latest boy wonder, 14-year-old Michael Rabin, whose rare gifts have created quite a bit of excitement among experts who have heard him.... The recital was of course the test, and from the point of view of sheer control and facility in handling the violin, he passed with high honors. He was applauded enthusiastically and bravoed by an audience that was larger than some of our big name violinists have been able to draw of late. He took this all in stride with the youthful unconcern that was about as astonishing as some of the technical feats he accomplished.

---

* Among the violinists present was Isaac Stern, who at an after-concert party hosted by the Galamians, inscribed his compliments in Michael's autograph book: "A memorable evening — the beginning of a great adventure in music — guard your great gifts and enjoy your music — with warmest wishes to talent rare and welcome." There was an amusing incongruity in Michael soliciting the autographs of his adult colleagues on the very evening they had come to pay him homage.

Having lauded the boy, Berger gently pointed out some of his weaknesses and ended his thoughtful critique on a prescient note:

> There is no doubt that Mr. Rabin is among the elite where violin virtuosity is concerned and that he is one of the most gifted and accomplished talents to come along in many a year. One might even venture the epitaph "Great" to describe his grasp of the instrument....
>
> It remains for him now to develop his own personality and broaden his musical horizon and his powers of interpretation.... The next step should be maturing as a person and musician and not the exploitation of his present phenomenal accomplishments and a concert schedule that might prevent such maturing.[27]

November 24, 1950, was a day of high drama for Michael and the Rabin family. All those hours of practice, those lonely, private hours spent away from school, friends, and peers; all those road trips and times of family separation; all those auditions for Jascha and Mischa and Uncle Arthur, for Messrs. Francescatti, Szigeti, Mitropoulos, Szell, and Koussevitzky, and all so carefully orchestrated by George and Ivan Galamian, had been but a prelude to this moment.

Michael was certainly old enough to appreciate the import of the occasion. He symbolically chose that evening to express how he felt for the man who had taken him so far. "To my beloved teacher Ivan Galamian," began his dedication on an Abresch photograph, "with greatest admiration, affection and deepest gratitude for all he has done for me. With love, Michael."[28] This heartfelt acknowledgement, publicly expressed, nevertheless awkwardly refers to Galamian in the third person, giving the sentiment a slightly detached feel. A grammatical slip? Or a reflection of the emotional distance between pupil and master? What is more certain is that Galamian cherished the photo and dedication.

Michael's parents and Galamian eagerly awaited the reviews of his debut. It was, after all, the stamp of critical approval that they had sought by Michael's venture onto the grand stage. When the morning papers came out the next day, there was praise enough to satisfy all parties.

But what of Arthur Berger's advice that care should be taken in allowing the boy to mature, that his wondrous gifts should not be exploited by too many concerts, and his oblique warning that failure to follow such a course ran the risk of hampering Michael's further development? Did the adults who loved Michael, who watched over him so intensely, who perhaps saw in him the embodiment of their own future hopes and successes, heed the caution together with the praise? Swept up in the escalating momentum of his career and flushed by superlatives that were being showered upon him, it would have been so easy for Michael's guardians to dismiss any whiff of criticism as nothing more than the perpetual gripe of those paid to find fault. If Michael had faced a critical moment in his young career before his Carnegie Hall debut, his minders faced just such an instant in the concert's heady aftermath. There is every indication that, unlike their precious charge, they were found wanting.

CHAPTER 5

IN PURSUIT OF PERFECTION

It is helpful to pause at this point in Michael's life, to stand back a little from the heady rush of success and his escalating concert commitments and take stock of his young life. He was fourteen years old. He had made a successful Carnegie Hall debut, was known nationally through his *Telephone Hour* broadcast, and had cut his first disc for Columbia Records. His technical expertise on the violin was fully formed and knew no limits. The sound that he coaxed from a succession of borrowed instruments already had the luscious, rich texture and powerful projection that would come, like his formidable technique, to define his musical legacy. While his repertoire appeared largely rooted in the romantic, virtuoso world of the nineteenth-century composer-violinists, in interviews he had hinted at a much broader range of works, all memorized. His talent had been endorsed by many older famous musicians, he had one of the largest and most prestigious concert agencies managing his engagements, and away from the spotlights, had a family that was not only musical and musically well-connected but devoted to him and his career.

"My mother always considered that being Michael's sister or mother or father was a very wonderful thing," recalls Bertine:

> And it was wonderful. Once I remember we were at the Rodzinskis and he asked me some kind of question like, "What do you want to be when you grow up?" and I gave some stupid answer like, "I'll marry a rich man," or something like that. My mother

said, "Oh you don't have to do that. You're Michael Rabin's sister."[1]

It is clear that talent alone had not been responsible for Michael reaching such an exalted position so quickly. Galamian demanded long hours of practice. "Work harder," urged Elman. "Strive for perfection," advised Francescatti. "With more work, a bright future beckons," opined Heifetz. Michael obeyed them all. Erick Friedman, a contemporary, recalls that while he was practicing six hours a day, Michael was doing eight or nine.[2] Jack Heller, another student of Galamian, remembers that whenever he walked passed The Lilacs, which was a fifteen-minute-stroll from the main house at Meadowmount, Michael would be practicing, always playing slowly during those marathon sessions.[3] Bertine's memory from this time is of her brother closeted in his bedroom with his violin for company. It was a life essentially devoted to music.

"My mother put a lot of pressure on us," noted Bertine:

> We always had to be the best, but we were never good enough. The pressures were verbal, physical, mental. But then she would go outside the home and she would tell everyone how wonderful we were. So I'd get the stories back and I would say, "I wish she would tell me." And this occurred all the time. We didn't dare disobey her in anything she told us to do. If we protested, she smacked us around a little bit. We weren't beaten, but I remember getting smacked in the face. I remember spankings. And Michael got that too. With him it was mainly related to work.[4]

Hard work was of course necessary, but in Michael's case, his childhood had been sacrificed on the high altar of artistic achievement. He may have been able to dazzle with Paganini, but he did not have a friend. In keeping him away from other children his own age, Jeanne and George had not only deprived him of friends, they had more importantly prevented him from acquiring the necessary social skills and confidence to make friends. Without his violin, away from music, Michael felt awkward and could not relate comfortably to other adolescents. Entering puberty and the turbulent teenage years, he was developmentally adrift, steered unwittingly into troubled and anxious waters by parents and a teacher whose blinkered mantras were "work, work, work." By ignoring the necessity of childhood play and peer contact, Jeanne and George had left their wunderkind ill-equipped for life as an adult. Soon adolescence would cruelly expose these deficiencies.

Galamian too was not without blame here. That Michael adored his teacher and was loved in return is without doubt. That Galamian initially took care in gently shepherding his protégé onto the concert stage cannot be challenged. But what is equally apparent is that Galamian never took George and Jeanne aside to urge a more balanced approach to Michael's upbringing. He would have been aware that Michael had been withdrawn from school and had no friends. He must have known that Michael was inhabiting, prematurely, the world of adults. But he said nothing and did nothing to alter this. In his relentless quest for excellence, in his pursuit of the perfection that Francescatti too had so fulsomely endorsed, Galamian appears to have lost sight of the little boy and his emotional needs. His praise and admiration for Michael were conditional, linked inextricably to the boy's mastery of a fiendishly difficult instrument and his ability to demonstrate that fact before the public.

"The combination of my mother and Mr. Galamian was bad for Michael," Bertine asserted:

> With Mr. Galamian, Michael's performances were never wonderful. My mother was like that too. It was always, "Now you'll improve it for next time." If you got a 99 on a test, well that's okay, but next time you've got to get 100. Mr. Galamian was very much that way too.[5]

If Jeanne had been more sensitive and responsive to her son's emotional needs, had the maternal pressures on Michael to perform been less intense and conditional, then Galamian's demands coupled with his largely cerebral approach to teaching would not have been so onerous. But that was not his way. Uncomfortable around emotional matters, Galamian was ill-equipped to offset the excesses of a forceful mother and guide his fragile pupil through the coming storm.

Similarly, George was no match for his formidable wife. A quiet, mild-mannered man, he appears to have deferred to Jeanne on all matters pertaining to his children. He was certainly less demanding when it came to practicing and was not averse to surreptitiously countermanding Jeanne when she left the apartment. "My father adored my mother," recalls Bertine. "My mother, I don't think, was adoring. With my father, the sun set and rose on my mother."[6]

George was not so accommodating with his siblings. The fractious Rabinowitzes had never really made peace after George's elopement, and residual resentment towards Jeanne persisted. For her part, Jeanne lacked a forgiving temperament and was unlikely to quietly ignore ongoing slights. Matters came to a head when George's sister Jean died. En route to the funeral, Sarah and her surviving children encountered Michael going off for a violin lesson. Old wounds quickly reopened and family bonds, weakened by years of skirmishing, fractured a second time.

So complete was the latest separation that when Sarah died and George and Jeanne attended the funeral, they were not recognized by one of their nieces. Judy Levin was thirteen at the time and recalls being introduced by her mother to an unknown uncle and aunt. She also remembers, with embarrassment, her mother admonishing George for his failure to attend a recent family celebration. "We wanted your presence, not your presents," were Grace's memorable words.7 An unfortunate consequence of this ongoing feud was that Michael was cut off from paternal cousins his own age, further cementing his social isolation.

Michael's parents were not totally oblivious to his need for peer contact. They did make some sporadic attempts to dilute his solitude, but these were few and tightly controlled, and missed the gist entirely of what their teenage son needed. Every Saturday Michael would take his seat at the back of the violin section of the Juilliard's Preparatory Division Chamber Orchestra conducted by Wesley Sontag. It was here that he first met Lewis Kaplan, another Galamian student three years his senior.

Lewis remembers being invited to a birthday party in 1950 at the Rabin apartment with a couple of other Juilliard students, all a good few years older than Michael.8 They had been invited to make up the quorum as it were, but none could be classed as friends. Lewis, whose rapport with Michael had yet to blossom, was aware of the strained and stilted atmosphere that afternoon on what should have been a carefree occasion. Michael's precocious talent had always meant he moved in an older social group, and in the contrived festivity of a birthday party among older children with age-appropriate social skills, his younger, awkward demeanor was even more painfully exposed. The astonishment Michael's talent induced in other children only added to his separation, another barrier to be bridged in what was fast becoming the increasingly remote and foreign, yet longed for, world of uncomplicated youth.

If Michael's peers were uncomfortably aware of his social unease, there is every indication Michael was starting to feel it too. "Although the mastery of music comes with awesome speed to most prodigies, life's other challenges may not be so easily met," noted cellist and teacher Claude Kenneson. "While balancing unusually advanced abilities in one area with more ordinary abilities in another, the working prodigy may begin to feel alienated from siblings and peers."9

The crowd that flocked to Carnegie Hall to witness Michael's extraordinary debut were privy to none of Michael's nascent conflicts. Incipient social anxieties vanished when the boy put a violin under his chin. The gauche lad who had struggled uncomfortably through his fourteenth birthday party was transformed into a scarcely believable, supremely confident young man in formal dress suit, who for two exhausting hours held the rapt attention of an audience of thousands. And lest they wonder about what kind of child could accomplish such a feat, there were the soothing blandishments put out by the Columbia publicity machine: the boy out on the street with his bike the day after Carnegie Hall; his love of chess, photography, airplanes and cars — in short, he was just like any other kid his age.

There were photographs to prove it. Mike with his bike and Mike with his model plane and Mike with his box camera — and in all these photographs, Mike looks out at the viewer, his expression a winning mixture of boyhood happiness tinged with modesty and a modicum of shyness. What the photographs could not show, however, and what his publicity gurus did not know or did not want to know, was that this gentle youngster blessed with a mysterious and wonderful gift did not have a friend. He was still as close as ever to Bertine, loved by parents and teacher, and admired by a growing coterie of fans, but on a peer level, at that crucial juncture in his social development, he was very much alone.

In January, Francescatti returned to his home in New York.* He performed the Brahms Violin Concerto with the New York Philharmonic and met up again with Michael. February found the Francescattis in Sweden, from where Zino's wife, Yolande, sent Michael a postcard greeting. Five days later Michael wrote back, his letter once again an expression of profound gratitude and unbounded admiration:

> You have been gone for only three weeks, but to me, it seems like a year because I do miss you and Mrs. Francescatti very much. November is really very far off, but I will have to wait that long before I can see you again. It will certainly be worth waiting for.
>
> Your wonderful performance of the Brahms concerto still rings in my ears. It was the most wonderful and the most perfect Brahms I have *ever* heard. I listened to it again on the radio on the following Sunday, and it was just as wonderful as ever.
>
> Mr. Judson has been planning some wonderful concerts for me. But before I can tell you what he said, I *must* tell you how

---

* He had bought an apartment in New York in 1939.

kind, understanding and helpful you have been to me. If it hadn't been for you I would never have gotten under the management of Judson, O'Neill & Judd. I also got to Columbia Records and "the Telephone Hour" through your help. I want to tell you now and always how much I appreciate your interest and how much love and respect I have for you.

Michael went on to tell Francescatti of some upcoming performances and the imminent release of his recording of some of the Paganini caprices, before signing off with "most affectionate wishes to you and Mrs. Francescatti from your friend. With much love — 'Mike.' P.S. I just received your postcard from Stockholm, today. Thanks loads."[10]

Michael's life had become a whirlwind of concert performances and social engagements. On February 25, 1951, he was invited by the Bohemian Club to perform at a dinner to he held at the Waldorf Astoria in honor of Dimitri Mitropoulos. It was a glittering event, the proceeds going to the Musicians' Foundation to assist those in the profession in need. After a sumptuous banquet — which included Key West turtle soup and breast of native guinea hen, Mirette potatoes and asparagus tips mimosa, followed by golden rum sabayon and petit fours — Michael picked up his violin and, with the guest of honor at the piano, played "Guitarre" by Moskowski, "Ave Maria" by Schubert (arranged by Wilhelmji), *La Capricieuse* by Elgar and the Introduction and Tarantella by Sarasate.[11]

On April 24 he was back at the Waldorf for another dinner, this time honoring Albert Spalding, who had recently retired. In the presence of Fritz Kreisler, Spalding, and other guests, he performed the former's Recitative and Scherzo and three excerpts from the latter's "Etchings." According to Michael's management, when he had finished playing, Harriet Kreisler ran up to her husband and the guest of honor, admonishing, "You should both be ashamed of yourselves. Go home and practice."* The same month, reviews started appearing for Michael's recording of eleven Paganini caprices, with the critics expressing wonder at his technical accomplishments. "Rabin Paganini Recording Bares Remarkable Artistry," read the headline of a review by music critic Elmore Bacon on the eve of Michael's performance with George Szell and the Cleveland Orchestra. He continued:

One is left in awe of this young man as he maintains a fervor, internal warmth and all the fiery brilliance of these Paganini

---

* "Dear Michael, I cannot tell you how much I enjoyed your playing tonight," wrote Kreisler in Michael's ever-present autograph book.

sketches. The shading is superb, the musical intelligence with which he sets forth these intricate scores is that of a violin wizard who has all the magic at his command.[12]

For his Cleveland concert, Michael used yet another borrowed instrument, as he informed Francescatti. "Mr. Emil Herrmann has lent me a wonderful 'Strad.,'" he wrote. "It sounds marvelous, and I don't have any trouble handling it. But the only trouble is, that as soon as I come back from Cleveland (2 weeks) he takes it back! So — that means again I have no fiddle. It *is* quite a problem, n'est ce pas?"[13]

Nothing, however, could dilute Michael's success with the Paganini concerto. "Comes another wunderkind," waxed Elmore Bacon. "Another budding Heifetz was our thought as we joined the overflow audience in cheering violinist Michael Rabin."[14] There were no dissenting voices. James Frankel in the *Cleveland Press* noted that:

> The customary self-controlled Thursday night audience at Severance Hall really let loose last night, and justifiably so. For nine thunderous curtain calls they cheered, stomped and clapped the young Michael Rabin, who will be 15 next month. Without benefit of formal dress, Michael in a dark business suit overwhelmed orchestra and audience alike with his uncanny skill, his amazing tonal beauty, his complete command over his instrument.[15]

The Francescattis were both very fond of Michael and kept the correspondence going, although their affection was expressed in more subdued tones. On March 8, while on tour in Amsterdam, Francescatti replied to Michael's latest passionate missive with: "A thousand good wishes to you and friendly greetings to your parents. Z. Francescatti."[16] In a letter dated March 26, Michael outlined the repertoire he was working on (Vieuxtemps's Concerto No. 5, Saint-Saëns's B Minor Concerto, Bach, Paganini, *Tzigane*, Brahms's D Minor Sonata, and Paganini's "Moto Perpetuo"). "Besides that I have five school subjects," he wrote, "so you can see I am kept busy all the time and have no time to waste. But I consider it important to write to you, because I promised you I would and I *do* keep my word." And then Michael concluded with a by-now-familiar refrain — his desire for friendship.

> How is Mrs. Francescatti in Marseille?... Please send my love to her and tell her I hope she is well.
>
> There is not very much more to say except that I do miss you and Mrs. Francescatti. I feel that you are my best friends and I am

sure you know how a fellow feels when he doesn't see his best
friends for ten months.[17]

Looking beyond Michael's overt adulation, there is a plaintive quality in
his letters to the older man. "Your friend" is how he saw himself in relation
to a man thirty-seven years his senior, while in turn he regarded the couple as
his "best friends." If Michael had had some friends his own age, then his
reaching out to Francescatti in this fashion would not have had the same
poignancy. In writing often and fervently to a man who had become his
patron, Michael was responding not only to his older colleague's generosity
but also to his warmth, accessibility, and a character devoid of artifice.

Perhaps some of the affinity Michael felt also stemmed from his identifi-
cation with a man who had had a difficult childhood. It cannot be a coinci-
dence that on May 2, 1951, his fifteenth birthday, Michael picked up a pen
and had this to convey to his esteemed colleague:

> Mr. Judson told me what a very hard life you had, how hard you
> worked and about your early sickness. Please don't think me to be
> too sentimental, but I just want you to know that I respect you
> (and love you). Mr. Judson also said that very few people who
> have reached your terrific height of fame and success are so sweet,
> kind and understanding and that I should *try* to copy some of
> your wonderful character. I honestly mean it.
>
> Please send my love to your wonderful (one in a million) wife,
> and tell her I think of her too.[18]

To a lonely boy, the personal qualities embodied by Francescatti must have
had an instantaneous appeal.

Fresh from his resounding success in Cleveland, Michael returned to New
York for a unique engagement, but one that he felt ambivalent about, suc-
cumbing in the end to pressure from his management to accept. He returned
the Strad to Emil Hermann and went over to Rembert Wurlitzer's studio to
pick up another fiddle that he would need for a daunting series of performances due to begin at the Roxy Theatre. "On May 9 to May 23 (two weeks)
the New York Philharmonic is playing at the Roxy Theatre under Mr.
Mitropoulos," wrote Michael to Francescatti:

> I have been chosen as soloist and believe me, it will be hard. I have
> to play 4 times a day for two weeks, in other words 56 times. The
> first week I play the first movement of the Paganini Concerto, with
> cadenza, and the second week I play Introduction and Rondo

Capriccioso.* At first we didn't like the idea of this engagement, but Mr. Judson thought it would be wonderful publicity and etc.[19]

In leaving the sentence unfinished, in using the *etc.* to reveal how he truly felt about this unwanted marathon undertaking, Michael, having just turned fifteen years old, betrayed the first signs, perhaps inadvertently, of cynicism in his dealings with those who controlled his every minute. He was now learning, in ways that were clearly uncomfortable to him, that pressures came not only from a mother and a teacher. A third master had to be obeyed — the manager. For the pending May performances, the orchestra would alternate with the showing of a movie: *I'd Climb the Highest Mountain,* starring Susan Hayward and William Lundigan. Young Michael could have been forgiven in thinking the film title referred directly to what was expected of him.

Judson, in pushing Michael to accept an engagement he and his parents and teacher did not want, was overreaching himself.† He was no doubt unaware of what had befallen the eleven-year-old piano prodigy Josef Hoffman, who in New York in 1887 had come to the attention of the Society for the Prevention of Cruelty to Children. After twenty-four successful concerts and with a further forty planned, the society intervened, and the boy was forced to withdraw from the stage for six years.[20] No such action was forthcoming in Michael's case, but in eschewing moderation when it came to shepherding its youngest artist through to a happy and successful adult career, Michael's management was setting a worrying precedent.

To his credit, Michael played very well at the Roxy. "I'd like to see the day when audiences go as mad for this boy as they went for MacArthur," Mitropoulos told an appreciative audience. "Then I will say that there will be no more wars."[21] The concerts did not, however, pass off without incident. "During the second week at the 'Roxy' the violin I was using opened at the right front top seam!!" Michael wrote to Francescatti. "I was so scared, but Mr. Wurlitzer had a special glue, and it was sealed again within two hours. That was very fortunate, and after that everything was all right."[22]

While engaged at the Roxy, Michael gave an interview to the *Daily Mirror.* Intermingled with his attempts at shoring up his persona as the all-American kid, he admitted to feeling lonely. And he took a verbal swipe at his mother. The *Mirror's* article appeared under a picture of Michael holding his violin with the caption, "The son outplays the father." "It's a toss-up whether he loves his violin or his shiny new bicycle the best," ran the article:

---

* Michael played the first movement of the Paganini concerto both weeks.

† Arthur Judson was also manager of the New York Philharmonic Orchestra (together with Bruno Zirato) at the time.

He even has a speedometer on his bike. "Burned up the road yesterday," he confided. "I got her up to 35 mph."… Mike is also an expert swimmer and a crack photographer. Like all true artists he knows what loneliness is and he's been conducting pen pal correspondence for over two years with a 19-year-old second lieutenant serving in the British Army in Egypt.

Switching tack, Michael disclosed how he felt about his mother. "She's not only my musical mentor, she's also my musical tormentor."[23] The clever wordplay could not disguise the sudden departure from his previously carefully scripted interviews. Michael's public disclosure hinted at newfound tensions in his relationship with his mother. Even allowing for some teenage spunkiness, it must have galled Jeanne to have him voice his views in such a public forum. How she responded is not known, but Michael is unlikely to have escaped unscathed.

Michael's ability and stamina had ensured his success during the Roxy fortnight. He had also demonstrated his resilience when challenged onstage by mechanical problems with his violin. All of this must have reinforced the views of Judson, O'Neill and Judd that the boy was ready for even greater challenges. For as Michael had told Francescatti in a letter of May 2, "Now here is something *really exciting!!!* Next summer (1952) I am going to *Australia!!* for four months. July, August, September & October. I will play 47 concerts of which 18 will be recitals and 29 orchestral appearances." Notwithstanding Michael's obvious excitement at the news, which owed much to the prospect of far-flung travel ("Imagine, I will be there for 17 weeks [including travel time]. It takes 36 hours one-way, by airplane! I will be 10,000 miles away from New York!!!"),[24] this was another grueling engagement. This time there were no objections from parents and teacher. Even Francescatti appears to have seen nothing remiss in the number of concerts proposed nor in the time that would be spent on the road. "Miss O'Neill told me that you thought it was good I was playing in Australia," Michael wrote to him on June 8. "I am glad to learn that you think it is good, because I respect your opinion very highly."[25]

After his Roxy exertions, Michael was looking forward to an end-of-season break. As usual he would spend time at Meadowmount, but his growing fame was starting to attract the attentions of the summer festival organizers. Two concerts were slated with the Chicago Symphony Orchestra conducted by Izler Solomon as part of the annual Ravinia Park series. In the first, he played Mozart's Third Violin Concerto and in the second, Paganini's D Major Concerto. "He senses the magnificent equilibrium of a perfectly sculptured phrase," wrote Seymour Ravin in the *Chicago Daily Tribune*. "He has an unbelievable feeling for pace for one so young, and solid understanding of punctuation, ornamentation and the other attributes of well cultivated musical speech." Amid this sea of praise, however, appeared some momentary anxiety. "He cannot fail," mused the reviewer, "unless fate plays some of the tricks it has turned out for some other gifted youngsters. Let us hope not, for too much would be lost here."[26]

The start of the 1951–52 concert season marked the fifteen-year-old Michael's first American tour. On October 16, he appeared in Philadelphia as soloist in the Paganini D Major concerto with the New York Philharmonic under Mitropoulos. "This was not the mere playing of a gifted prodigy who may or may not weather the public's favor, but rather the performance of a young man who already has a style in a manner quite his own, and legitimately so," was the comment in the *Philadelphia Evening Bulletin*.[27] Three days later, Michael was back behind the microphone for the *Telephone Hour* in a performance of Heifetz's transcription of Leopold Godowsky's "Alt Wein" and the first movement of the Tchaikowsky Violin Concerto, which Michael dedicated to all the young violin students who were practicing the work.[28] From New York he set out for concerts in Allentown, Dayton, and St. Louis, where he played the Paganini D Major Concerto on successive days with the St. Louis Symphony conducted by Vladimir Golschmann.

In an interview, Michael spoke on a theme that would come back to haunt him a few years hence. "I am never nervous when I play a concert," he said. "I go out to play for people who go to hear good music. That's what I'm here for. So what is there to be nervous about?" He then divulged his three great ambitions: his first was to get hold of at least $25,000 in "hard, cold, freezing cash" with which to buy a first-rate violin, the second goal was a car, and the third was to be a great concert violinist, at which the ubiquitous Jeanne broke in to say, "You can borrow a car or a violin. You can't borrow a career or a reputation."[29] Faced with this withering logic, Michael could only acquiesce.

From St. Louis, Michael traveled to LaCrosse, Wisconsin and played two recitals accompanied by his mother. Another followed in Montreal before he returned to New York, well in time for his miniseries of four concerts with the New York Philharmonic and Mitropoulos at Carnegie Hall that began on November 29. Two performances each of the Paganini D Major and Wieniawski F-sharp Minor concertos were scheduled. "His career has been handled very carefully," wrote Harold Schonberg in the *New York Times*. "Next season his parents have accepted a limited number of engagements for their son. 'Relatively few recitals, mostly orchestral appearances,' said Mrs. Rabin. 'There's no rush.'"[30] What Jeanne and George had not told Schonberg was that they had just signed up their son for a four-month, eighteen-recital, twenty-nine-orchestral tour to Australia that translated into three concerts a week over sixteen weeks. And that was only part of the story. For inspecting Michael's flight log reveals that in the months that lay ahead, even before he was due to step on to the DC-6 that was to transport him across the world, his management had booked concerts for him in a dozen cities.

Looking at the pace at which Michael was now concertizing, it also seems astonishing that George could have told Schonberg earlier in the same interview, "You see, [Jeanne and I] are both professional musicians. We've been through the mill and know what a professional's life is like."[31] On the one hand, both parents were voicing their concerns to an eminent music critic about the pressures faced by musicians, and yet on the other hand, they were subjecting their child to the very stresses they warned about. Were Michael's parents being deliberately disingenuous? Did they harbor concern, perhaps even some guilt, at failing to slow the rapidly escalating momentum of his career and thus feel compelled to ply Schonberg with selected facts? Or did they truly believe what they had said? If the latter, it implied a worrying insensitivity to the potential consequences of their actions.

Jeanne in particular was deeply embroiled in Michael's career, which curtailed her ability to view events with the objectivity the situation demanded. Certainly, Michael's talent and his seeming capacity thus far to soak up the pressured demands of the itinerant life of a virtuoso may have lulled them into a reassuring complacency. As Michael had said to Harold Schonberg, playing the Paganini concerto in front of an audience of thousands was "a lot of fun." And lest that subjective emotion be taken as little more than youthful bravura, this is how Mr. Schonberg's no less distinguished colleague at the *New York Times,* Olin Downes, appraised Michael's Carnegie Hall performance with Mitropoulos and the New York Philharmonic:

> Mr. Rabin appears to us to have simply everything. He is so completely the master of every technical problem that a passage of superlative difficulty is merely an excitement and a stimulus to him — an additional incentive to make music.
>
> It was Franz Liszt who remarked that youth is the time of virtuosity. Mr. Rabin, his virtuoso equipment being already such that it can be taken for granted, is at the stage and in the frame of mind to give not only brilliance but give a melodic beauty and romantic glow of a Paganini concerto, as he might not be in later and soberer years....
>
> All rejoiced in his achievement."[32]

Faced with a review like this, Jeanne and George may well have concluded that things were coming along very nicely indeed. And from that standpoint, it is not hard to extrapolate that they saw this fulsome praise as a validation of their approach to their son's career. This may help explain how Michael's parents, aglow in the happiness of his critical acclaim, set the tempo of his concertizing to come by abandoning prudence while simultaneously giving voice to it.

Olin Downes noted that Michael was very much at home playing the concertos of the composer-violinists of the nineteenth century. Here, his admirers were legion. "Did you hear the boy? That's it. That's the only way to play it!" Elman had exclaimed when he heard Michael's broadcast of the Wieniawski F Minor Concerto.³³ At fifteen years of age, Michael was supremely confident of his abilities, and his playing reflected this. His enormous natural talent had been skillfully molded by Galamian over the space of seven years into an iron-clad technique. There was simply nothing technically the boy could not do on the violin, and this astonishing fact was proudly brandished via conduits such as Paganini and Wieniawski on the great concert stages of North America.

Together with this confidence came the cockiness of youth, not an arrogance, but a refreshing sassiness imbuing his playing with an infectious liveliness that immediately transmitted itself to the listeners, forcing them to sit up, take note, and ultimately marvel. For Michael's violin playing represented far more than mere technical excellence, impressive as that was. It was prodigious technique combined with a unique sound: big, voluptuous, energetic, audacious, and distinct. When Michael played the violin, conversation ceased, heads turned, people stopped what they were doing to listen. What emanated from a succession of borrowed violins riveted attention. No less an authority than Schuyler Chapin, Commissioner of Cultural Affairs for New York City and for a time Jascha Heifetz's road manager, recalled that when a Rabin performance came over the radio, the playing held one captive.³⁴ The big technique, the rich timbre, the uncomplicated confidence of youth all coalesced, the whole greater than the sum of the parts and bearing the unique stamp of a blessed boy.

CHAPTER 6
AUSTRALIA:
TRIUMPH AND TROUBLE

*M*ichael made his second Columbia recording on March 5 and 18, 1952, this time accompanied by Artur Balsam at the piano. The repertoire of largely virtuoso showstoppers was once more designed to display his extraordinary technical command. A visual record of the two-day session remains courtesy of Columbia recording engineer Fred Plaut, who was also a keen amateur photographer. In some of the photos we see the boy wonder in high spirits, laughing, having a drink, munching a donut. In others he appears somber, intensely engaged in the music under the watchful eyes of Galamian, Jeanne, and Balsam.

Michael's burgeoning career, so vividly captured in Plaut's photographs, now meant that his days at Juilliard were coming to an end.* Among his peers were Van Cliburn, John Browning, Daniel Pollack, and Leontyne Price, but he had little if any contact with them, and no friendships formed. His main interaction with other students took place in the Juilliard Preparatory Orchestra. "Michael in his younger years really needed attention all the time," recalls Lewis Kaplan:

> In fact, it might even have been true of him in his twenties. So, whenever there was a break in the orchestra, there was Michael launching into a Paganini caprice, to the chagrin of the conductor. He was very imaginative in finding ways to draw attention to himself. [1]

---

* The Juilliard Preparatory School.

In the early 1950s, Michael and Lewis would also meet at Galamian's summer camp, and "the few minutes we would spend together were just fun," reminisces Kaplan. Like many of the children who attended Meadowmount in the early years, he retains a vivid memory of Michael eternally practicing under the vigilant gaze of Jeanne:

> Once in a while he would dash out when he saw me, and he was pretty well grabbed back by his mom and told to get back to work. It was clear she had taken control of him at a young age. Even then and later he would say, "My mother sees me as the career she always wanted." He knew that.[2]

The role models Michael were encouraged to emulate were all adults who had stellar careers in music. Nothing less was expected of him, too. Not surprisingly, references to past and future "'great successes" peppered his letters to Francescatti.

In April 1952, the friendship between master and acolyte culminated in a joint *Telephone Hour* performance of the first movement of Bach's Concerto for Two Violins. In preparation for their broadcast, Francescatti had written to his young friend:

> Dear Mike,
>   …It is a long time now we left New York and I start to yearn for my home. I am very happy we will play together — take the first violin of the Bach and we will adjust our bowings early April when I'll be back. I am sure you have wonderful success and you keep going on the high way [sic] to perfection. Our best greetings to your lovely family and affections for you.[3]

Partnering Francescatti on such a high-profile event was another singular accomplishment for Michael. It was also fun. The publicity photos reflect this, showing the two of them together as colleagues, violins in hands, smiling broadly as they look over the Bach score. Michael's admiration for Francescatti was by now starting to manifest beyond the praise he expressed in letters. "He took a lot from Francescatti," recalls Lewis Kaplan, "including the 'sort of swaying from the knees' which was exactly a replica of him."[4]

Two days after Michael turned sixteen, there was fresh evidence he was well set on the "highway to perfection." Hunter College announced that three violinists would perform in their forthcoming season — Heifetz, Milstein, and Michael Rabin. But first an Australian odyssey beckoned and there was some important business to take care of. At the top of the list was the need to find a violin of his own. Until then he had played on a succession of instruments borrowed for a concert or two from Rembert Wurlitzer, Emil Herrmann, or the estates of Huberman and Godowsky. With a four-month tour imminent, such an ad hoc arrangement was no longer tenable. Michael had recently spoken of his wishes in this regard, in the process revealing a lively sense of humor. "He has of course a fiddle of his own," noted an interviewer from the *Toronto Telegram*, "but not exactly what he wants. 'You see, a fiddle is something that costs less than $10,000,' [Michael] explained. 'After that it becomes a violin. I want a violin for Christmas.'"5

Given the pressure of an encroaching departure deadline, a feverish search ensued. Adding to the stress was the fact that a good violin cost a lot of money and spending many thousands of dollars with an eye on the clock was not an activity that came easily to a middle-class family with a tight monthly budget. Frustration within the Rabin family at their inability to locate a suitable instrument increased when the *New York Times* ran an article on April 20, 1952, lauding Fritz Kreisler for donating a Guarnerius del Gesù to the Library of Congress.6 In response, Bertine wrote the *Times* an indignant letter bemoaning the fact that so few good instruments were available. Placing one behind glass in a museum was a travesty. The letter was not published.7 Michael, however, was by now earning not inconsiderable sums from his concerts, and the anticipated revenue from his pending Australian tour made a purchase possible. Once again it was Rembert Wurlitzer who came to the rescue, with a violin purported to be by Guarnerius del Gesù circa 1724. In January Wurlitzer had sold the violin to a Joseph Rosenberg of Brooklyn, but in May the sale had been cancelled. The 1724 label was not considered original, and the violin had not been played in sixty years, but it was decidedly not a "fiddle," despite the $8,000 price tag. Four days before Michael left for Australia, the violin was his.8*

Michael's upcoming tour would test his endurance once more. To help him through it, his parents had approached Josef Seiger and asked if he could travel with Michael as accompanist, chaperone, and general factotum.9 But Seiger had to decline—he was locked into an exclusive contract with

---

* According to the records of William Moennig and Son, to whom Michael consigned the violin for sale seven years later, the instrument measured 35.3 cm. in body length with the area between the F-holes reinforced with a breast patch. Furthermore, there were four long strips of wood glued into the upper bouts and two long strips into the lower bouts, presumably because the back had been "thinned" previously. (Moennig never had the violin apart and their information was derived from drawings and the documentation supplied by Herrmann and Wurlitzer.)

Elman — so the Australian pianist Raymond Lambert was engaged instead. In preparation for Australia, Michael did not concertize in May, devoting his time to learning new repertoire and completing his final month of home schooling. In similar vein, his days at Juilliard were almost over and with them his exposure, limited as it was, to other children in Mr. Sontag's orchestra. Michael had now reached a watershed in his young, eventful life, and the vestiges of childhood were relinquished. It had been a truncated, watered-down youth to be sure, and he was still only in his mid-teens. But by the time he left La Guardia on June 11 for San Francisco, en route to Honolulu, Canton Island, Fiji, and Australia, the final impediments to a full-time career as violin virtuoso had been stripped away and his life given over to a blur of airports, airplanes, trains, stations, concert halls, and recording studios.

It was with a sense of keen anticipation that Michael arrived in Sydney with his mother on June 14, 1952. His hosts shared in the excitement of the occasion. Audiences and critics were curious to see and hear the youngster billed as the next Jascha Heifetz, and comparisons were already being made with a visit twenty years earlier of the other great American prodigy, Yehudi Menuhin, who had left such a memorable impression.[10] Yet by the time his tour ended on October 23, Michael could not wait to see the back of Australia. For in the intervening months he had confronted, what was for him, an entirely new phenomenon — a hostile press. It had taken a few impulsive and injudicious comments from a teenager to rouse the Fourth Estate to a jingoistic fury.

Michael's first impressions of Sydney were not positive, as he noted to Bertine five days before his first concert:

> Now that I've had 24 interviews and all the stuff that goes with it, I'm beginning to take a look around me. I'm not particularly in love with Australia. Sydney is a very quiet town. After 6 o'clock absolutely nothing is open.... And I've been told that Sydney is the brightest town in Australia. But I'm pretty sure that when I start my concerts (June 25) I'll be plenty occupied.[11]

Despite his initial disappointment at the quietness of Australian urban life, the musical part of the tour started well enough. Michael trotted out his trusty war-horse, the Paganini D Major Concerto that had never yet failed to win over an audience. The *Daily Mirror, Sydney Sun,* and *Sunday Telegraph* were all suitably impressed, with quotes that mirrored their American counterparts: "Sydney this week has applauded the extraordinary violin playing of Michael Rabin. It seems almost impossible that at age 16 anyone could have achieved such perfection in so little time."[12] Familiar-sounding words boded well for the months ahead, but embedded among all the praise was an early warning sign of the churlish provincialism that lay in wait. "He left us in no doubt whatever that he could fiddle all the bugs off a sweet potato vine," whined the critic of the *Sydney Morning Herald.* "But even at that he could not make the work sound any less of a bore."[13]

There followed a series of interviews that skimmed over Michael's musical ability, choosing to focus rather on his youth and highlighting the impetuosity and immaturity of a sixteen-year-old boy. This is how the *Adelaide Mail* perceived him:

> A handsome, dark-eyed youth hailed in America as the greatest talent since Heifetz, Michael interviewed us with unshakeable aplomb and continuous chewing of gum.
>
> "An American custom" he explained.
>
> …Michael himself informed us he never suffered from nervousness, stage fright or air sickness. "And actually" he said, shifting his chewy, "I'm most interested in people. You might say I'm a student of people.
>
> "Right now, my main ambition is to shake one of your Aborigines by the hand."
>
> He chewed this over, and then added in some alarm… "I don't know.
>
> "Are they the kind of people that might pick up one of those boomerangs and bong you on the head with it?" The thought almost gave pause to his chewing.[14]

The tone of an article in the *Sydney Bulletin,* dated July 2, was marginally more flattering:

> Michael Rabin, the 16-year-old prodigy from New York who plays the violin so beautifully is an enfant terrible in the drawing room. At the reception given for him by the Sydney Symphony Ladies Committee, one really hesitated to sit down for fear he had put a tack on the chair. Wearing a huge camellia bud in his buttonhole, he flitted about, and although rather large to flit — he did have some Pucklike quality about him — Puck and Billy Bunter if you can imagine it. He seems quite without timidity, nervousness or even self-consciousness. He also seems, however, to be without guile, ill will or gloom, which makes him quite likeable.[15]

It was left to his hosts, the Australian Broadcasting Corporation, to give a more generous interpretation of his obvious high spirits. Referring to him as

"The Genius Violinist of Tomorrow," lifting Mitropoulos's generous praise, the ABC noted:

> Some of the advanced publicity from the United States gave the impression that he was typical of many Australian conceptions of American teenagers: brash, opinionated and inclined to be overbearing.
>
> Not once did he give that impression. True, he compared Australian and American oysters to the disadvantage of the former, but he did so not as a chauvinist, but as one who knew a good oyster. When he spoke of oranges his findings were the reverse, backed by good sound reasoning.
>
> "Ask me about my forefathers" he begged when I used the word "ancestor."
>
> When I obliged he exclaimed in glee, "But I haven't got four fathers, I've only got one!"[16]

Away from the character sketches, the reviews for Michael's recitals turned equivocal. The music critic for the ABC weekly noted that:

> this was the most astonishing violin playing I've ever heard. Never at any time was I moved. Perhaps this was the fault of the music? But for complete command of technical resources, the instrument combined with ease and fluency of execution, I have not heard playing to surpass it. Perhaps Heifetz and Menuhin played like this when they were boys. I don't know. But surely Rabin, even now at his age, must be regarded as one of the greatest players of the instrument in living memory. How he will develop musically time will disclose.[17]

To another reviewer, however, the verdict was less charitable:

> Young Rabin is not, for all his technique and virtuostic attributes, the quality of violinist music lovers of 1932 heard when Menuhin, a year younger than Rabin, gave those magnificent performances of Elgar's concerto. I hope Rabin will again tour Australia, perhaps in eight or ten years when he could easily have developed into the Heifetz he now so much admires.[18]

The general theme that Michael possessed a masterful technique but lacked musical depth had taken hold early in Australia.

The equivocation continued. Two reviews in the Australian music journal the *Canon* expressed divergent opinions. The first grappled with the old problem of having to explain the origins of genius within the limited confines of language and knowledge. "When rational reasoning does not explain, when intelligent argument produces neither solution nor compromise, we reach a point where we ... just have to bow before nature and accept facts."[19] It was, however, the second review that left Michael reeling:

> What does the virtuoso find when the technical problems have been overcome? After the tricks and techniques are mastered, what then? This is the question raised by the playing of Master Rabin. He gave four programmes of orthodox virtuoso standard, but of the most unorthodox virtuosity, neither faltering at mechanical difficulties nor rising to them, but merely fiddling on as if they were not there. But Brahms sounded like Cesar Franck, and Bach (almost) like Chopin/Milstein. Beyond the solution of technical problems there was nothing, not even the raised hand of another problem — just vacuity. Surely this is not the real solution, this emptiness: it was not, at any rate, with the sixteen-year old Menuhin, whose prodigiousness is supposed to have been eclipsed by Rabin.
>
> Already it seems that this youngster has started to become bored with his own facility, finding nothing further to do with the violin. He plays the Chopin/Milstein with a tendency to relish and exaggerate the absurd double-stoppings and lascivious slidings, and he treats the Concerto of Tchaikovsky (at the Rite of Spring concert) with contemptuous nonchalance, compressing note values, telescoping phrases, abbreviating rests, accelerating and drawing back — all with the most superb competence. No, this is not a solution of problems: it is not even essentially musical, merely decorative.[20]

Michael had never received such damning criticism before. To a young man whose professional life thus far had been defined by a succession of superlatives, the shock must have been great. And the humiliation did not end there. Even his choice of repertoire was running afoul of some critics: "the [Glazunov] concerto, despite its pretty finale, says little that had not been said before. The gentleman in the southern gallery who decided to read the newspaper had our sympathy, if not our approval."[21]

Praise was still forthcoming from other sources, but with little more than a month of his tour completed, Michael had run into stormy waters, unanticipated and beyond his capacity and that of his mother to fully comprehend. After taking it on the chin for four difficult weeks, Michael answered back in a way that made a difficult situation immeasurably worse — he took a leaf out of *The Devil's Dictionary:*

> There is a land of pure delight,
> Beyond the Jordan's flood,
> Where saints, apparelled all in white,
> Fling back the critics mud.

> And as he legs it through the skies,
> His pelt a sable blue,
> He sorrows sore to recognise
> The missiles that he threw. [22]

On July 14, an irritable Michael left Sydney and flew into Melbourne, where he met the press. Displaying his annoyance proved disastrous and showed that he had completely misunderstood the character of those who had criticized him thus far. The Australian media were feisty. Interspersed among the knowledgeable were the parochial and the chauvinistic. They loved controversy and relished a fight. Their easy access to the general public gave them power and they were not shy to use it. Arrayed against them was a sixteen-year-old boy, far from home, out of his depth socially and culturally. The first signs of trouble appeared the following day in the *Adelaide Advertiser* under the title "Young U.S. Violinist is Not Impressed":

> "Australians are just so smug. They think they know everything, but they don't," said visiting child prodigy, sixteen-year-old violinist Michael Rabin…. "Americans are more unassuming, although they know a lot more," he added. "And it's just hilarious the way Australians don't know a thing about music. They are so ignorant they applaud in the middle of Beethoven and they just don't know whether it's the middle or the end."
>
> Young Master Rabin said he brought a $25,000 violin with him. "It's a Guarnerius del Gesu. I don't suppose any of you guys can spell that? No? That's the trouble with you Australian reporters. You can't spell. Americans can." He's got no time for music critics either. "Most of them don't know a thing about it," he said. "I figure I know my own business better than any critics. When I am playing badly they say I'm good and if I'm good, they

say I'm bad." He's already played to concert audiences in Sydney and Brisbane and was not impressed.

He is a keen baseball fan, but will not go to see matches here. "What's the use?" he asked scornfully. When told the Brooklyn Dodgers would visit Australia he was more interested, but thought it was funny that any of our teams might have a hope of beating them. He said this about hotels. "Hotel life is pretty awful anyway, but your hotels are the worst of all. Especially the one I was in at Sydney. The elevator even stopped between floors."[23]

Did Michael really say all these things to the national press? He undoubtedly voiced some criticisms, letting off steam at what he perceived was his unfair treatment to date by certain sections of the media. But it no longer mattered whether the report contained facts, misperceptions, exaggerations, or fiction. Smelling blood, the journalists gleefully turned on him. A day later, their riposte appeared and was distributed nationally:

Young Master Rabin has come from America to entertain us with his playing of the violin.... Although of course we are paying him through the ABC for his work, we can still be grateful that he is giving our money's worth and much more, musically. Much may be forgiven one who can play like Master Rabin. Perhaps his parents did not believe in corporal punishment. Whether and for how long they retain that belief is something on which we can only speculate, chuckling. But whatever the facts are which have produced the boy as he is now, there can be no doubt that Master Rabin is a believer in the practice of free speech....

We are glad to know that Master Rabin can laugh, even if it is only at other people. That's a start and it may be that when the years have mellowed him, he will be able to laugh at himself....

The boy is a keen baseball fan but scorns our ball games. He thinks it very funny that any of our teams might have a chance of beating the Brooklyn Dodgers when they visit Australia. Possibly he's right. But I suppose its America's national game and not ours. But both countries share a love of tennis and Master Rabin possibly knows that we poor Australians haven't done so poorly in open competition in that sport. Doesn't an Australian Frank Sedgman, at the moment, hold the American Singles title? And in cricket we can hold our own. We may have hotel lifts which, like Master Rabin, don't know when to stop. But in these stern times poor untutored savages must be grateful to Master Rabin for giving us another chance for laughing, even if it's a laugh at ourselves. And he really can play the violin, even if he's very juvenile in some ways.[24]

These articles were only the start of the furor. The press photographers added their insults too. On July 16, the *Argus* published an uncomplimentary picture of Michael eating, caught with his tongue out of his mouth, and ran the caption, "Michael Does Not Like This." The article went on to state that "Michael Rabin, 16-year-old violinist (all the way from New York) yesterday summed up Australians in a word. The word is SMUG*!!*"[25] The *Sydney Sun*, under the heading, "We Do Get on Michael's G String," embellished what the naive youngster was supposed to have said. "Smug" became "darn smug" and new insults were added to his list of purported earlier gaffes. "He summed up our hotels in one word — ham. Michael claims that he hasn't seen any pretty girls since he arrived in Australia.... Asked, 'What made you take up the violin at the age of 8?' Michael replied, 'What made you be a newspaper man?'"[26]

It says much for the fragile nature of the Australian psyche at the time that the remarks of a sixteen-year-old boy could have produced such a national outpouring of anger. In one snarling mass, the press rose to the defense of the motherland. Michael's hosts, the ABC, were appalled. Readers sent letters to the editor berating Michael. Attendance for his concerts dropped. "The unfortunate prelude to Michael Rabin's season here," noted the *Australian Musical News,* "brought him much hostility [and] certainly played havoc with his solo recital audiences."[27]

As controversy engulfed Michael's tour, one or two voices rallied weakly to his side. "I've got a horrible suspicion Master Rabin could be right," opined one defender.[28] However, the most mature view of the whole kerfuffle, and the one that came closest to appreciating what had occurred, was expressed by the Melbourne critic John Sinclair. "Personally, I've considerable sympathy for Master Rabin over the incident of that press interview. Here was a 16-year-old boy answering explosive questions — and not a boy with a normal background, but one who had lived the strained and highly unnatural life of a child prodigy."[29]

Notwithstanding these supportive comments, Michael's tour was in trouble. Consequently, after a series of hurried crisis meetings, the ABC moved quickly to settle the nation's hurt pride. Michael was instructed to issue a series of public apologies. Faced with this difficult situation, he tried squirming his way out with an ingenious revisionist interpretation of what had occurred. He told the *Australian Musical News:*

> I was sitting at a table taking coffee and sandwiches while about 16 newspaper people fired questions. Just as the lady passed me the sandwiches and asked what I should like, someone asked me, "What do you think of our hotels?" To the lady with the sandwiches, I replied, "Ham," and it was reported that I had given that reply on hotels. Questions came thick and fast. "What do you think of Australians?" I said they appeared reserved. At that someone snapped, "You wouldn't say we are smug would you?" and it was reported that I said Australians are smug. At the same time as another asked, "What is your opinion of our trams?" someone from the other side of the group asked, "What about our critics?" To the inquiry on trams I replied hilarious and was reported as saying the critics are hilarious. I am a guest in your country and my business here is a series of 46 recitals. As young as I am, I fully realize that the most important thing is to have 46 successful concerts, both musically and financially. Had I said the things in the way reported, I really don't see how a success could be made, for many people would feel insulted by comments such as these coming from a visitor, and stay right away from my recitals.[30]

The baying critics were buying none of it. Michael's convoluted explanation had shifted the blame onto them. Meanwhile public opinion remained inflamed. According to the *Sydney Sun,* hundreds of people had complained to a Melbourne newspaper about the "spoiled little boy and a very ill-bred young man." Michael would have to eat more humble pie. A second, more explicit apology was offered up:

> I would like to express my deepest apologies for any rudeness that may have occurred at the press interviews yesterday. I was rather tired and cranky when I arrived in Melbourne and I really did not have a chance to collect my thoughts before I spoke to them [*sic*] at the meeting. I must say that people have been very wonderful to me and I think it is a wonderful experience to be able to play for the audiences here. They are really very good ones. I hope we can be friends and not have any bad feelings. I'm very glad I've been able to stop in Melbourne on my tour of Australia and it is

indeed a very beautiful city. I hope I shall be able to give some people pleasure with my music.

This time the hacks were partially mollified — "Michael in Tune Again" ran the *Sun*'s headline.[31] But many in the media would not forget what they saw as a slur on their country. In the three remaining months of Michael's tour, they would never let him out their sights and, on more than one occasion, gleefully slipped the knife into their chastened and wounded victim.

Michael's tour had started disastrously. How had such a situation come about? Unquestionably, he had said some foolish things to the press, failing to recognize that diplomacy was called for. He was a guest in a foreign land and social niceties demanded a certain decorum and respect for his hosts, which translated into holding his tongue and voicing his displeasure in private. What befell Michael in Australia signaled a lapse in judgment. But in mitigation, he was barely sixteen years old and prey to all the impetuosity and impulsivity of adolescence. Which begs a further question: where was Jeanne all the while? For eight years she had tightly controlled her son and his career, until that one day in Melbourne when he suddenly slipped through her hitherto impervious net, plunging his tour into crisis. According to Bertine, Jeanne responded to the media attacks by privately lambasting Michael long and hard for his behavior. Even after their return from Australia, her mother's criticism did not abate.[32]

To make matters worse, the media now turned their attention to Jeanne with an eye on parody. What emerged were a malicious series of embarrassing family portraits. "Mrs. Jeanne Rabin … told us this week that we must never, never refer to her son as a prodigy," noted one reporter. "'Michael doesn't like it and I don't like it.' Mrs. Rabin said prodigy sounds like a flash in the pan, something that's only going to last a short while. 'Besides, I've always tried to keep Michael as normal as possible.'" Jeanne was described as a short, rotund woman whose thin lips had a carefully defined cupid's bow and whose eyes were hidden by gold-studded glasses with bright blue rims. When asked whether she too had been a prodigy, she was reported as saying:

> I don't know what I was. I've played the piano ever since I could remember. I could play everything by the time I was four.
>
> I played everything my sister had learned by ear. I had my first piano lesson when I was five, but it wasn't until I was in my teens that I studied.
>
> I married soon afterwards. That's the usual thing that happens to a talented woman.

This unflattering introduction in the *Sydney Sunday Sun* was, however, but the preamble to a contrived character assassination of both mother and son.

"Michael's got such a delicious sense of humor." Jeanne was quoted as saying. "He is always teasing and fooling. He'll do all sorts of pranks if you'll let him. He can think up plenty of good ones."

What, we asked, were some of the good ones.

Mrs. Rabin said. "I really can't think of any. You think of some of your boyhood pranks. I'll bet Michael's been up to them."

We told Mrs. Rabin we had heard that at a Sydney press conference Michael had grabbed photographer's flash bulbs and pushed them down the front of women's dresses.

"That sounds like Michael alright," said Mrs. Rabin. "Such a wonderful boy. Always ready for a joke.

"Its nothing for him to put a big spoonful of salt in the sugar basin.

"I don't try to curb his sense of humour because he's always had to work much harder than other children."33

An extraordinary interview that appeared in *Woman* magazine in early August continued this trend:

When asked about music Michael responded, "Well, I don't know how I feel. I don't feel nervous at concerts — there is really nothing to be nervous about…. But I do think when I am standing up on the platform playing away … what a good target I am for a gun."

"There you are," says Mrs. Rabin. "He's always joking. It would serve him right if you printed that and made him stop being funny."

Michael said that when he knew he would be coming to Australia he had read a few books about the country.

"Then I figured, why bother reading about the country when I'll be there anyway, so I gave the books away." He turned to his mother.

"Mom, for goodness sake, take off your hat. You never look relaxed when you're wearing a hat."

Mrs. Rabin removed it.

Asked if Michael was critical of her appearance she said, "Michael is critical, period."

Said Michael, "I don't like my mother to go out looking cheap. She's got to look good. Now, that suit she is wearing. I hate that. It's comparable with a 1929 Ford model."

"It's just a suit I have for wearing around the house," interrupted Mrs. Rabin.

Michael went on, "Now see that grey coat hanging behind the door? My mother's in love with that coat, but I simply despise it. She says it's practical. I suppose that's why we have a grey car at home."

At this stage Mrs. Rabin suggested Michael went off to practice. As he was going he said, "My mother can wear any colour she likes, but not red. My main problem here in Australia is going to be to look after my mother and see that she doesn't get into trouble. In the plane it was easy because she was asleep all the time."

"Practice Michael," said mother. Michael went, but came back a few moments later to warn his mother that her clock was 15 minutes fast.[34]

Publishing the article was clearly designed to hurt the Rabins. The usual tone of respect and admiration that attached itself to interviews with visiting virtuosos was turned on its head, and instead what emerged was a cruel exposé of a tense relationship between a mother and her adolescent son, under siege from a hostile press and trapped in a grueling succession of concerts. There were no attempts to dilute the unflattering images by introducing one of the many positive aspects of Michael the musician, attributes that the American, Canadian, and Cuban press had had little difficulty seeing and writing about. The rawness of the verbatim quotes, the lies (Michael had never pushed flashbulbs down women's dresses), the uncomplimentary physical descriptions — it was clear old scores were still being settled. And in focusing on Jeanne as well, the press had found an irresistible target that offered rich material for caricature. These interviews, with their shameless mockery of an awkward youngster and his blunderbuss mother, temporarily derailed the emotional equilibrium of Michael's tour.

What makes these Australian interviews so striking is that the tone and content are the very antithesis of what American journalists were saying. The same month these character-damning pieces appeared in Australia, an article entitled "The Making of a Violinist" appeared in the United States. In the interview, Michael spoke of his introduction to the violin, his daily practice routine, his attention to correcting faults in his bow arm by practicing in front of a mirror, and his gratitude for having musical parents supervise his practice routine. The article concluded with Jeanne giving her thoughts on musicality:

"I believe that genuine musicianship is definitely a matter of inborn feeling. You can teach a youngster what to do — you can't teach him what to feel." Even George, so often silent, had his say: "I disagree that mere increase in age makes for artistry. Look at Mozart and Mendelssohn." The article was accompanied by a picture of the Rabin family, smiling, making music. There was no sign of rudeness or disrespect from Michael. He came across as a thoughtful young man, happy within his family and meticulous in his work habits.[35] Comparing this article with the Australian portrait of the artist as a young man, it seems barely credible that the subject was the same individual.

The ABC tried to counteract the negative publicity with a series of charity events. Michael was photographed signing Braille programs for three blind boys. A picture appeared of Michael playing table tennis with a messenger boy. Michael gave a concert for 400 psychiatric patients in an asylum and another to raise money for orphan children in Israel. The press noted these with less enthusiasm than they paid to Michael's verbal gaffes, but these good deeds helped restore some calm to his tour. By September Michael was starting to receive the kind of praise he had garnered back home. On the road, he met up with Paul Badura-Skoda and they played sonatas. The pianist was having his own difficulties with the Australian critics, albeit of a less personal nature. "In works demanding continuous energy and strong development of climax," ran one of his reviews, "his lack of technique led to senseless scrambling, ugly tone and a plentiful supply of wrong notes."[36] Whether the two artists commiserated with one another is not known.

In a letter to Bertine, Michael confided that he was not enjoying himself:

> You have no reason to envy me just because I'm in Australia. Believe me, you can't imagine how dull it is, and how anxious I am to get back home. But it won't be for 8 weeks yet. Next week I go to Canberra and then to Brisbane. This week I am playing the Prokofieff Concerto No. 2 (your favorite) with the Melbourne Symphony, instead of the Mozart. It will be a wonderful experience. So far I've done 28 concerts and have 19 more to do, but this tour is gradually coming to an end.[37]

The pace of his concertizing was also starting to tell. Critics noticed his gathering fatigue. "Was Rabin Tired?" asked one reviewer, who stated that "it is not possible for a 16-year-old boy to give four good recitals in one week" and that "tiredness undermined Master Rabin's shortcomings."[38] He also came down with a bad cold in Adelaide and had to miss a reception in his honor. When asked a question about a "spent youth," he admitted that his career was "a steady upward grind, and to reach the top you must make sacrifices."[39]

Michael's letters home were not a litany of complaints, despite his many trials, responsibilities, and obligations. What shines through are his resilience, humor, boyish high spirits, and love of family and teacher. Writing to Bertine, he observed:

> According to Daddy's letters, you and he have been having a mar-velous summer. I bet you don't miss me at all. I think it's wonderful that you have learned to type so well. Perhaps if I pay you a high enough salary, you will be my secretary. In that case, I would have a very beautiful secretary with all the usual feminine equipment. Savvy??…
>
> How is Mr. Galamian? I wrote him 7 letters but only got one reply 3 weeks ago. Give him my love and tell him that I am really working. Even now, my program for the Telephone Hour on Nov. 10 is really in tiptop shape. Since it will be my first performance back in New York it's *got* to be as perfect as possible. So even at this early date I'm working hard at it.[40]

As Michael's tour entered the home stretch, winter in the southern hemi-sphere gave way to spring. With warmer weather, friendlier audiences, and a few weeks left before departing home, Michael wrote again to Bertine in high spirits:

> Dear Bert,
>
> Here we are in Brisbane and really getting some hot weather and plenty of sunshine. The people of this city match the weather, because they are most kind and friendly. The attitude of the people is different in each state of this country, as the people differ in the states of our country. In this state the audiences are very warm — last night I played the Glazounoff with the Brisbane Symphony Orch., and had seven recalls, but I must admit that I *did* play unusually well. Now with 10 concerts to go, returning to New York seems more of a reality than it did in July. Then it seemed that I would never get home, but time never stops. In about 5½ weeks I'll be gliding in for a landing at LaGuardia. Yippee!!

The letter also provides a window into the mind of a child prodigy, high-lighting the juxtaposition of precocious ability and childlike innocence. The Michael who could entrance an audience with his musical prowess was the same boy whose great passion was model airplanes and who would exclaim "whoop" when happy. Continued Michael in his letter from Brisbane:

> QANTAS = Queensland and Northern Territory Air Service. That is a very big Australian and English Airline. In all my interviews in this country, I always mentioned that I was crazy about model aircraft. Well, Bert, they presented me with a tremendous model of a Boeing Constellation, in return for a few publicity shots.... It's a peach....
>
> Incidentally Bert, that Webster automatic record player that I have, is yours, because you are so sweet and I love you. It's in one of the closets in my room. Look around for it. I hope you enjoy it. I'll buy you a stack of records when I get home.
>
> With love to you, the most beautiful and wonderful sister I could want,
>
> Mike.[41]

Michael's bright spirits and enthusiastic endorsement of the Brisbane audiences could not disguise the fact that his tour had been a very difficult one. The press trouble that had dogged his first month in Australia had left a pall, and while the second half of his visit had been more successful, it had not been enough to leave him with a positive view of the land and its peoples. On October 24, Michael and Jeanne left Sydney for Hawaii en route home. Only now, with his ordeal finally over, did he feel relaxed enough to let his sister know his true feelings:

> We've only been in Honolulu for 10 hours, but we've already had a good look around, and believe me, Bert, it's paradise. The weather is hot and balmy and there really is a romantic atmosphere about the place. But after Australia, anything is better....
> The last week in Sydney was so awful for us, that if [some cousins of a New York acquaintance] hadn't been so wonderful to us, we would honestly have gone crazy. I don't think I was ever as happy as I was yesterday morning when I saw the Australian coast slipping away in the background. As you can see from the mileage on the top of this letter, we are just a bit more than half way home. But in 6 days, 2 hours and 14 minutes I will be home. I can't believe it.[42]

CHAPTER 7
HOLLYWOOD

When Michael returned from Australia on October 31, he had been away from home for almost five months. He had barely enough time to recover from the flight and fifteen-hour time difference before he appeared on another *Telephone Hour* program, playing Sarasate's *Zigeunerweisen*, Chopin's Nocturne in C-sharp Minor (arranged by Milstein), and *La vida breve* by de Falla (arranged by Kreisler). The Bell publicity mentioned that Michael's appearance marked his first performance since his return from a highly successful tour in Australia. It was fortunate that Australia was a long way away. News of the hostile critics and Michael's unhappiness Down Under did not make it into the American press. The bad times were glossed over, and in all subsequent promotional material, the tour was billed as a triumph.

Before leaving in the new year on his tour of the Midwest and West Coast, Michael returned to the Columbia recording studios on 30th Street in New York City. He was joined by the Columbia Symphony Orchestra conducted by Donald Voorhees, and on January 29, 1953, they recorded Sarasate's *Zigeunerweisen* and the "Perpetuum Mobiles" of Paganini and Nováček. Six days later, mother and son began touring, leaving behind George and Bertine. In their teenage years, the siblings were united by a new bond, one of mutual support in managing a difficult relationship with their overpowering mother. "I hope you are having some fun," Michael scribbled en route to St. Louis. "Especially since mother's not around. Lucky you."[1] Another card followed from Iowa City, where by chance Michael had met up with his teacher:

> Dear Bert,
>   The trip so far has been perfect, and even though everything and everybody is wonderful, I'll be looking forward to getting home. But that's not until March 13. Mr. Galamian told me to send you his love and he told me that you are very beautiful. How right he is![2]

The occasional cryptic reference to Jeanne here and there represented ongoing rumblings of insurrection from Michael, although the kind of openly expressed hostility recorded with such schadenfreude by his Australian detractors had not yet manifested back in America. The pressures inherent in his tour Down Under had brought these tensions to the surface. Now, with the restoration of a more familiar routine on home soil and the diluting presence of Bertine, George, and beloved cat Kiki, a little space was inserted between Michael and Jeanne. An uneasy truce settled over family life.

Michael made his West Coast debut in February, playing the Tchaikowsky Concerto with the Los Angeles Philharmonic and Alfred Wallenstein. When he had last played this work, he had attracted the opprobrium of the Australian press. It is unlikely that in a few short months Michael would have significantly revised his interpretation, and yet in Los Angeles, his playing aroused nothing but admiration. Where the Australian critics had heard "compressed notes, telescoped phrases, abbreviated rests" and witnessed "contemptuous nonchalance,"[3] to American ears, such as those of the *Los Angeles Times* music critic, Michael was "an instinctive musician … endowed with taste far beyond his years. All the invitations to excess that the Tchaikowsky Concerto contains were artfully evaded. It was brilliant, but brilliance was not the primary aim; it had sentiment but it never lapsed into sentimentality."[4]

Michael loved California. The warm weather and more relaxed pace of life appealed to him, but he could not linger. A series of concerts awaited him in the Midwest as he slowly wended his way back home for an important recital at Hunter College. On the evening of March 22, 1953, accompanied by David Garvey, he gave the tenth and final recital in a series that had seen Jascha Heifetz and Nathan Milstein precede him. Michael's program comprised works that had become standards in his repertoire: Handel's Sonata No. 6, the adagio and fugue from the G Minor Sonata of Bach, Brahms's D Minor Sonata, Vieuxtemps's Concerto, No. 5, and Ravel's *Tzigane*.

The New York critics, like their Los Angeles counterparts, were impressed. "Mr. Rabin has arrived," signaled a reviewer from the *New York Tribune*. In a succession of superlatives, Michael's technique, interpretation, and poise were praised. "By instinct, by training the violinist is everywhere suited to his calling. And his present trumpets well his future."[5] Noel Straus writing in *The New York Times* was no less impressed, and noted that "Mr. Rabin had but to play the opening Adagio of his first offering, Handel's Sonata in E major, to make one aware that here was a performer of more than ordinary sensitivity and imagination."[6]

Michael, at the top of his form, took the same program to Chicago for his March 31 recital, where the impression his playing created was overwhelming. "Hear Rabin and Know the Gods Have Not Forgotten the Violin," read Claudia Cassidy's headline. She continued:

> I sometimes wonder if up on Olympus the gods ever sit around with their after-dinner nectar and perhaps a reminiscent cigar, and look down benignly on the world of music. If so, I think that not so long ago they might have said, "Let's see. It's been a long time since we sent down a really big talent for the violin ... well, let's see what we can do." Fanciful? No doubt. But give me a more logical explanation for Michael Rabin, who played his Chicago debut recital last night in Orchestral Hall.[7]

Praise of this magnitude was too good to be left gathering dust in a newspaper's archives. Michael's management lifted Ms. Cassidy's words verbatim and, for the next decade, used them whenever and wherever the opportunity presented.

Michael efficiently dispatched his commitments for the first half of April, including a performance for the National Federation of Music Clubs, which four years earlier had awarded him a scholarship. The trustees of the federation must have noted with satisfaction that young Rabin's progress in the intervening years had more than vindicated their belief in him. Given all his accomplishments, it was astonishing that his age still overlapped with those of the children in the audience.

It was also a sign of Michael's peripatetic existence that one week would find him in the company of children and another cavorting with film stars. By April 19, Michael was back in Los Angeles buoyed by what awaited him — seventeen days on the MGM set in Hollywood to record the soundtrack for the movie *Rhapsody*. The film was based loosely on Henry Handel

Richardson's novel, *Maurice Guest*. Produced by Charles Weingarten and directed by Charles Vidor, it starred Elizabeth Taylor, Vittorio Gassman, John Ericson, and Louis Calhern. A succinct description of the plot ran as follows:

> Romance of poor-little-rich-girl and violinist who dedicates his life to music…. Set principally in Zurich, Switzerland, the film is a conflicting mixture of fine music and shallow soap opera. Elizabeth Taylor, continental playgirl, falls in love with poor but talented musician Vittorio Gassman. His career is almost ruined because he neglects his violin for Taylor, but he recovers in time to become the toast of Europe. On the rebound, Taylor marries aspiring pianist John Ericson, turns him away from music. When she later learns there is still a chance for life with Gassman, she helps Ericson back to his former genius, planning then to divorce him. Instead she finds he is the one she really loves.[8]

Michael's job was to record a series of well-known violin works with the MGM studio orchestra conducted by Johnny Green, who together with Bronislau Kaper was a codirector of the film's music. The repertoire was familiar to him and included modified versions of the Paganini D Major, Tchaikowsky, and Mendelssohn violin concertos; Saint-Saëns's Rondo Capriccioso; Sarasate's *Zigeunerweisen*; Brahms's D Minor Sonata; and Debussy's "La plus que lente." Claudio Arrau performed the piano parts. Fun as it was to be on set, Michael saw through the hoopla attached to Tinseltown and his head was turned by none of it:

> The MGM lot is really something. You see movie stars walking around and they look just like ordinary people. However, I personally think they look much better on the screen when they're all painted up. My God, you should see Elizabeth Taylor — is she an idiot. She goes around in a tremendous *pink* Rolls Royce and has two big British flags attached to the car. Naturally she has *two* white French poodles with her, and smokes cigarettes from a $1,500 gold mouthpiece which is about 15 inches long. At the studios they say she's a brat and is impossible to work with and is terribly conceited. How common she makes herself look….
>
> However, aside from the studios, I'd much rather live out here than in New York…. I'm getting to like New York less and less all the time.
>
>   I've already done several recordings for the sound track and so far it's all been very good. Today, we're going to record the

"Michael, with love, John Barbirolli," New York Philharmonic Orchestra's Christmas party, 1937.

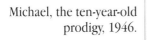

chael and Bertine, 1938.

Michael, the ten-year-old prodigy, 1946.

, age seven, c. 1931.

Clara Weiller (nee Rabinowitz).

From left to right: Bertine, George, Sarah, and Michael, c. 1945.

From left to right: Jeanne, Bertine, George, and Michael, 1936.

From left to right: Jay and Jeanne with her parents, Bertha and Michael Joseph, c. 1928.

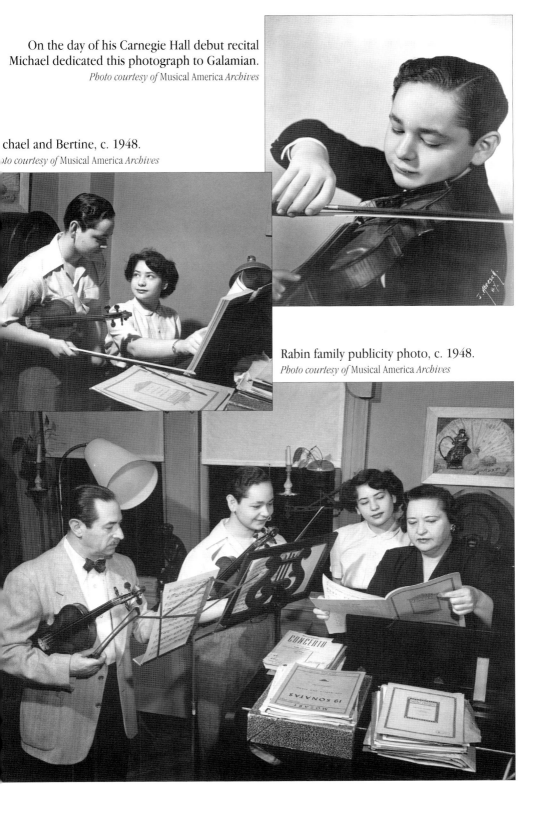

On the day of his Carnegie Hall debut recital
Michael dedicated this photograph to Galamian.
Photo courtesy of Musical America *Archives*

chael and Bertine, c. 1948.
oto courtesy of Musical America *Archives*

Rabin family publicity photo, c. 1948.
Photo courtesy of Musical America *Archives*

"Lilacs," the house rented by the Rabins during the summer at Meadowmount.

Michael flanked by Dimitri Mitropoulos (left) and George at his debut with the New York Philharmonic Orchestra, 1951.

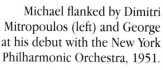

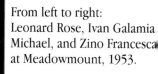

From left to right: Leonard Rose, Ivan Galamia Michael, and Zino Francesca at Meadowmount, 1953.

om left to right: Arthur Rodzinski, Michael, and
an Galamian, 1949.

anne with Arturo Toscanini on tour with the
ew York Philharmonic Orchestra, 1930.

From left to right: Michael, Ivan Galamian,
and Josef Szigeti at Meadowmount, 1949.

From left to right:
George, Bertine,
and Michael,
c. 1954.

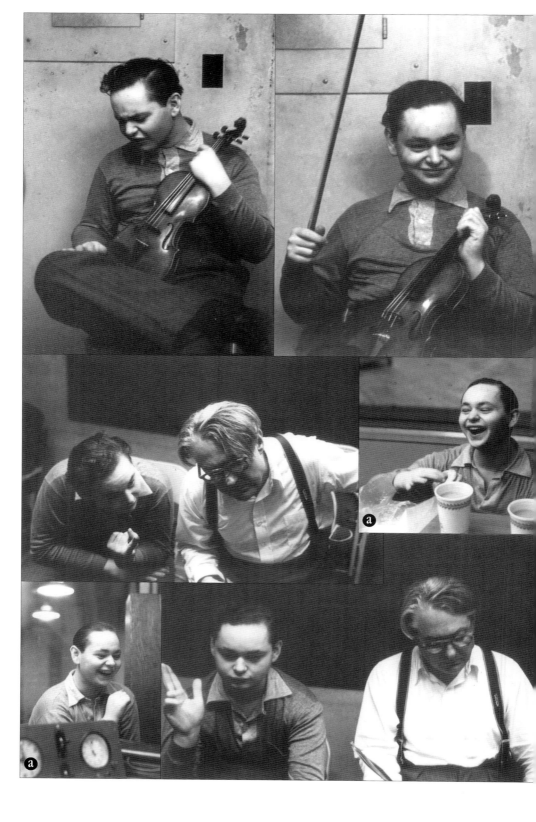

Michael in the Columbia Records 30th Street
Studio in 1950 (*a*), 1952, and 1953: with
(facing page) Donald Voorhees; (top, right)
Artur Balsam (on the left) and Ivan Galamian;
and (left) Ivan Galamian. *Photos from Frederick Plaut
(The Frederick and Rose Plaut Archives, Yale University
Music Library)*

Michael and Jeanne Rabin off to Australia, June 1952. *Photo courtesy of* Musical America *Archives*

Michael in a promotional photograph for *The Telephone Hour*, Cincinnati, 1953.

Arthur Judson and Michael. *Photo courtesy of* Musical America *Archives*

Playbill for Michael's Carnegie Hall debut, November 24, 1950.

Tchaikowsky concerto, and on Thursday, Danny Kaye is coming
to watch and listen to me record. I bet we will have fun....
    There's nothing else of interest to tell you, so I'd better sign
off.9

However, it was clear from a series of photographs, both formal and spontaneous, that the letter's phlegmatic ending was somewhat contrived. MGM
publicity shots show Michael with the studio orchestra and Michael accompanied by Johnny Green on the piano. The caption to one photo read:
"PLENTY OF TALENT HERE... That's beautiful film star Esther Williams looking
over the $30,000 violin of Michael Rabin and also congratulating him on his
17th birthday." Williams did indeed look beautiful, while Michael appeared
very dapper in a double-breasted suit with silk tie and matching pocket hand-
kerchief. The value of the violin, however, had been inflated to almost four
times the purchase price. There were clearly some aspects of Hollywood
hyperbole that Michael could neither control nor avoid.
    Away from the movie set, Michael and Jeanne traveled around with the
Arrau family. Michael had brought his box camera and the black-and-white
snaps captured, as they did in Westport over previous summers, the select
social circles he was moving in. There were pictures of Michael with Arrau,
Arrau with his family, Jeanne with Piatigorsky, the Szigetis, Johnny Green,
"Bronie" Kaper, Esther Williams, and Bill Judd with Claudio Arrau, among
others. The weather was balmy, the smiles were broad, and the sessions were
going well. The day Michael finished his recordings, he turned seventeen, and
a party was thrown for him on the set. Esther Williams, Kathryn Grayson,
Jane Powell, Jean Simmons, Stewart Granger, Spencer Tracy, and Elizabeth
Taylor were on hand to wish him well. With his involvement in the movie
over, Michael headed home.
    Filming continued in California and thereafter Europe during June and
July 1953. The movie previewed at MGM studios on February 11, 1954, to
mixed, and at times amusing, reviews. Writing in the *New York Post,* Archer
Winsten observed that Vittorio Gassman "is a man whose bony ascetic face
is peculiarly right as that of a violinist. He looks more like one than Heifetz
or Kreisler." As for Gassman's co-star, Winsten noted that she "is as stunning
a creature to contemplate as ever, and now there is more of her too."10 What
the tempestuous Ms. Taylor made of this double-edged appraisal is not
known. *Newsweek's* assessment was that "in the language of the trade, this is
a 'woman's picture' deluxe."11 In the end, however, any movie that contained
three success stories, one suicide attempt, two complete changes of character,
and a happy ending could not be taken too seriously. The offscreen contribu-
tions of Michael and Arrau were either praised or passed over. From Michael's

perspective, the visit had been fun and largely stress-free. His artistry had enhanced the film, and in turn his career benefited by having his name on the credits and linked closely to some of the biggest names in show business. He also joined a long list of violin virtuosos* who had either made the sound-track of a movie or appeared in the film itself.

In a postscript to his Hollywood adventure, Elizabeth Taylor revealed that she did not reciprocate Michael's damning character assessment. On his eigh-teenth birthday, a year after he had recorded the soundtrack, a telegram arrived backstage at Carnegie Hall, where he was due to play the Glazunov Concerto:

> We know that because of your brilliant playing how responsible you are for much of the musical success of our film "Rhapsody." Let me wish you additional success with your Philharmonic Symphony appearance today and very special greetings for your birthday which we all celebrated a year ago at studio on set of "Rhapsody." I'll be listening to your broadcast and send you all good wishes.
> Elizabeth Taylor, MGM Studios, Culver City, California.12

Michael returned to a sticky and humid New York. In June the family decamped for Elizabethtown, where he worked on new repertoire for his fall tour. Francescatti visited and so too did Raymond Lambert, who had accepted an offer to become Michael's accompanist. Their fall itinerary got off to a good start in Petoskey, Michigan. "Well, the first concert is over and both Raymond and myself think it was quite successful," Michael noted to Bertine. "Poor Raymond hates to fly in the DC-3 and today we have to fly on 3 of them. But he is really getting to love the US and is already thinking about coming here for good. After Australia, I couldn't blame him at all."13

Michael liked Lambert and welcomed his company on tour, but he still felt lonely. Jeanne's viselike grip was making matters worse and resentment was burning afresh. After a concert at the University of Wisconsin, she hauled him away from a table tennis game despite his obvious enjoyment. "He seemed eager, even desperate, for interaction with peers," recalls David Schoenbaum, one of the students who had invited Michael to play.14 But Jeanne was simply relentless in exerting her will. "You know what my mother calls me?" Michael asked Jack Heller, a fellow Galamian student. "Michael. *Michael!!!*"15 Distinct echoes of "George, *George!!!*" Except that here the object of her verbal harangues was a child more easily subdued.

---

* Heifetz, Elman, Stern, Campoli, Menuhin, and Seidel.

When Michael next wrote to Bertine, from South Bend, Indiana, he confided:

> At this stage, I'm all mixed up. I'm homesick and yet I hate to come home. I don't know what the hell's the matter with me. And as you know, mother dear doesn't make things any better. You know her cunning tactics.
>
> I'll be seeing you on October 31 and will have a few nice things to tell you.[16]

By the time Michael put pen to paper again he seemed a little more upbeat. " I hear you had a terrific time at the Steinway party," he wrote from St. Louis. "Champagne and all the works — the real McCoy! It's a lucky thing that I wasn't there because I probably would have gotten terribly drunk. But I'm glad you enjoyed yourself…. The programs are going well and I'm having good success."[17]

The seesaw in emotions captured by Michael's letters on tour illustrate not only the vicissitudes of life at that turbulent age but also how his truncated youth had left him ill-equipped to deal with the social demands that he confronted after a concert. "Last night I played the first of my two St. Louis recitals and it went very well," he wrote a couple of days later in high spirits:

> After the concert … believe it or not, I danced with about six lovely girls. One especially was a knockout, a real blond, what a baby she was — the real McCoy. Hot stuff!! Although I don't know how to dance I did — after a fashion. I just pushed the gals around in rhythm to the music. I was able to get on, but *please* Bert, when I get back home, I want you to teach me how to dance. Please. I've found out that to know how to dance is a real social asset, and anyway it's about time I learned.
>
> Those girls were very nice to me and said that with a little experience I'd be an excellent dancer, especially since I do have good rhythm. But it certainly was a nice experience having a girl in my arms and pushing her around. To be perfectly truthful though, none of them were quite as beautiful as you are. You undoubtedly would have had all the boys drooling. All in all, the concert and the dance were wonderful — especially the dance.
>
> I am now working harder and better than I have in the last two years — really. I don't know what's gotten in to me. I'm just practicing and practicing. The concert last night wasn't my best,

but you should have heard the concert in Royal Oak, Mich. It was lousy from the first note on. Luckily for me there was no critic present. But I feel that if I continue to work hard now, there's no telling how much improvement I can make. Only time will tell.

On Monday we are flying down to New Orleans. I'm anxious to see it and tell you about it....

With love and you know what,

Mike[18]

What Michael could not see was that his resurgent energy and his renewed enthusiasm for practicing were the direct products of his newfound happiness. He had met some girls. He had danced with some hot stuff. They had liked him, complimented him. This brief interaction had been an emotional tonic. To a seventeen-year-old boy starved of friendship, the kindly words of a few Missouri schoolgirls had done more to lift his mood than the combined praises of the critics. Had he been left to play an evening of table tennis in Milwaukee, had the half an hour with a girl in St. Louis been allowed to extend into an evening date, Michael would have had the social contacts he so craved. Finding himself locked into an existence that was at odds with his physical and emotional needs left him distressed and frustrated.

Jeanne too had written to Bertine from St. Louis, the day after her son's fleeting social success. "This is a very tiring trip," she confided, "and although Michael is behaving surprisingly well (all facts considered), it's a great strain for me, and I am constantly under terrific nervous tension — never knowing what the next minute will bring." Having brought her tribulations to her daughter's attention, she launched into a detailed description of a cute kitten she had seen in a local newspaper, before concluding with love and kisses and the following postscript: "The concert last night was ... about 38 miles from St. Louis. The headmaster in charge drove us out and back and it was very tiring — but everything went very well."[19]

The letter deserves close scrutiny, both for what it says and what it omits. No one could dispute Jeanne's complaints of tiredness, but she failed to acknowledge the possibility that her young son felt likewise. There was no mention of what a strain it must have been for a seventeen-year-old to traipse out on stage, night after night, and work his way through the most demanding of repertoire on an unforgiving instrument. There was not a whisper of satisfaction that Michael had enjoyed himself meeting some girls his own age. Rather, her sole mention of him was a backhanded complement, laden with negative overtones. The only positive observations were reserved for a photograph of a cute little kitten she had seen in a local newspaper. She had begun her missive by drawing attention to her fatigue and for added effect closed the same way.

From Marshall, Texas, Michael's letter to Bertine gave some indication of the long hours and short nights that were now demanded of him. "Things are going to be a bit tough for the next day or two," he noted: "Tonight I play the recital here then catch a train at 4:10 AM which gets me into Waco tomorrow at 4:15 PM (there's a five and a half hour wait in Ft. Worth) and the concert is tomorrow night in Waco. So I had better get some shut eye in the train."[20] His worries were well founded. In Waco he took ill on stage. "You probably heard about the unfortunate incident in Waco," he wrote home on November 26, "when during the middle of the concert I was forced to stop because of excruciating dizziness."[21] Overcome by exhaustion, Michael simply could not finish his program. It had taken his collapse on stage for Jeanne to get an inkling of something amiss, although her explanation fell short of addressing the central issue of why her son was being subjected to such an enervating schedule. She confided to Bertine:

> Michael gave me quite a scare in Waco. No doubt you've heard about it. He seems to be OK now, and I think it was fatigue plus the horrible hours, smoking, bad choice of food, all combined to make him feel that way. At any rate, when we get back I'll make him have a thorough check-up. As should you. This life is strenuous and one must be in good physical condition to be able to take it and do a good job. He does not realize that.[22]

On tour in Texas, however, there were few concessions offered the overburdened boy — the abandoned concert in Waco would have to be made up even if it meant cobbling together the kind of travel schedule that had precipitated his collapse in the first place.

Notwithstanding his fatigue and gruelling schedule, Michael's performance standards seldom faltered. The self-administered rebukes that crop up intermittently in his letters should be seen in the context of a young man whose teacher and mother had inculcated a hypercritical self-appraisal. To the critics and audiences alike, his playing continued to induce a fevered mix of adulation and awe. Furthermore, there were many aspects to life as an itinerant musician that Michael enjoyed, not least of which was his exposure to new sights and cultures.

After grinding to a physical halt in Waco, he bounced back in El Paso, his next stop. "I love [the place]," he declared from his room at the Hilton. "It's part Spanish, Mexican, Texan, and Western. And the climate is dry as a bone.

No matter what you touch you get an electric shock. When I play I actually see the sparkles going along the strings. I hope to give an electrifying performance of the Paganini."23 Three days later, he confirmed his high opinion of the town:

> I'm really enjoying myself here….
>
> Yesterday we crossed the border and went to a city in Mexico called Juarez. It's about 1 mile from here, but oh brother, what a different atmosphere. You'd think you were in the heart of Mexico. However, it's purely for tourists who want to unload some money. We had a good steak dinner there and it was marvelous. You can get a good Grade A 2½ lb. T bone for $1.50. So when you want a steak dinner you just cross the border and go to town.

It was not only the touring that had suddenly become more enjoyable — the music making was more fun too. "The conductor, who is Italian, is very good and a hell of a nice guy," he noted in his letter. "His name is Orlando Barera and believe me, I wish every conductor would be as easy to work with as he is. He takes away all the tightness and strain and just lets me enjoy myself."24

As Michael's tour proceeded through Dixie, not everything he saw pleased him. "Down here in the South the White-Negro problem is very noticeable," he informed his sister:

> In trains, buses and all public conveyances and public places the white and colored people must be separated. In Port Arthur the concert hall had a separate section for the colored people. It was full, too. But that sort of thing really burns me up. We complain about wars and yet we fight so bitterly among ourselves. It's really very childish and stupid. Naturally, it only makes the Negroes hate the whites more.25

Further evidence of his awakening social conscience emerged in a letter dated December 7 and posted from New Orleans:

> Today is a day on which I think and wonder. Just 12 years ago the Japanese air force attacked Pearl Harbor, H.I. And yet today we seem to be on such palsy-walsy terms with Japan. It's really something I think about. I just wonder — when will the whole damn thing start up again if ever? How do you like McCarthy's latest

pranks? He's such a lousy bastard. I wish some crazy loon would assassinate him. Good riddance, I'd say. You'll see Bert, he'll get his lousy neck broken yet. Just you wait and see. He's way overdue.[26]

By the time Michael had reached Louisiana, he was tiring once again and had taken ill. "I have a hell of a cold — it's so bad that I haven't been able to breath through my nose for the past three days. As you can imagine, it was quite difficult to play my recital in Baton Rouge with my mouth open…. Fortunately, no foreign agents entered my maw while I was on stage!" Loneliness had also resurfaced:

> I'd love to hear from you once more before I get home. Bert, please. As soon as you get this write me a newsy *air*-mail letter to the Roosevelt Hotel in Waco and I'll love you. It's so wonderful to get letters when you're traveling in strange places. It makes me feel so important to know that someone cares.[27]

Coming from a boy who was touring with his mother, this last sentence inadvertently hinted that all was not well on the road.

Confirmation of this would not be long in coming. After a short holiday season break that included the annual Columbia Christmas party, much enjoyed by all the Rabins, Michael took to the skies again. It was a bitterly cold winter, and there were a number of Northern stops to visit before he could enjoy the warm California sunshine once again. By now a veteran traveler, Michael had developed a discerning eye and did not pull his punches when it came to his assessment of small town America. "This particular town is a real stink pot," he wrote from Storm Lake, Iowa. "The hotel looks and is like an old converted manure warehouse, and to a certain extent smells as such. Fortunately, I leave it in 36 hours and go to Salt Lake City, Utah, which is supposed to be marvelous."[28]

Moving from place to place also had its ups and downs. "I hate the trains and Greyhounds," he confided in Bertine, "but as you know I love the flying. It relaxes me so completely that it's hard for me to understand why some people get tense and afraid of planes."[29] But there was a good reason why many of Michael's fellow artists did not share his enthusiasm. Survival. Ginette Neveu and her accompanist brother had died in an air crash in the Azores five years earlier,[30] Jacques Thibaud had met his end when his plane came down in the Alps on September 1, 1953,[31] and less than two months later, William Kappell, the young American pianist, was killed when his plane flew into a mountain.[32] This spate of accidental deaths had prompted

Menuhin to swear off airplanes until such time as on-board radar was fitted in civilian aircraft, something that was still seven years away.33

The soothing joys of air travel were not enough, however, to offset Michael's loneliness or diffuse the escalating friction with his mother. Two weeks into his tour, having arrived in Seattle, he gave voice to a cathartic out-pouring of pent-up emotions. Careful to let his sister know the time by jot-ting it down alongside the date ("very late at night, 3:20 AM. Sunday in fact"), Michael returned to familiar themes: "Thanks a million for your letter. It was very sweet of you to write and when I get mail, especially from you, it makes me feel better because the only mail I ever get are the hotel confirmations." Health problems secondary to the cold dry weather ("I'm having a terrible attack of dry skin on my hands") may have contributed to his irritability, but the real source of his frustration was Jeanne. "As far as my diet is concerned, I'm not starving myself, but I am being much more careful than I used to be," he wrote:

> Mother isn't watching her diet at all and I'm sure that if she doesn't, she'll get sick. She eats too much and too much of the wrong foods and has a continual heart burn. I suggested she should buy the Alka-Seltzer factory and thus save a great deal of money!! But I really pity that woman. She makes fights with Raymond all the time and she's always picking on him and he gets terribly mad. And I'm in the middle all the time. I am going to refuse to play concerts after the European tour if she travels with me. I'll be old enough then to go on my own and A.J. heartily agrees on that. In any case, there will have to be changes — and soon. I can't take it very much longer. God damn, you'd think I'm an infant the way she treats me and makes the fool of me in front of people. It's embarrassing and belittling.34

Having vented his sense of frustration and humiliation, the emotional floodgates opened completely and Michael began flailing at his sister too, dis-placing all his anger from Jeanne onto Bertine, the one person who had been able to sympathize with his difficulties. "But I doubt whether you'd know or even care about my troubles," he railed on. "It's not like you to think or worry or feel sorry for people. Not even your brother. With you, all that matters is Bertine Rabin and what she wants, cares for and thinks is right. Oh well." Having hurled that accusation, Michael's anger was spent and he turned con-versational, seemingly oblivious to the content of his outburst:

> I hope you'll write again very soon and you may be sure that I'll do the same. I'm really sorry I'm going to miss Francescatti and

Heifetz on the Telephone Hour but be sure to give them both my best regards if you go down to the studio. And of course my love to Mr. Voorhees…. Be good and take care of yourself.

Love,

Mike.[35]

Michael's fragile emotional state did not intrude into his concertizing in Seattle. The reviews for his recital, in which he played Beethoven's "Kreutzer" Sonata, Stravinsky's Divertimento, and Tartini's "Devil's Trill" Sonata, among other works, were good. His ability was likened to that of his idols Francescatti and Heifetz, and it would not be long, reasoned the critics, before he began challenging other violinists such as Isaac Stern and Josef Szigeti for supremacy.[36] Always sensitive to the opinions of the critics, Michael was buoyed by these positive reviews, but they did not lessen his fatigue. On February 3, 1954, he arrived in Los Angeles from where he penned a short note:

> After a really hellish week … [we] were damn glad to get here. I'm pretty tired as I've played three recitals in the past five days and the connections to the small towns are really awful. But I'm sure that by tomorrow night I'll be set for the first of my three concerts with the LA Phil.[37]

Within a week, Michael was in San Francisco for three performances of the Mendelssohn Concerto with William Steinberg conducting, and then it was back to Los Angeles for a series of recitals. He complained again to Bertine:

> I've really been having a hell of a tough schedule, and it will be tough until I get home. This is by far the most exacting and demanding tour I've ever had and I can feel the after effects every day — I don't think I've ever been so tired in my life. And the traveling is too hard and there is too much of it…. Oh well, what can I do about it anyway?

It was at times like these, far from home and overcome by exhaustion, that Michael felt a nostalgia for New York that not even the balmy weather of the West Coast could negate. He wrote to Bertine:

> On the 22nd [February] I finally leave California and gradually start working my way back East. Although I've been in cities that I like much more than New York, it will be very nice to get back home — even though it'll only be a week.

San Francisco is a wonderful city and I really made a big success with the symphony there. As a city it is perhaps nicer than Los Angeles, but I'd rather live in Los Angeles than "Frisco." Personally, I think the most beautiful residential area I've ever seen in my life is Beverly Hills. When I play in the Hollywood Bowl this coming summer I'm going to insist that you fly out with me and see it and the entire Los Angeles area for yourself. It is something you shouldn't miss.[38]

Before leaving Los Angeles, the Rabins had dinner at the home of Larry Weingarten. "He ran off the film [*Rhapsody*] for us and it was a *very* disappointing picture," he noted to Bertine. "The music was okay, but I didn't care for the film at all." Meeting Greer Garson at the producer's home impressed Michael far more than the 115-minute movie. "She was very sweet and she's going to send me a photo!" he gushed. Michael's enjoyment of his tour to California was, however, tempered by his workload. "I was so horribly busy during the 3½ weeks I was in California that I didn't get much chance to do anything," he wrote the day after leaving Los Angeles. "Do you realize that I played 14 concerts in California alone. So you can easily imagine how tough it was and how hard I was working."[39]

But getting home was no simple matter, as his letter from Grand Island, Nebraska made clear. "After a hell of a day yesterday we finally arrived here at 10 PM," he groaned to Bertine:

We had to get up at 5:30 AM and we took the airport bus at 6:30 — the bus broke down on the way to the field so the plane took off 1½ hrs late — And it was so bumpy that we could hear the baggage being thrown around in the hold below us. After six hours of that we finally touched down in Omaha, then we took a lousy cow train to here — Believe me, sometimes the traveling can be murder.

Away from California, Michael's enthusiasm for the towns he had to play in plummeted, and he was back to the sharp-tongued descriptors that he had employed so liberally on his way out West. "Have two recitals to do in this joint — tonight and tomorrow night — this town sure is a dud. And I'll be really happy to get on to Kansas City, St. Louis and New York."[40] It was a tired and irritable young man who climbed off TWA flight 58 at La Guardia airfield on March 1.

The two-month tour had been physically and emotionally punishing. This leitmotif appears time and again in Michael's letters. Wherever he decamped, he picked up a pen and told his sister how tiring it all was. For a young man blessed with such a wonderful gift, the paucity of joy in his correspondence was disconcerting. It was as though a heaviness had settled on Michael early in the tour and never really left him. There were the occasional moments of enthusiasm that broke through the fog of exhaustion — his fondness for Los Angeles, meeting Greer Garson, his love of airplanes, a concert well played. But his joy was fleeting and quickly retreated behind a surplus of complaints. Nevertheless, difficult as the tour was for him, it should not obscure the fact that it had been a musical triumph. From venues big and small, the critics praised him with a list of superlatives that taxed the thesaurus. It said much for his resilience that he had never let his subjective distress intrude onto the concert platform. No matter how hard he was pushed by his management or how much he was goaded by his mother, Michael at seventeen years of age was the consummate professional, able to suppress any outward manifestation of distress once he stood before his public.

Bertine recalled that the excitement of mother and son returning from a tour had by now given way to tension. Michael was rebellious:

> He resented my mother and her domination. He was happy with his music but he was not really happy with his life. I think he didn't quite know what the matter was. He would say, "I hate her, she's always telling me what to do. I can't do this, I can't do that. I don't want her to travel with me." I think he started feeling that he was being closed in a vice and that he had no free will. It was the beginning of Michael looking out on the world and saying, "Look, I can't do what I want to do." It was enormously frustrating for him.

There were some rousing fights. Michael would throw objects. He ran away from home and disappeared for days, phoning Bertine to let her know he was safe but not divulging his whereabouts. Jeanne responded by clamping down further. At times she would lock Michael in his room. Dissent within her family was simply anathema to her. "We were taught to present a facade to the outside world," Bertine remembers. "And there was also a sort of facade inside the family too. You weren't supposed to get angry, yell at people, that kind of thing. But it was especially enforced outside the home. We had to be like this model family. I remember that so clearly."[41]

Publicity pictures from this time were designed to reinforce the persona of the all-American family—Mom and Pop and the two kids, successful and happy. Columbia distributed a series of photographs showing a seated George pointing to a spot on a large, unfolded map while eager, smiling Jeanne, Bertine, and Michael avidly follow his direction. "The family project—the Michael Rabin project" as Bertine described it, now captured in photographs. It would be inaccurate to imply the images were a fabrication—indeed, there was much truth in them, particularly early in the decade. There was no shortage of love in the Rabin family, even if, in Michael's case, it appeared conditional. They were an extraordinarily talented family, the children were good-looking and photogenic, and Michael's success was great. None of these ingredients changed as the decade progressed, but imperceptibly at first and later with a gathering momentum, one constituent altered. Michael's happiness gave way to frustration that fomented rebellion and, in time, hostility.

What was difficult for Jeanne and George to understand was that Michael's insurrection was not "bad" behavior but rather the signs of frustration in a young man growing up, wanting to be independent, and as Bertine saw it, "pushing against always having to be perfect."[42] The pressures on him were not those confronted by most adolescents. The quest for autonomy unfolded stormily alongside the inordinate strains of concertizing, the loneliness of a life without friends, and the exhaustion of incessant travel. Michael's parents had snippets of insight here, but their rare attempts at helping him smacked of the very things that were infuriating him. One example was their approach to his dearth of friends. Michael certainly knew many people, and while he moved in an adult circle, his time at Juilliard and his ongoing attendance at Meadowmount in the summer brought him into contact with a sizeable peer group. He had much in common with them, not least their shared love of music. Michael had, however, always been whipped away from orchestral rehearsals the moment they finished, preventing further social contact.

In the early 1950s, Jeanne and George contrived to fix this problem by reintroducing Michael to the very same peer group they had separated him from. But this time, mixing would be in a situation of their choosing and subject to the same stultifying controls they imposed on his daily routine. Rather than let Michael out of their sight, instead of encouraging him to venture forth with some fellow students, his parents selected one or two of them and invited them over for an evening of chamber music under their watchful eye. In doing so, they completely missed the gist of what was wrong. Their son was practicing eight hours a day. When on tour he was concertizing at a rate of one performance every two or three days. The last thing he wanted in his free time was more playing, particularly with Jeanne looking on. Jack Heller remembers those evenings in the Rabin apartment on West End Avenue very well. He was one of the invitees. Michael would soon lose interest in the music and drift away from the quartet. An embarrassed George would hastily take over to save the evening. But the evening, of course, was already lost.[43]

For the last leg of Michael's American tour, Jeanne was replaced by George. Precisely why she had momentarily stepped aside is not known. She may have felt too fatigued, or Michael may have followed through on his demand to Judson for some breathing space. Whatever the reason, a change was felt in order. Michael toured the south for a week, during which George wrote four postcards to his daughter. If Jeanne was windy in her letters, George was the opposite. A few lines sufficed — the tour was going very well; the weather was hot, humid, and rainy; and the girls in Birmingham, Alabama were the most beautiful in all the South. There were no murmurs of discontent from his son.

Michael returned to New York on April 3 to prepare for the world premiere of Richard Mohaupt's Violin Concerto, due to take place with the New York Philharmonic and Mitropoulos at Carnegie Hall. Mohaupt had completed his three-movement work in 1945, six years after his arrival in America. It was not destined for success. "There are three kinds of violin concertos," wrote one critic, "those that are great music and also good for the violin; those that are neither great music nor good for the violin; and those that are good for the violin without being great music. Mr. Mohaupt's belongs to the last category."[44] It was left to Olin Downes, the finest of the New York critics, to sum up performer and composer most accurately when he wrote that "Mr. Rabin sacrificed himself generously upon the altar of a work that is difficult and showy enough in the solo violin part to reflect eminent credit upon a capable performer, but that on account of its inherent dryness brings little that favors the fortunes of its interpreter."[45] Michael repeated the performance the following afternoon, after which Mohaupt and his concerto fell rapidly into obscurity. Michael never played it again.

At age eighteen, Michael's life was a paradox. On the one hand, he felt stymied socially and howled against his entrapment in a tightly spun maternal web. On the other, he held a unique position in American cultural life. The prestige he had attained came from many sources. Concertizing alone could not have led him to such exalted heights so quickly, even if he was performing at a frenetic pace. By his late teens, Michael had already acquired a show-business persona. Although his role in *Rhapsody* was off-screen, the publicity generated by MGM Studios had boosted his name immeasurably. Furthermore, he had appeared on the Milton Berle show, had played at Eddie Cantor's sixtieth birthday, and had been photographed with movie stars. He performed regularly on the *Telephone Hour*, his recordings for Columbia were highly praised and widely available, and he had given one world premiere of a violin concerto. Articles on him appeared regularly in all the big American broadsheets in addition to magazines such as *Time* and *Newsweek*.

There was no other violinist of Michael's generation whose public profile matched his. What made this achievement even more extraordinary was that it occurred during a golden era in violin playing, a period in which there was no shortage of competition from a phalanx of older, celebrated virtuosos. Kreisler's career may have been over and Elman's star on the wane, but Heifetz still performed and would do so for another sixteen years. Milstein was at the height of his powers, Stern was in top form, Francescatti had a home in New York, and Arthur Grumiaux, who had first toured the USA to critical acclaim in 1951, was a regular return visitor. Menuhin — the violinist Michael had most often been compared with — had yet to forsake America for Europe, Szigeti remained active, Ida Haendel and Erica Morini continued to dazzle, and rumors of Leonid Kogan's great talent had filtered through the Iron Curtain. So crowded was the field that when David Oistrakh made his American debut at Carnegie Hall the following year, he was one of three violinists to appear on stage that day, sandwiched as he was between Mischa Elman's 2:30 PM concerto performance and Nathan Milstein's 8 PM recital.

It was in the midst of this plethora of remarkable instrumentalists, each unique in his or her own way, that Michael's talent had announced itself, demanding to be heard. In the hard, competitive, and unforgiving world of the virtuoso violinist, it had taken a boy of very special ability to come this far so quickly.

CHAPTER 8
THE GRAND TOUR

*M*ichael's elevation to the upper echelons of violin virtuosos was based primarily on the opinions of the critics back home. For his career to move forward, others further afield would have to hear and judge him too. Two years had elapsed since his Australian tour with its mixed results, and the time was now right for him to venture abroad once again. Much of the summer was therefore given over to preparing repertoire for a lengthy European tour that would begin in the fall.

There were also a few outdoor concerts commitments to attend to. On June 24, 1954, he teemed up with Sir Adrian Boult for a performance of the Tchaikowsky concerto at the Lewisohn Stadium. It was a propitious collaboration — Sir Adrian would feature prominently in Michael's recording career soon to blossom. In July he traveled to the Ravinia festival in Chicago. Bertine went with him. It was the first time she had accompanied her brother on tour, something he had always wanted. "Now that your first plane trip is a fait accompli, you have another experience to your credit," George wrote:

> I'm glad you seized the opportunity to go, and you will know what constitutes a concert tour.... It has been dull and lonesome since you all left home.... Sometimes, Michael gets restless and bored between concerts, so you must do all you can to help mother keep him out of mischief.[1]

The biggest upheaval that month, however, was away from the stage. The family moved into a spacious three-bedroom apartment at 110 Riverside Drive.

Michael's first European tour had been organized by the English agency Harold Holt Limited. Holt, an ex–South African, had built up the premier concert agency in the United Kingdom, looking after the interests of artists such as Heifetz and Menuhin, among others. He had been pivotal in organizing the English debut of the Polish wunderkind Josef Hassid in 1939, and it was thus fitting that his agency would be involved in introducing the next great violin prodigy to the English public.[2]

When Holt died on September 3, 1953 (his obituary appeared in the *Musical Times* under that of Jacques Thibaud),[3] responsibility for Michael's arrangements passed to Ian Hunter. Even before Michael set foot in England, his tour ran into difficulties.[4] The problem was that in 1950s Britain, visiting artists appearing for the first time were not given a labor permit until they had satisfied the anonymous apparatchiks in the English bureaucracy that they were good enough. Even then, after passing first muster, they would be allowed to perform just twice. These draconian restrictions, instituted to protect local musicians, were waived in the case of "international celebrities" from abroad. Michael, according to the Ministry of Labour, was not one of them.

An irate Ian Hunter wrote an open letter to the *London Times* deriding the ministry's policies. He pointed out that if Michael was forced to organize his own debut, the costs would relegate the event to a small hall, the least spectacular and important way of introducing an artist to Britain. Furthermore, Hunter believed that the ministry was completely wrong in its assessment of Mr. Rabin's credentials. The fact that three distinguished conductors, Sir Malcolm Sargent, Sir John Barbirolli, and Rudolph Schwarz, had invited him to appear as soloist with their orchestras should have been testimony enough. Barbirolli in particular came to Michael's aid, with a letter that combined understated style with compelling content. "As you know," he wrote to Hunter, "we of the Hallé were among the first to engage him, and, if I may say so, this is not without significance as to his quality, for we are rather sparing of soloists as a rule."[5] The matter did not end with Hunter and Barbirolli's letters. The General Secretary of the Incorporated Society of Musicians added his angry voice to the *Times* correspondence, and the tart exchanges continued until the eleventh hour, when Hunter got his way.[6] The young American was classed officially as an "International Celebrity."

Michael would tour with his mother and Raymond Lambert. How this triumvirate would fare in the months ahead was cause for concern, given the conflict earlier in the year. But qualms gave way to excitement when, in early October, Michael and Jeanne boarded the transatlantic liner *Liberté* in New York bound for England.* Jeanne, with her natural gregariousness, immediately felt at home in the relaxed social milieu of the ship. "Mr. and Mrs.

---

* Lambert traveled separately and would join the Rabins in London.

Freddie Mann are on board and have been very sweet and kind to us," she wrote to Bertine. The Manns, wealthy Philadelphia philanthropists, would soon finance a new concert hall for the Israel Philharmonic Orchestra in Tel Aviv, and meeting them at sea was fortuitous. The importance of social networking was not, however, foremost on Michael's mind. "[He] is very restless and wishes he had flown," noted Jeanne. "He's afraid of the boat."[7] Michael, for his part, saw things a little differently, as he confided in Bertine. "My ocean trip to England on the *Liberté* was a good one but I don't care for boats at all. I had a constant headache from the side to side rolling and ate like a horse and got plenty sick. But I played at the Captain's Gala Evening and he gave me a special medal!"[8]

The first concert was scheduled for Sweden, and on October 5, the Rabins and Lambert flew from London to Stockholm. From the very beginning, Michael loved Scandinavia, and the affection was reciprocated by his audiences. "Please don't be mad at me for not writing sooner than this," he apologized to Bertine on October 15, "but I'm sure that my negligence has a good excuse, and that is the unusual experience I'm having here in the Scandinavian countries." What Michael was obliquely referring to was the novel sensation of thoroughly enjoying himself:

> Let me start telling you what I've done in reverse. Now I'm in Oslo, which is truly a marvelous city. It is spotlessly clean, has wonderful climate and the hotel and concert hall are perfect. I rehearsed with the Philharmonic this morning and it really is a fine orchestra.
>
> We left Stockholm two days ago and I was really sorry to go. It is such a beautiful city and has that clear-cut atmosphere that is typical of these Northern countries. I also played in a town in Sweden called Gothenburg and it was also very charming."[9]

Michael spent almost a month in Scandinavia and his recitals and orchestral appearances were a huge success. He invariably felt the need to top up his Mendelssohn concerto with a few Paganini caprices, and the normally restrained Swedes and Norwegians thundered their approval.

While in Stockholm, the Rabins ran into Yehudi Menuhin in the foyer of the Grand Hotel where they were all staying. "He was so very sweet and friendly," noted Jeanne. "He is playing tonight — a recital and invited Michael and me to come to his concert. How very friendly he was and what lovely manners he has. Even Michael was impressed by his behavior and cordiality."[10] Despite this dig at her son, Jeanne and Michael were getting along well — a notable feature of his correspondence was the absence of rancor towards his mother. In fact, he never mentioned her. Earlier in the year, in response to her vigorous appetite and subsequent heartburn, he had caustically suggested she buy the Alka-Seltzer factory. Now he remained silent in the face of a fresh set of gastronomic challenges faced by his mother, who had half-complained to Bertine: "the food is good and the pastries are out of this world. One has to exercise terrific self control—it is so easy to succumb."10

Jeanne's copious letters were full of concern, advice, and love for her daughter. She was also not insensitive to the demands faced by Michael. She urged Bertine:

> Please darling, write to him directly and tell Daddy to write him *often*. You have no idea how upset he gets when he gets no mail. It's a very hard life and can be very lonesome in a strange place— not knowing the language etc. And it's wonderful for the morale to get letters from loved ones. I can take it better than he—so please write to him and tell Daddy to write him often, as often as to me. Also, please tell Mr. Galamian to write to him. Michael is making Mr. G. famous everywhere he plays.11

On November 3, Michael, Jeanne, and Raymond Lambert left Copenhagen for Italy. The more leisurely pace of travel and concertizing in Scandinavia gave way to a frenetic cycle of concerts in Rome, Florence, Turin, Genoa, and Milan. "Dear Bertie, I feel like such a bastard for not having written to you in the last three weeks," confessed Michael:

> but if you saw my Italian itinerary you'd know why. I think it was the toughest tour I ever had—11 concerts in 16 days and 10 of them were recitals. The only orchestra concert was with the Rome Philharmonic. So you may be sure it wasn't easy, and traveling conditions in Italy are really terrible.* So now I've done 20 concerts and have 12 more to do before I get back to New York. So I still have my work cut out for me.

Despite the pressure of relentless concertizing, Michael was enjoying Italy too. "Now I'll tell you a few interesting things," he wrote to Bertine:

> Italy is wonderful, but my favorite cities are Florence and Rome. The latter is really something (unfortunately, I didn't see much of

---

* In Italy, Michael moved between cities by train.

the cities I played in, but I think I got some terrific movies). Milan is awful. I hated that city, but I did have a terrific success at La Scala Opera House. But Rome is definitely *the* city in Italy. So far the two cities that I've really loved were Oslo, Norway and Rome."[12]

Coincidently, while Michael was touring Italy, news was announced of the discovery of the manuscript of a Paganini violin concerto, listed as his fourth, and missing for the past 123 years.[13] The concerto was performed for the first time on November 7 in Paris by Arthur Grumiaux, creating considerable interest.[14] Paganini was considered a national treasure by the Italians, and the premiere of a lost concerto, coinciding with Michael's performance of some of his caprices in Genoa, Paganini's city of birth, focused the public's attention on the young American. "Michael played in Genoa and created a sensation," Jeanne wrote back home. "They loved him and the critics praised him to the skies. It's a lovely seaport town on the Mediterranean. We've met some wonderful people who dined and wined us. We visited the city hall and saw Paganini's violin in its glass case."[15] Public interest in the American phenomenon remained high, and when Michael played Paganini's D Major concerto in Rome on November 17, he was complimented by no fewer than eight different reviewers.[16]

There was no letup in Michael's performance rate, which reached a peak in Brussels. Yet the griping over workload that had so dominated his American correspondence earlier in the year was absent now. "I just arrived here in Brussels so I can't pass judgment on it yet," he wrote to Bertine. "I'm playing 6 times in 5 days here with the Philharmonic, so that won't exactly be a party either. But that's my profession and I should be glad that I have the work to do. Others, less fortunate, would die to play a few concerts." One additional, nonmusical fact may have contributed to his improved mood and newfound equanimity. At eighteen years of age and earning a good living, he could at last indulge his great passion and purchase a car. "Have you seen the 1955 Plymouth Belvedere Sport Coupe?" he asked Bertine. "It's terrific and I can't wait to get mine. Daddy sent me the catalog."[17]

No sooner had Michael arrived in London and checked into his hotel at Marble Arch than he took stock of his professional life. He reported to Bertine:

> Now I've got the greater part of this European tour over, considering that I've done 26 concerts, and I'm really looking forward to returning to America with very great eagerness. I really miss it very much and am sorry that I'll only be home for 10 days. If I make

good plane connections out of London, I could be in New York
on January 8th, but I leave for my American tour on the 18th. So I
will, unfortunately, have a very short time at home.

On looking back and ahead, my schedule(s) is as follows: In
Europe 32 concerts — In USA — 37 concerts, which makes the
total for the season 69 concerts. That's the hardest season I've ever
had and I think it really is too much. Next year I'm not going to
do more than 35 concerts. But of the total of 69 I've only done 26,
so there's still plenty to do.

Michael had been on tour for two months, and the excitement of yet
another new and great metropolis was wearing a little thin. Nostalgia also
seemed to invoke a newfound fondness for his home city and awaken his
patriotism. "From the little I've actually seen of London, there in no doubt
that it is a great city," he wrote:

Of course it is so different from New York and there are so many
customs which seem strange to me … but I'll keep New York.
Believe me Bert, there's no place in the world like New York, and
we are really lucky to live there and be Americans. I think I can
appreciate these circumstances very well because I travel so much.
I can't wait to get back. It's just a month now.[18]

Hunter had arranged four concerto engagements in England, one apiece in
London and Birmingham and two in Manchester. Coincidentally, David
Oistrakh was making his first tour of the United Kingdom and Szigeti was in
town giving a two-part recital of the Bach unaccompanied sonatas and partitas.

Michael's first concert was set for Sunday, December 12. Two days before
this, he went with his mother to hear Yehudi Menuhin again, this time at the
newly opened Festival Hall. Menuhin had teamed up with his brother-in-law,
the pianist Louis Kentner, in a concert devoted to Beethoven sonatas. The
venue rather than the soloist impressed Jeanne. "The new Festival Hall is a
gorgeous place," she wrote. "It's located on the river and so much of the
building is glass — it's really fabulous inside. It's the last word in modern ele-
gance."[19] What Michael thought of the building and Menuhin's playing that
night is not known. His thoughts were focused on a different venue. "The
famous Albert Hall here is a very fine concert hall," he informed Bertine. "It
seats 6,200 people. I'm playing there Sunday (Tchaikowsky) and it's one of
my most important concerts in Europe. I'll be playing with the BBC
Symphony under the famous Sir Malcolm Sargent. Wish me luck."[20]

It was unusual for Michael to solicit good fortune for a performance. The grandeur of the Albert Hall, a famous conductor on the podium, his debut in England, the importance of the concert highlighted by his English management — all these factors united to make the event a special one and reminiscent of his Carnegie Hall debut four years earlier. Michael was not, however, fazed by the big occasion. "There was some trouble this autumn about the labour permit for Mr. Michael Rabin, a very young American violinist," wrote the music critic for the *London Times*, "but he proved yesterday afternoon, even in a single concerto, that he is already qualified as a true international celebrity."[21] Milly Stanfield, writing in *Violins and Violinists*, reported that "there was some murmuring prior to [Michael's] appearance that his engagement as soloist at a Sunday Celebrity Concert at the Albert Hall made mock of the title of the series." Even his age, caught between wonderchild and mature adult, was against him, she noted. However, by the time he had played the final note, he left the stage with the "plaudits of a thrilled public thundering in his ears, regarded as one of the most promising instrumentalists of the day."[22] From mockery to high praise, all within half an hour; this suggested either Michael had played very well, or else the public was notoriously fickle. Common sense pointed to both.

Illness forced Michael to cancel his performance with the City of Birmingham Symphony Orchestra, but he recovered in time for his recording session at the Kingsway Hall. "I suppose you know that I had my 'Angel' recordings to do in London," Michael wrote to Bertine.* "Well, they're finished now. I did the Glazunoff (I know you love this concerto) and Paganini with the Philharmonia Orchestra [conducted by Lovro von Matačić] and I must say that it's going to be a terrific recording. It's a 12" LP — finally."[23] Walter Legge, the Director of EMI International and founder of the Philharmonia Orchestra, made a point of dropping by to listen to the American sensation. He liked what he heard. Michael was to receive five percent royalties on each sale, his rate half that of Legge's wife, Elisabeth Schwarzkopf, also on contract to EMI. In addition, there was an advance of £595.19, in accordance with the stipulated American union rate. Von Matačić received £50 per concerto.[24]

The day after completing his recordings, Michael flew to Paris, where he expressed himself singularly unimpressed by the City of Light, despite settling into a hotel on the Champs-Élysées. "It was nice to leave London after being there for two weeks, but after I got here (Sat.) I wished I were back in London. Believe me, London is a million times better than Paris in every

---

* Angel was an American subsidiary of EMI.

way."[25] His glum view of the city did not affect his playing. According to Jeanne, who was offended by the choice of venue:

> Michael's concert last night was a great success artistically. He played beautifully and the people who were there cheered him no end. Michael is not used to playing under such circumstances (small fee — chicken feed and small hall), but nevertheless he gave a wonderful concert.[26]

By now mother and son's homesickness had become acute. Michael let his sister know that he was so anxious to get home he was actually counting the hours. "At present it's only 448¼ hours to wait! I hope I'll have the patience to wait it out."[27] Jeanne shared his longing, but preferred to express herself in more forthright terms with culinary overtones. "By this time I've had my fill of Europe and hotels and restaurants and I'll settle for a simple hamburger at home."[28]

After a recital in Lisbon on December 27, Michael returned to England and his final two engagements with the Hallé Orchestra conducted by Sir John Barbirolli. Sir John was known to the Rabins from his tenure at the New York Philharmonic, where he had succeeded Arturo Toscanini in 1937. He was a gentle, nurturing musician who enjoyed collaborating with talented young musicians, and now he had an opportunity to welcome the pick of them. The letter he wrote to George after Michael's performance was a heartfelt and moving tribute to father and son.

> My Dear Rabin,
>
> Last night Michael made his debut with the Hallé in Manchester and I am writing immediately to let you know what a truly great success he had. He is really a beautiful violinist and I was greatly touched by his playing of the Mendelssohn which was not only technically fine but was played with a grace and charm (and thank God, not too fast) which is sadly lacking amongst the younger violinists, of today.
>
> He seems a sweet boy too, quite unspoiled as yet and I pray he remain so.
>
> With his lovely modest and humble attitude towards his art the great gifts which God has endowed him should carry him very far.
>
> Believe me, my dear friend, that nobody was happier or prouder of him last night than your old Maestro.

Lady Barbirolli joins me in the warmest good wishes to you, for this coming year.

Yours very sincerely,

John Barbirolli[29]

It was a fitting conclusion to a happy and musically successful tour, one that had passed without recriminations and in good cheer.

CHAPTER 9
FIRST LOVE, REBELLION

Schuyler Chapin, later Mayor Giuliani's Commissioner of Cultural Affairs for New York City, was part of Columbia Artists Management during the 1950s. Chapin knew all about violinists. For three years he had been Jascha Heifetz's tour manager. "I heard Heifetz night after night in every city and state and territory and God knows where else," recalls Chapin. "When I first joined Columbia, I knew vaguely of Michael Rabin, but then in 1954 he was sort of plumped into my lap to deal with. But I found that when I heard him play, there was something extraordinary there, quite musical and exciting." Over a five-year period, Chapin would see Michael two or three times a week. Comparisons with Heifetz were inevitable. "Heifetz, whether you liked his playing or not, was *the* giant, perhaps of all time, in terms of the instrument," recalls Chapin:

> You have other great players, Mischa Elman and Isaac Stern and others that you could basically divide into the Russian and non-Russian Schools. Michael, with his unique talent, seemed to be the pick of the next generation of young Russian players. He caught my attention because he commanded the instrument and also with his musicianship. There seemed to be an extraordinary musical intelligence, even though Michael didn't give you the impression of that kind of intelligence when you were dealing with him. Because he was a big sloppy kid. I can't describe him

any other way, and he was very much in need of affection. He used to deal with me as if he was a son and I was the father.[1]

Chapin thought Michael's career was being managed very well. He had not been around when the sixteen-year-old boy had been exposed to an exhausting Australian itinerary, but here it is germane to point out that having been Heifetz's road manager, he would have seen little remiss in a season that contained seventy concerts. That was the pace at which the great virtuosos concertized, and if the nineteen-year-old Michael wanted to play in that league, long, arduous road trips through small town America were de rigeur.

Michael had coped well with a two-month trip to Europe, the novelty of the old world counteracting his exhaustion and homesickness. Nevertheless, on his return, he felt moved to tell the *Wichita Eagle*, "It is so good to get back to the country that I never want to leave it again."[2] The joy was short-lived. Approaching his nineteenth birthday, Michael was starting to appraise his life differently, and he was not comfortable with what he saw. "It was so sweet of you to write me such a sweet letter from New York," he let his sister know:

> It is also nice to know that you were glad to speak with me on the phone and nice to know that you miss me, because I don't know of anyone else who does miss me.
>
> I thought your most mature outlook on life at 21 was wonderful. For me, it is more than just food for thought, because as you know, in my business I can't act as 18 or 19 or play as if I were 18 or 19. I think I can safely say that I'm more mature than my years.
>
> Now this is no bull — I am seriously thinking of giving up the violin as a profession at the end of this season. That's in 7½ weeks. During this 54/55 season, I've got 70 concerts of which I've done 51, so there are a "mere" 19 to do yet. This is not a decision which I've thought up overnight, but one which has been tormenting me for a year and a half, and I don't think that this kind of life is for me. As a matter of fact, I'm quite sure it isn't. The only big problem facing me is what can I do? But this so called life of glamour is over come May. I shall try and start off my 20th year doing something with a future, if possible.
>
> I'm glad that you're not going to let mother interfere with your life. I know what she is capable of doing and I refuse to be dominated by her any more.

Please stay well and please write to me before I leave here on
March 10th.

    With my love and a big hug,

    Michael 3

It was not easy for Michael to pursue life independently. Despite his ear-
lier resolutions to travel alone, Jeanne still accompanied him, and Schuyler
Chapin's observations confirmed her dominant role. "I had gotten to know
Michael fairly well," he recalls:

> and then I ran into, of course, his mother. I knew his father a
> little, who really seemed a gentle, sweet man, but the mother was
> obviously a huge and overpowering presence in Michael's life. I
> had a feeling that the mother ran the roost, ran the father, ran the
> daughter, and especially ran Michael. She was a dragon when it
> came to anything to do with Michael, as near as I can detect. And
> of course, the arguments and discussions that I overheard between
> mother and son were outrageous. That is the only word for it.

To Chapin, the pervasive influence of Jeanne was clearly harming
Michael's fragile self-esteem. "Her attitude towards Michael was petulant and
demanding," he remembers:

> I'm certain it was based on affection and pride, but I'm quite sure
> she was in charge of what Michael should do and how he should
> behave. So while I did deal with Michael, I also had to deal with
> his mother, who was the one pulling the strings. I went a couple
> times to have a meal at the Rabin household, and it was the
> mother who commanded the scene. My reactions were that it was
> interfering, grasping, unpleasant — I kept thinking, boy, if this
> was me, I'd have to find some way of being able to muzzle this
> incredibly forward, pushy woman. But the overall effect on
> Michael was an increased sense of insecurity.4

The lack of self-assurance that was so apparent to Chapin had not
intruded onto the concert stage. Michael's reviews from his 1955 season were
consistently laudatory. But even in the one domain where he felt at home, he
was dissatisfied. Ten days after he had written to Bertine and confided his
desire to give up the life of a traveling musician, he reiterated his conviction.
From Nashville, Tennessee, he poured out his anguish:

Sorry I didn't write sooner, but I've been so Goddamned busy with my Great Career that I haven't had much time. Well, tonight's concert is no. 21 so there are only 15 more to go. Big deal —

I'm still quite determined that after this lousy season is over, I'm going to put the violin away, and do something worthwhile. So, I've got about 6½ weeks to go and I'm counting the minutes....

Believe me Bert, I'm really feeling the pinch and frustrations of not having any social life, especially with girls. Don't forget, in five weeks I'm going to be 19, so I'm not imagining things, and I think about it all the time, and I'm not working well, and I'm not playing well. I just don't know what I'm going to do, and besides not having any real friends and being very much alone, I'm scared as hell. I want to live a normal life and at the moment (and the past three years) it's hell on earth. Believe me, it really does exist.[5]

Approaching the end of his teenage years, Michael found himself in territory not unfamiliar to prodigies. Martha Argerich arrived at just such a point at the age of twenty-one and reacted by suspending her talent, withdrawing from the piano for three years, and spending her days watching television in her New York apartment.[6] Midori, on reaching her early twenties, was admitted to hospital with anorexia nervosa and contemplated giving up music and studying psychology instead.[7] Janos Starker, beset by doubts at a similar age and disillusioned with the life of a concert artist, stopped playing concerts for seven months and rethought his future.[8] Three examples in a long list of emotionally troubled wunderkinder. With the prodigy years behind them, the young artist awakens to find that much has been sacrificed along the way. A childhood has slipped by unrecognized, friendships never cultivated, education neglected.

Michael's crisis of faith was of the same order, that of a young man whose personal development had been hobbled in the relentless pursuit of career. It is in this context that one should read his two letters of March 1955: his emotional life was in rebellion against the unnatural restrictions he had been forced to endure for most of his teenage years. Earlier that year, in an interview with the *Miami Daily News,* he had addressed, more circumspectly, a similar theme. The one thing he missed in a life filled with music, he had said, was an association with people his own age. Asked about any romantic interests he pointed to his violin and replied dejectedly, "I don't know if I can have both."[9]

In 1955 Michael did not stop playing the violin. He did not even slow down the pace of his concertizing. To Jeanne, it was inconceivable that her son would suddenly quit. And Michael must have reached the same conclusion when he sat down to seriously think about the future. He had been raised to play the violin — the past decade had been devoted to nothing else, and the trajectory of his life, seemingly preordained, did not allow for diversions. He may have sarcastically deprecated this in his letter home with his capitalized reference to his "Great Career," but what his emotional distress could not obscure, at least for the time being, was just that — his truly remarkable career. Much as he fumed against the constraints of his life and bemoaned the absence of friends, Michael could not walk away from his life as a violinist. The momentum of his success did not allow for it. Like the gravitational field of a large terrestrial object, it held him fixed, orbiting in uneasy alliance with his parents, management, recording company, teacher, and a growing public.

Michael returned from his road trip on April 23, 1955, and that week gave an interview in which he advised other teenagers to aim for the concert stage "only if you feel there is nothing else in the world."[10] This bleak view did not stop him from accepting an invitation from Donald Voorhees to be part of the *Telephone Hour*'s sixteenth anniversary celebrations, joining Lily Pons, Brian Sullivan, José Iturbi, and Eileen Farrell. Within a month, he was back at the *Telephone Hour*, but this time with a new concerto in hand.

June 13 marks the day Michael first performed the Brahms Violin Concerto in public. He chose the third movement in what was a warmup for the full work, which he played nine days later at a summer concert in Lewisohn Stadium with Mitropoulos conducting. "Mr. Rabin, now 19 years old, is developing into a great violinist," noted the *New York Times*. "He has amply demonstrated in previous appearances that he has all kinds of technique and natural facility. His musical outlook, at the present time, continues to broaden. His approach was serious and that of a thorough musician."[11]

That summer Lewis Kaplan returned from army duty as soloist and concertmaster with the Seventh Army Symphony Orchestra in Germany. The two Galamian students, although fond of one another, had not corresponded during Lewis's two years abroad. "In my absence, Michael had become famous," recalls Lewis. "I got out of the army and went backstage [after his *Telephone Hour* performance at Carnegie Hall] and he wrestled me to the floor with hugs. I was astounded. I was thinking he was not going to remember me…. We went off to Meadowmount together." At last Michael had a friend, someone who understood him, admired him, but most important of all, liked him. "I saw Michael as real fun," reminisced Lewis. "We went swimming together. Whatever troubles he was having were not huge at that point. We were carefree that summer. He had bought his first car, which was a very modest Plymouth."12

Apart from his Bell and Lewisohn performances, Michael gave only one further concert over the summer. On August 6, in the gymnasium of the Elizabethtown-Lewis Central School in Elizabethtown, he was joined by a new accompanist, David Poliakine, in a charity recital. On a hot and humid evening, Michael raised over a thousand dollars for a local hospital and half as much for Meadowmount, prompting a warm letter of thanks from Galamian.13 It was truly a return of the prodigal son. With fulsome praise from his teacher, a new car, and a rediscovered friend, life was again sweeter, and his earlier angst and desire to retire from the stage was put aside.

Six happy months passed, swimming, playing table tennis, and exploring Upstate New York in his beloved "Plymmie." Michael exulted in his new-found freedom. The cellist Peter Schenkman, a contemporary who met him for the first time at Meadowmount that summer, remembered Michael as a very bright, opinionated, and impetuous young man, who was always generous in his dealings with colleagues, enjoyed chamber music, and drove very fast, almost recklessly, weaving in and out of traffic. He was struck by the boldness of Michael's violin sound, which in its intensity and high edge recalled that of Leonid Kogan.14

The summer idyll was interrupted once more in September for a recording session devoted to works for unaccompanied violin: Bach's Sonata No. 3 and two of Ysaÿe's Six Sonatas for Solo Violin, Op. 27, No. 3 (dedicated by the composer to Georges Enesco) and No. 4 (dedicated to Fritz Kreisler). In two days Michael was done, and with summer fading, he jumped back into his car and went looking for Lewis, cramming in as much driving and friendship as time allowed before the start of the next concert season.

In October, the reviews came out for Michael's Angel recording of the Paganini and Glazunov concertos. Ricci's version of the Paganini had been released around the same time, inviting comparisons. The *Gramophone* magazine favored Michael's — the recording was considered rounder and fuller, the orchestra more polished, the violin tone larger than life. "And then one realizes just how astonishing Rabin's playing in fact is," enthused the reviewer:

> His technique sounds as effortless as Ricci's and his intonation is
> actually better—the purity of his harmonics and thirds has to be
> heard to be believed. Were it not for a fidgety habit of slowing
> down every time a lyrical phrase comes along — possibly true to

Paganini's period, but so destructive of continuity — this would be a really wonderful performance.[15]

A subsequent review in the *New York Times* confirmed the superiority of Michael's intonation but preferred Ricci's fervor.[16] As for the Glazunov recording, the *Gramophone* stated that Michael's performance stood comparison with Menuhin's, while the *Times* considered it flawless.

The reviews came out just as Michael began his 1955 season. It was a time of change for him and his family. Bertine had announced her engagement to Ivan Lafayette and would soon be married and out of the home.[17] Gone was Raymond Lambert, replaced by Dutch-born David Poliakine. Gone too was Jeanne. And with his mother's departure, Michael found a new resilience. "The traveling has really been indescribable, but thank God I've got the strength to put up with this nonsense," he wrote from California:

> Tonight's my 8th concert of this tour and I've got 12 more to knock off before I get home....
>
> Incidentally Bert, I don't know how to explain it, but I'm playing better now than ever before. Almost without really trying, it sounds terrific. I didn't tell this to Mother or Dad because they probably would think I'm kidding.[18]

This letter, dated November 10, 1955 (and begun at 17:34, as he compulsively noted), would be Michael's last to his sister for many years, his uncharacteristic epistolary reticence perhaps a reflection of his reluctance to intrude into Bertine's new life.

The impending loss of his sister as confidant was partially offset by Lewis Kaplan's reappearance and the beginnings of Michael's first real friendship outside his family. The two young New Yorkers complemented one another by bringing to their kinship different attributes that each found appealing. To Lewis, there was Michael with his prodigious ability on the violin, whereas to Michael, there was a friend who was at home in the world, socially adroit and comfortable around people. Within months of reconnecting, Lewis arranged a date for Michael. And his friend fell head over heels in love.

The woman who so captivated him was Adrienne Rosenbaum, a violin student at the New England Conservatory. When Lewis had first mentioned Michael as a possible date, she had expressed some trepidation, as he was by then famous and she felt awed by his reputation. She was also slightly hesitant for another reason — she was in love with the conductor Kenneth

Schermerhorn. But in the end, her curiosity won out, and she agreed to meet Michael at an aunt's apartment in New York City in December. Whatever anxiety she was feeling before the date immediately disappeared when she answered the doorbell and saw a "terrified" Michael standing there. She did what she could to put him at ease. No sooner had Michael calmed down than fear gave way to love. He was immediately smitten with a woman who not only shared his interest in music and the violin but was also very beautiful. So taken was Michael that forthwith he informed her his surname had, once upon a time, been Rosenbaum too. Adrienne saw little need to disbelieve Michael's harmless but slightly clumsy way of endearing himself to her.[19]

No sooner was their date over than letters from Michael started arriving thick and fast. On January 3, 1956, he wrote stating he would soon be playing the Beethoven Violin Concerto for the first time in public and wanted to dedicate the performance to her. In the same breath, he told her he could not wait the sixty-seven days before they were due to meet again.[20] Another letter followed from Rochester three days later,[21] and a third from the Lord Nelson Hotel in Halifax, Nova Scotia, dated January 20, in which he passionately declared his love, confessing that he dreamed of her and thought of her while he was performing.[22]

Not only did Michael speak of love, he also offered to help Adrienne with her playing by arranging an interview with Galamian. In time, the meeting took place, although it was a social occasion and Adrienne never played. What she remembers of the evening was Galamian's charismatic eyes and how those eyes were for Michael only. "Galamian would look at Michael with great fondness and love," she recalls, "and witnessing that was one of the most moving experiences of my life." That evening she was content to sit back and listen as master and pupil reminisced about the early years of their association. At one point, Michael turned to her and sheepishly confessed that when younger he had occasionally misbehaved at a lesson, like the time he had kicked Galamian in the shins.[23]

Adrienne was initially bemused and a little overwhelmed by the intensity of Michael's ardor. The two started dating, but fond as she was of him, it did not translate into love. There was also the complicating factor of Michael's busy career, which kept him on the road for much of the concert season.

His letters to her describe not only his most intimate feelings, but also his concert itinerary. Rochester, Hartford, Portland, Boston, Halifax, and New York filled January. His performance of the Beethoven Concerto with the Hartford Symphony, dedicated to his first love, received a fine review. Not so his early February performances of the Brahms Concerto with Mitropoulos and the New York Philharmonic. He had already played the work in the more informal surroundings of Lewisohn Stadium the preceding summer, essayed the third movement on the *Telephone Hour*, and given a number of other full performances outside his hometown. Despite laying such thorough groundwork away from the exacting and at times pernickety gaze of the big-venue music critics, his performance on the Carnegie stage was found wanting. "Mr. Rabin might have [tried] something less taxing" was the *Times*'s pithy rebuke.24

In fairness to Michael, his tepid reviews may have had more to do with the critic's fatigue than his paltry musical insights. By that stage in the New York season, the critics had already sat through four different artists playing the Brahms concerto, while the year before they had had to listen to no fewer than six different interpretations. Familiarity, if not breeding contempt, may have induced a certain blasé attitude, with Michael the scapegoat for jaded appetites. It would not have escaped Michael's notice that seven months earlier he had played the Brahms to critical acclaim in the same city, but away from the searching Carnegie spotlight.25

Whatever qualms Michael had about his performance and the reviews, within two weeks an event took place that overshadowed everything. He spelled out what had happened in a letter to Adrienne, written from Beaumont, Texas:

> I'm awfully sorry that you haven't written to me for the last two and a half weeks, because I would have been very happy to hear from you. I just hope you dislike writing letters and that it is nothing personal.
>
> …Now my plans are as follows. If my plane is on schedule I'll be in New York City tomorrow evening, and I'm supposed to pick up my new car from the dealer sometime on Wednesday. I expect to drive up to Boston on Friday, as originally figured, and hope to be at your place by 3 o'clock….
>
> Adrienne, there are many things that I must discuss with you when I see you. I respect your intelligent judgment, and … I feel that I can tell you things in confidence that I could tell no-one else.
>
> I did not want to tell you (and I have not told *anyone* else) what happened to me during my four day stop in New Orleans until the crisis was over. I arrived in New Orleans on Feb. 17th and that same night I was walking along the main street about 8:30 PM and I tripped on something on the pavement and fell down. After I caught my breath back from the shock, I looked back and realized

that there was nothing I could possibly have tripped over. Well, I started walking back to the hotel and I started to shake violently all over my body. At the hotel, I saw the house doctor and he said I was suffering the last stages of a nervous breakdown. He said my way of life was finally catching up with me. It's a bit better now, but my nerves are terrible, and of course, I now get horribly nervous when I play. That's something that never occurred to me before.

Sit tight and I'll see you soon. We have lots of catching up to do, and I'm sure we have lots to tell each other. Until Friday....
Love,
Mike. 26

A tiny grain of vulnerability had intruded into Michael's life back in Waco, Texas; when overcome by exhaustion, he had developed incapacitating dizziness while on stage. That concert was cancelled. Now, a second sign of frailty had appeared — anxiety penetrating a chink in his formidable stage armor. As a fifteen-year-old wunderkind, his photograph had appeared in *Time* magazine beneath the caption "Stage Fright — What's That?"27 Now, for the first time in his professional career, Michael knew what those chilling words meant. Despite the dramatic tone and content of his letter, the review of his Glazunov performance in New Orleans made no mention of any discernible stage anxiety.28

Subsequent concerts in Shreveport and Beaumont also passed with good reviews and no mention of unsettled nerves. And when Adrienne met up with Michael a couple of days later, she too saw no trace of residual emotional distress. "When Michael came with his new car right after that letter was written," she recalls:

nothing was said about that event. I'm certain I brought it up because it was not like me to let anything of that magnitude pass. But the car really eclipsed anything negative that occurred. He was truly thrilled to have it and have a semblance of normalcy, dating, riding in the car. There was much discussion about that car and it was given the name "Little Bomb" after me.29

Michael had to cancel a March 20 performance of the Tchaikowsky Concerto at Carnegie Hall with familiar collaborators Leon Barzin and the National Orchestral Association after claiming to have caught his hand in a subway door the previous day. But Michael had improved sufficiently by April 6 to take the place of an indisposed John Weicher, concertmaster of the

Chicago Symphony Orchestra, in a performance of the Beethoven Violin Concerto with resident CSO maestro Fritz Reiner on the podium.

The reviews he received, apart from that of the consistently awestruck Miss Cassidy, repeated the criticisms leveled by New York critics at his playing of the Brahms Concerto earlier that year. "Privately, I cannot believe that Michael Rabin knows why he plays a certain passage in a certain fashion other than he has been instructed to do so," was the comment from the *Chicago American*'s critic.30 "The first concerto by Wieniawski, the fifth Vieuxtemps, one of the two Paganini concertos could have given Rabin an honest triumph — but Beethoven is no music for a fledgling" was not something a violinist approaching his twentieth birthday wanted to hear.31

Nevertheless, Michael appeared to shrug off these criticisms. He was preoccupied with winning Adrienne's affections. And there remained the distraction of his new six-cylinder Plymouth coupe. Sally Thomas, a fellow pupil of Galamian and later his assistant, recalls that when Michael purchased his coupe, he gave his first Plymouth, no more than a couple of years old, to his parents as a gift. The cars were black and white and when parked alongside one another resembled skunks. When she asked Michael why he had bought a six-cylinder car for himself but handed over a four-cylinder model to his parents, he replied with an absolutely straight face that now he could get away from them faster.32

Adrienne's presence had given a much-needed fillip to Michael's enthusiasm for his career. On April 17th, he wrote from Washington telling her that he loved life as a concert artist, moreover stating that he was "lucky to have [had] a good head start." A sudden change in his concert schedule had forced him to cancel a meeting with her, but rather than berate his full agenda as in days of old, he demonstrated a surprising volte-face and declared fervently that "not to have concerts is a living hell."33 Love was proving invigorating indeed, but whereas Michael doted on Adrienne, her responses were cooler. "His greatness lay in his playing," she recalls. "He was not a particularly interesting person to know, but when he picked up the violin, it was pure magic. I wish he could have continued it into his conversation."34

The day before Michael turned twenty, his recordings of the solo Bach and Ysaÿe sonatas were released across the nation to critical acclaim.35 A month later, he set off for London with Jeanne to make some more records — this time collaborating with Alceo Galliera and the Philharmonia in the Tchaikowsky Concerto and two Saint-Saëns works, *Havanaise* and the Introduction and Rondo Capriccioso. EMI, who also had their eye on Christian Ferras and Johanna Martzy, now considered Michael the pick of the young American violinists.36

After one of the recording sessions, Michael and Jeanne were invited back to a party at the Golders Green home of the impresario Paul Fishman. Formerly a furrier, Fishman had switched to concert management and was on close terms with many of the day's great instrumentalists, including Casals and Elman. Present that evening at Fishman's house were David Oistrakh and Max Rostal, the famous Austrian violin teacher, pupil of Carl Flesch, and later his principal assistant. Dr. May, a physician friend of Fishman's and a talented amateur cellist, needed little prompting to complete a makeshift quartet, with Michael on first violin, Oistrakh on second, and Rostal on viola. A single, grainy black-and-white snapshot captured that brief moment in violin history, a gathering of violin luminaries no concert audience was ever likely to see: the music stands arranged in a circle in front of a grand piano; a smiling Oistrakh chatting with Fishman; Michael seated with his back to the camera, left hand raised with sheet music; Dr. May standing with cello in hand; the head of violinist David Wise in the bottom right hand corner; and at the far left of the picture, caught in profile, the taxi driver Alf Levy.

How a London cabby came to find himself in such company spoke to his remarkable personality. Levy and the Russian-born Fishman had been friends for many years, their association going back to the days Fishman worked as a furrier. Both shared a passion for music. Levy was a regular concertgoer. Moreover, he knew that many musicians had established accounts with the London Taxi Service and, by memorizing which account numbers were associated with which musicians, made sure he was on hand to take care of their transport needs when their calls came through to the central booking office. In that way, he had over the years met many of the famous singers and instrumentalists that passed through the city. A born conversationalist with an encyclopedic knowledge of classical music, he quickly endeared himself to his illustrious clientele. Many were the musicians who, after overcoming their surprise at meeting such an erudite cab driver, ended up signing autographs and programs for him and on occasion inviting him in to their rehearsals, performances, and even recording sessions. When Michael and Levy met at Paul Fishman's home, their rapport was instant.

Levy retains vivid memories of that evening. "What fascinated me," he recalls, "was that the four of them put the music up and just played it as though they had seen it all their lives." Michael, as was his habit, was prone to dashing off some fiendishly difficult bit of Paganini in the lull between pieces, and in response to a passage of crystal-clear double-harmonics delivered with nonchalant ease, Levy remembers Oistrakh turning to Fishman and saying in Russian, "I can't do what he's doing." [37]

The brief meeting between Michael and Oistrakh took place at the height of the Cold War, when cultural exchanges between the two superpowers were few. Six months earlier, an article had appeared in the *New York Times* mentioning that negotiations were in progress to get a group of American musicians that included Isaac Stern and Michael Rabin to visit Russia.[38] Stern had in fact visited in May 1956, a month before Michael met Oistrakh in London, but nothing ever came of plans by the Soviet Ministry of Culture to organize a similar visit for Michael.

The social gathering at Fishman's house was warm and convivial, although Levy recalls that Jeanne was convinced the house was under surveillance by the KGB and CIA, and would frequently peer out from behind the curtains to look for the presence of secret service agents. Her agitation was regarded with benign amusement by those present, with Oistrakh in particular inured to his security shadow.[39]

On Michael's return to New York on June 15, Angel Records published an interview with their young star in which he was quoted as saying that his immediate plans involved nothing more strenuous than hopping into his new Plymouth and driving until the tank ran out of gas, stopping wherever his fancy led him.[40] His life, of course, was never so simple or carefree. On the immediate horizon was a performance of the Brahms Concerto with the thirty-seven-year-old Leonard Bernstein at Robin Hood Dell, summer home of the Philadelphia Orchestra. Bernstein, soon to succeed Mitropoulos in New York, would record the Brahms concerto in 1961 with Michael's mentor Zino Francescatti. But first, it was the younger man's turn to perform under his direction.

"The most enthusiastically received concert of the season took place last night at Robin Hood Dell," reported the *Philadelphia Daily News*. "Such is always the case when people's choice Leonard Bernstein comes to make music. But this time there was an added factor named Michael Rabin. It was the first Dell appearance for this 20-year-old violinist. Few debuts in recent years have been so successful."[41]

Summer also meant time spent at Meadowmount, where Michael met up with Lewis. That year the Rabin family had taken a house in New Russia, approximately fifteen miles from Meadowmount, and Jeanne invited Lewis to come stay with them, which he did for a couple of weeks. "I woke up the first morning," he recalls:

> and I heard a terrible noise. In fact it woke me up. I couldn't understand what it was. I walked out of the bedroom and looked over the railing down the steps and just at that moment there was Jeanne Rabin chasing George Rabin out the house with a frying

pan saying, "George, I'll get you." Can you imagine this woman chasing him out of the house with a frying pan?

But apart from that one rocky episode, Lewis remembers his stay with great affection. "It was fun being with Michael," he reminisced:

> He was a lot of fun, with a great sense of humor. And Jeanne was kind to me. And at the time I admired her, because I think that any violin student would have liked to have been Michael Rabin or had the career of Michael Rabin. She called all the right shots, it appeared. She made him practice, she did this, she did that, and here's Michael playing all over the world.

Lewis had frequent opportunities that summer to view Michael's playing close up:

> We practiced some. When his mother was out shopping, of course, down went the violins, and then with a big laugh he would say, "Here she comes," and pick up the violin and pretend he had been practicing all the time. My impression was of a violinist totally in charge of the instrument. He had a real presence with the violin. He was at the top of his form. His playing had progressed from an adolescent, although a wonderful violinist, into more of a mature artist. But along those lines, Michael was very insecure about what he was doing musically.[42]

With the passage of time, Lewis took a less charitable view of Jeanne. He came to view her invitation to New Russia not as a gesture of friendship, but more as a premeditated attempt to control her son by keeping him at home with his friend as the bait.

Contact with Lewis allowed Michael the opportunity to talk about girls and tell him how things were progressing or faltering with Adrienne. The voluminous flow of letters to his "Dear Princess" continued. Adrienne's replies were far fewer, which had the effect of further increasing Michael's anxiety about how she felt about him. It was a sign of how emotionally estranged Michael was from his parents that he could never tell them about Adrienne. Not only did he love her, she had all the right personal attributes that made her a good catch — young, pretty, never-before-married, musical, artistically talented, and most importantly, not the dreaded *shiksa,* that quasi-mythical demon who haunted the nightmares of many a Jewish mother. But

Michael held back, perhaps fearing that should Jeanne not approve, she would scupper the relationship. As he laughingly told Adrienne, his mother had her eye on Susan Strasberg as a future daughter-in-law.[43]

Given Jeanne's cloying presence, a meeting with Adrienne was just a matter of time. It finally occurred when Michael traveled to Boston in November for an afternoon recital. Adrienne was in the audience and after the concert went backstage to say hello. She found Michael signing programs. "When Michael saw me, he pushed through the crowd, grabbed my hand, and started pulling me out the building," she recalls:

> At that point, I heard a very loud voice yell out, "Where are you going? Who are you?" Michael turned very red in the face. It was Jeanne, who then rounded on me in public, shouting at me that I did not understand who Michael was, what his obligations were, what kind of public figure he was, and so on. I felt humiliated and could only respond by stammering something foolish, like "I am a nice girl, I come from a good family." Michael stood there crimson, crestfallen, and silent.

The agony for the young couple did not, however, end there. Jeanne demanded to know where they were going and, when Michael replied he was taking Adrienne for dinner, insisted on joining them. "Michael had by now become very agitated," remembers Adrienne:

> and I was struck by the fact that his mother never once paid him a compliment about his playing or told him how well the concert had gone. And it had gone very well — the audience loved him. At dinner I did everything I could to normalize the situation so that he would relax. When the time came to say goodbye, Michael looked at me with the saddest expression you can imagine and said "See!" It was heartbreaking to witness, it really was.[44]

CHAPTER 10
FRIENDSHIP, LOVE LOST

When Angel released Michael's recordings of the Tchaikowsky concerto and the Saint-Saëns Rondo Capriccioso in North America in time for Christmas 1956,* he inscribed a copy, "To the most wonderful woman in the world, all my love," and sent it to Adrienne. Mrs. Rosenbaum's propriety was offended. Her daughter was just twenty years old. So she erased the word "woman" from the album's cover.[1] In the opinion of the *Washington Post,* Michael's playing was "hardly to be bettered by anyone anywhere on records,"[2] while to Harold Schonberg, "music like this was just made for a virtuoso like Rabin, who sweeps through it with remarkable control and musical surety."[3]

More recording sessions were scheduled for New Year's Day 1957, necessitating a return visit by ocean liner to the UK. Jeanne went with him. The orchestra was once again the Philharmonia, but this time Sir Adrian Boult was on the podium. Michael had first collaborated with Sir Adrian at a summer concert in New York two years earlier and felt comfortable working with him, which was fortunate because within four days they had to record the Mendelssohn Violin Concerto, Bruch's *Scottish Fantasy,* the Wieniawski Concerto in F-sharp Minor, and Ravel's *Tzigane.* On January 2, in the midst of the recording sessions and homesick as always, Michael wrote a passionate love letter to Adrienne. "Without you my heart is a void," he professed, adding that he couldn't sleep and was burning up with love.[4]

---

* The England release was scheduled for April 1957.

On the brighter side, a visit to London was an opportunity to meet with Alf Levy once again. Michael lapped up the emotional warmth of the Levy household, where his affectionate welcome and the kindness shown towards him by his hosts were the perfect antidote to impersonal hotel rooms and his perception that no one really missed him when he was away from home. "We would cook him a meal," remembers Levy:

> and then afterwards he would join me in the kitchen, wiping up as I washed the dishes. Can you imagine that? Once the phone rang and it was a good friend of mine, and I said to him, "You won't believe me, but I have one the world's greatest violinists in the kitchen with me, and you know what he's doing? He's helping do the dishes!"[5]

After completing his recording sessions, Michael embarked on his second European tour. From Oslo he wrote to Adrienne praising the Philharmonic and the Norwegians in general, calling them wonderful.[6] Not so the Swedes, he griped from Stockholm, who were like the British and lacked warmth.[7] Neuritis in his bow arm led to the cancellation of three concerts in Sweden and Finland. A brief visit to Germany for a radio broadcast of the Prokofiev G Minor Concerto produced some grudging praise for the speed with which the Germans had rebuilt their cities after the war.[8] Performances of the Mendelssohn and Glazunov concertos in England and a week of concertizing in Italy went well. His insecurities, however, were never far below the surface, as a letter penned from Genoa in February to his friend the cellist Dorothy Reichenberger reveals. "It must be a wonderful experience for you to attend a fine college and I do envy you," he wrote. "That I never had a complete education will be one of the leading factors which give me my inferiority complex. (As it is, I have more than enough complexes, but this just adds fat to the fire). So try and enjoy your good fortune," he advised, "and never fail to appreciate it and its lasting values." For as he ruefully confided, "My main difficulty and frustration is that I try and solve the problems of the world and not my own. Believe me, this can and does lead to much confusion."[9]

Michael's reference to a troubled world may have been sparked by his pending trip behind the Iron Curtain where three concerts had been scheduled in Czechoslovakia. He never wrote from Bratislava, fearing his letters would be censored, so his impressions of life in the Communist state have not survived. But an indication of how the audiences responded to his playing was provided by the American Ambassador to Czechoslovakia. "Dear Michael, I'm sorry that because of the crowd attempting to see you following the concert last night I was unable personally to congratulate you on your splendid performance," he wrote:

You may be interested in knowing that the reception the audience gave you greatly exceeded that given David Oistrakh who appeared here last fall. You can also take satisfaction in having done much for your country in again demonstrating to these people our high standards of artistic excellence.[10]

Michael, patriotic as he was, no doubt took some pride in those words.

From Bratislava, it was a short hop to Vienna and then home via Shannon. Looking back, the tour had been a mixed bag. The successes lay in the recording sessions for EMI, his ongoing extraordinary popularity with Scandinavian audiences, the political portent of his triumph in Czechoslovakia, and his first modest foray into Germany that promised bigger rewards in the near future. On the debit side, neuritis had halved his Scandinavian tour, always a favorite series of venues for Michael, and the English had failed to warm to him. But to gauge from his letters, toting up the successes and failures was of secondary importance. For hanging over it all, like the London fog he so detested, was the pall cast by unrequited love. In a series of letters from each European city he visited, he poured out his heart to Adrienne. From Oslo he wrote that playing the violin had become an "uphill struggle," full of "melancholy and nostalgia."[11] From Stockholm he noted ruefully that it was 383 days since they had first met.[12] From Milan he gently scolded her for not writing frequently enough, declared his love for the umpteenth time, and after adding up the miles that separated the two of them, threw in the news that his air ticket home from Vienna to New York cost $476 and was worth every cent.[13]

On his return, he immediately sought out Adrienne. She found him brimful of patriotism — the more he traveled outside America, the more he appreciated his own country. But Michael's love of homeland was complex and frequently ambivalent. No sooner was he on the road than some of the towns and hotels began reminding him of manure factories and dumps. Similarly, New York was either praised or denigrated, his ambivalence a reflection of his varying moods and levels of exhaustion. But now that he was in love, his antipathy to venues in the Midwest and Southern USA softened somewhat, coinciding with a more seasoned appreciation of the vicissitudes of life as an itinerant violin virtuoso.

For Michael's 1957 tour, Poliakine had given way to Leon Pommers. Fauré's A Major Sonata, Bloch's "Nigun" from the *Baal Shem Suite,* Mozart's Adagio in E Major, and Suk's "Burleska" were added to the repertoire. The *Symphonie espagnole* of Edouard Lalo was reintroduced alongside the Brahms and Mendelssohn concertos. Among the slew of glowing reviews from Springfield, Tulsa, Plainfield, and South Bend, a curious observation could easily have been overlooked. A March 10 write-up of Michael's concert in Indianapolis appeared under the subtitle "Soloist Seems Shy." "Mr. Rabin, who appeared shy and somewhat worried about his fiddle being in tune, stood slightly aft of the podium for his solo," noted the *Indianapolis Times*'s critic. "This may have been for better ensemble effect. I am not certain it was well advised. For the rich Rabin tones should have projected more boldly into the auditorium."14

Michael's unusual stage position had little to do with musical effect, however. Rather, the anxiety that had so overwhelmed him in New Orleans a year back had resurfaced, not as strongly, but with an added twist. In El Paso, while on stage, Michael had feared that dizziness would lead to a fall. In New Orleans he did fall. And now in Indianapolis, a new anxiety surfaced, namely, a fear of falling off the stage. His position aft of the podium was the first public manifestation of his developing phobia, and his first instinctive response was to avoid the source of his fear. So he stepped back from the edge of the platform and took shelter within the orchestra, partly behind the conductor and the protective barrier afforded by the podium. Michael's phobic anxiety was, at that point in his career, mild and intermittent, which meant that by the time he reached Tulsa a week later and walked out onto the stage, it had largely subsided and there was nothing remiss with where he planted his feet.

In trying to understand the genesis of Michael's slowly emerging phobia, the importance of what occurred in El Paso and New Orleans cannot be minimized. At the same time, the clock needs to be turned back to a singular event that befell George, many years before Michael first picked up a violin. For if the case is to be made that Michael's prodigious musical abilities were in part inherited from his parents, in particular George, then it is also possible that his anxiety stemmed from a similar fear harbored by his father. Bertine can recall an episode from her childhood — she was perhaps seven or eight years old — when on returning from school she was instructed to be very quiet. Her father had taken ill, and she and Michael were not permitted to play inside for that week. It turned out that George had suffered a nervous collapse. He recovered quickly enough, but from that time on always preferred the inside seat at his first-violin stand.15

The audiences who came to hear Michael that year knew nothing of his anxiety — his playing remained unaffected. Passing through Kansas City, he took time out from concertizing to visit Harry Truman. "He's a regular fellow" was his assessment of the ex-president. According to *Musical America,* they agreed on favorite composers: Mozart and Beethoven.16 The choice was testimony to Truman's formidable political powers of persuasion. Michael disliked Mozart's music. Meanwhile he kept the letters flowing to Adrienne, whose enthusiasm for the relationship was rapidly waning. When Michael proposed marriage and suggested going to live in Big Sur, Adrienne turned him down. The idea of simply heading off west into rural California was clearly impractical, and she saw it as nothing more than a flight of fancy.

April 1957 found Michael back in New York. On the 16th, he wrote to Adrienne complaining that the city was "terribly empty, sad, overcast, like Uranus. I can't write dear, it's too hard."17 On another occasion he admonished her: "Do you think that my desire to be with you is strengthened by the fact that you ignore me so magnificently and for such long periods?"18 On April 23 he wrote again, dolefully noting the date — the tenth anniversary of his first-ever public performance in Providence, Rhode Island. There was to be no celebratory concert, and the anniversary was passing unnoticed by all except him. There should be a party, he complained, but instead he was contemplating going out alone to a bar and getting drunk.19 Underlying many of Michael's complaints was his frustration at failing to win over Adrienne. If first love was proving painful, Uranus had its happier side, and it would be a mistake to view Michael at this juncture as a Pagliacci-like figure, the brokenhearted artist masquerading behind a public facade of enforced happiness and contentment. That very same April he appeared on stage with Jack Benny at a benefit concert to help save Carnegie Hall and had a lot of fun.20

Lewis Kaplan's memories of Michael at this time also paint a different picture from the love-lost suitor. "Although he would still draw attention to himself in public, particularly when he was with people he was not comfortable with, which was most everybody," he recollects:

> Michael was never that way with me. He was completely natural, never any pretensions, never any strutting around as the famous virtuoso. He was very giving, not wrapped up in himself. I remember around that time moving into a small apartment off Riverside Drive on 80th Street. I had a large refrigerator that I had to get up to the third floor without an elevator. My brother was helping me move, and I had one other friend, and as we turned a corner on the staircase, we couldn't get this damned refrigerator any further. So, it's now 10 or 11 PM. I called Michael and he comes tearing over to help. There we are, all laughing, just like a bunch of guys would laugh. That's the way I knew Michael. Despite his insecurities, he was a guy who laughed a lot.21

The impression of a young man in good humor was confirmed when Michael arrived in Tel Aviv on June 10 for his first tour of Israel. It was also his first visit abroad without his mother, and he was met at the airport by Frederick Mann and Isaac Stern. To a reporter from the *Jerusalem Post*, he appeared "tall, robust, pink-cheeked and smiling and full of American wise-cracks … completely unlike the common conception of an internationally famous violinist and one, moreover, who has won rave notices all over the world."22

Michael's tour to Israel, organized by the America-Israel Cultural Foundation, had been in the balance because of the Suez crisis the year before. Nasser's nationalization of the Suez Canal and the Egyptian blockade of the Straits of Tiran had pushed Israel into the 1956 Sinai War, and political events were anxiously watched by many abroad, including the Mann family back in Philadelphia. "I suppose the opening of the Mann Auditorium in Tel Aviv may depend a little on that big fat pig Nasser," Sylvia Mann had written to Michael in January, "but if that horrible maniac does anything to hurt that new building I think I will personally have to fly over and take care of him myself. This may sound very humorous to you: in fact, the situation in Israel is very serious."23

Notwithstanding the anxious times, the auditorium had been completed just prior to Michael's arrival, and he was taken to see it. He found the omnipresent Isaac Stern in attendance. An account of what happened next was given by the *Jerusalem Post*'s reporter:

> While the talented young American violinist Michael Rabin, who will appear shortly as soloist with the Israel Philharmonic Orchestra under the baton of Walter Susskind, played ... Isaac Stern skipped in agile fashion over the heaps of rubble and sacks of cement to the furthermost corners of the hall to gain some impression of the acoustics.
>
> When he came back to the stage, Rabin began playing Bach's double Violin Concerto, and Isaac Stern, on hearing this, took up a borrowed violin and spontaneously took up the second part to the delight of the group of builders wearing their [hard] hats, who listened spellbound."24

Stern made no mention of this incident in his autobiography, where the only reference to a Rabin is that for the Israeli Prime Minister, Itzhak.25

In the five weeks Michael spent in Israel he played nineteen concerts, all with orchestra. The Paganini and Brahms were his chosen vehicles, the former receiving rave reviews, the latter suffering from the familiar complaint that he had failed to fully understand the music. He enjoyed his visit, although his relationship with the management of the Israel Philharmonic Orchestra, in particular Henry Haftel and Abe Cohen, was never relaxed. Michael's letters revealed his dissatisfaction over travel arrangements, his performance fee—which at $1,000 averaged out at $52 a concert,* his repertoire (Michael wanted the

---

* This situation was not unique to Michael. Artists who were invited to perform with the Israel Philharmonic Orchestra generally waived their usual fees as a mark of support for the orchestra.

Brahms concerto, Haftel and Cohen preferred the Glazunov), and the inability of the IPO to arrange recitals despite their assurances to him in this regard.[26] When Michael left the country and still had not been paid, he turned to Josef Seiger, a frequent visitor to Israel, and asked him to intercede on his behalf.[27]

In October a batch of new recordings of the Tchaikowsky Violin Concerto were released. Michael's version, now almost a year old, was compared to those of Heifetz, Grumiaux, Campoli, Gitlis, and Erica Morini. Schonberg favored Heifetz but felt that Michael ran him a close second.[28] Irving Kolodin, in the *Saturday Review,* thought otherwise. "I can only state that where Tchaikowsky is concerned I would rather have young Michael Rabin playing it than any of the others."[29] Angel Records was delighted. However, Michael did not fare so well three months later when the pre-Christmas reviews of new recordings came out. Stern had just released the Wieniawski No. 2 and Francescatti the Vieuxtemps No. 4 concertos, and their choice of repertoire had escaped the critic's ire, but Michael's coupling of the Wieniawski F-sharp Minor Concerto and Bruch's *Scottish Fantasy* did not. "Young Mr. Rabin is altogether impressive in his violinistic command," wrote Schonberg, "and the recorded sound is exceptionally faithful; but who, outside competing violinists, would want to hear such chromos these days?"[30]

Despite these pettifogging views, David Bicknell, the Artistic Director of EMI and husband of Gioconda de Vito, was keen to extend Michael's contract until 1960. Sales had been "quite satisfactory," he informed Leo Kepler of Capitol (Angel) Records in Hollywood.[31] In his reply, Kepler said he felt that Michael had the potential to be built into a major recording artist for the American market and was optimistic that the violinist would agree to the extension.[32] Walter Legge was also keen for Michael to remain with the company, for artistic and political reasons. "It seems to me that we should keep Rabin," he wrote to Capitol:

> but far away from the classical repertoire; there are still some virtuoso concertos for him to do. Angel is not rich in violinists; they depend almost entirely upon the Russians and whilst I rank David Oistrakh above all other violinists in the world, and Leonid Kogan a great fiddler, we can never be certain these artists will be consistently available to us.[33]

Negotiations, however, bogged down. The situation was also a semantic nightmare. EMI had taken over Capitol (Angel) Records, and while the merged entity was theoretically one company, contracts were issued separately. Michael was hoping for an extension under the aegis of Capitol. While his patriotic leanings and antipathy towards the British may have influenced his decision, a practical consideration, namely the option of recording at home, was likely to have played a bigger part. EMI was not happy with this. In principle, both Legge and Bicknell did not want EMI artists transferring their contracts to Capitol because of their fear that one day, as a result of antitrust action, Capitol would break away from their parent company. Notwithstanding their concerns, Michael held firm. He renewed his contract with Capitol, and in June 1958 Michael's EMI (US) contract was allowed to lapse.[34]

The beginning of 1958 found Michael back on stage at Carnegie Hall for a recital, his first in the hall since his debut in 1950. Leon Pommers was the accompanist. Harold Schonberg's review encapsulated much of the previous year's critical opinion. Technically, Michael was faultless.

> The three Paganini caprices — no. 9, 16 and 24 — were taken at a hair raising tempo and tossed off with insulting ease. Mr. Rabin's left hand flew over the fingerboard, negotiating fingered octaves, sixths, scales and pizzicato effects without losing pitch or rhythm. At such a tempo the playing was a stunt, like walking on a tightrope over Niagara Falls. But what an exhilarating attack, and what brilliant playing! Similarly, in Ysaÿe's unaccompanied Ballade, opus 27, no. 3 played in commemoration of the one hundredth anniversary of Ysaÿe's birth, Mr. Rabin displayed a wonderful command of the technical problems. This is the kind of music he understands.

But that was where Schonberg's praise ended. What followed was becoming a familiar refrain. "Apparently all of Mr. Rabin's training has been slanted towards a command of the violin, rather than an examination of musical problems." The Brahms D Minor and Hindemith sonatas were the main casualties. Summing up the evening, Schonberg said he hoped that in time Michael's musical development would approximate his technical skills.[35] It was an uncomfortable rebuke, and it came from one of the most respected and perceptive of critics, who had followed Michael's career from the very beginning and had been fulsome in his earlier praise.

Back on the road and away from the great concert halls, Michael's reviews reverted to unqualified praise, even if at times the sentiments expressed were a little overwrought. From Sarasota came this magniloquent assessment:

> The great emotional shock of the evening, in an artistic way, was Ernest Bloch's Nigun improvisation from the Baal Shem Suite. It was a racial lament from the downtrodden of a sensitive race,

mighty even with no more than these two instruments. It wrenched the heart and stirred sympathy and wonder as well on behalf of the Hebrews, who have suffered and yet have risen.[36]

Michael's attention was not, however, focused on music making and what the critics had to say, as his letters to Lewis made clear. From Clearwater, Florida, he gave an early indication of what he was thinking. "I'm very excited about getting my place," he wrote:

> And I don't imagine living in a movie-type bachelor's apartment. I know that you'll be surprised how well it's going to be and I know that I'm going ahead with it. I gave [my parents] 21 years of my life and the rest is for me, and I divvy it up the way I want.... Outside of my usual pangs of loneliness, I'm in a good frame of mind, because I'm doing constructive thinking. I'm not going to worry about Russia — I'm thinking of *me* and I'll worry about the bombs when they come. I've got such wonderful plans.[37]

When Michael reached Ottawa in the depths of the Canadian winter, he wrote again and reiterated his plans to find a place of his own. "I get home on March 19, and as soon as the plane lands at La Guardia, I'll be scanning the real estate section of the NY Times. Wish me luck, and you'll be the first to have the new address and phone number." He also handed out some worldly advice to his friend. "I strongly suggest that you should concentrate on three very important matters — they are: conducting, violin playing, and women. These things should really keep your mind wholly occupied.... You must be concerned with *You*." Michael also mentioned that he was practicing hard — "It helps me forget things I don't want to remember and incidentally, it *does* keep my playing in good shape!"[38] The alluded-to unhappiness was his unraveling relationship with Adrienne.

His next letter from Los Angeles, brimful of optimism, picked up where the last left off:

> Wow, what a hell of a schedule I'm running on now. Concerts flying at me like mad, with four orchestral performances thrown in for fun. Oh well, it's really much better than sitting around doing nothing and it sure as hell beats 110 R.S.D. At the moment I can only think of very few people and very few things I miss in New York, but you are on that list. And it's going to be a long time before I get back, and when I do, *operation survival* shall go into

effect as soon as it is reasonably possible. It's really different now, because this time when I return to New York I've really got something exciting and wonderful to look forward to ... and that it won't take too long for me to get used to my new way of life. Just wish me luck, and the rest is up to me and hundreds of little intangibles and circumstances. I have a feeling way down deep that it's going to work out just beautifully.[39]

What were the "hundreds of little intangibles" that Michael was referring to? What were the diverse factors preventing a twenty-one-year-old, financially independent man from living on his own? The answer was that these envisioned obstacles were really a smokescreen for one major impediment — his emotional enmeshment with his parents, and Jeanne in particular. It could hardly have been otherwise given the way the past two decades of his life had unfurled. The rites of passage loomed like an impenetrable maze before him, generating excitement, but also anxiety. In repeatedly mentioning his plans to Lewis, in the perseverative content of his letters, one senses Michael talking up his own courage to act.

Michael soon became anxious when Lewis was slow to reply. A thread that ran through all his letters to those he felt close to, be they Bertine, Adrienne, or Lewis, was his belief that if they wrote to him, it meant they cared for him. In his lonely existence as a peripatetic musician emotionally estranged from his parents, letters were a tangible proof that he was missed and loved. And so he wrote often and in turn hoped for, indeed expected, frequent replies. Invariably he was disappointed. None of his correspondents could keep up with the pace he set. They were not as emotionally needy — their lives were more balanced.

Three days after Michael's letter to Lewis, he was once again at the typewriter rebuking his friend. "I'm awfully surprised that I haven't heard from you in all this time." But as always, the reproach was gentle, tinged with longing and a palpable lack of self-confidence. With the reprimand out of the way, Michael reverted to musical matters. Gone was his angry repudiation of the "Great Career," replaced by a hunger for critical acceptance and a self-effacing pride in his accomplishments. He had come a long way in a short time.

Well, the performances with the Los Angeles Philharmonic are over and I really had great success with the Glazunoff concerto. As soon as the last concert was over the manager of the orchestra said to me that I'm re-engaged for the season after next to do the Brahms' concerto. Believe me, it's awfully flattering to have an orchestral manager talk to you that way. There were some laughs after the first of the subscription concerts when Jack Benny came backstage and put his arms around me and gave me a big hug. He invited me over to his house for dinner and as he put it, "a big talk." This could mean anything.

Before signing off, a momentary dark cloud drifted back into his thoughts. "I've seen much unhappiness and uncertainty in my young life.... *Please write* Lew."[40]

A week later it was a mollified Michael who sat down again at the type-writer, reiterating his resolve to find his own apartment because of a deterio-rating home situation:

> The more I think about my plans for moving at the end of this month the more I like it, look forward to it and know now beyond a shadow of doubt that I'm really going to do it, and I'm also com-pletely convinced that it's the only sensible thing for me to do if I want to give myself a chance to live and enjoy it. As you are fully aware, my relationship with my parents has even further deterio-rated to a very low point since the recital last January 17th* and if they don't know the way things are at this point I shall have to feel sorrier for them than at any other time, but my plans shall go ahead regardless of their problems. To detour now would be cer-tain to kill any initiative on my part and I refuse to let circum-stances put me in such a position.†

The correspondence between the two friends had become an intimate exchange of support and advice. Michael, constantly beset by domestic diffi-culties, was always alert to maintaining a balanced friendship, one in which he dispensed counsel in proportion to that received. "I shall never doubt at any time your honesty as a friend," he reassured Lewis.

> As for me depending on you there is no need for you to worry on this point. Depending on you in the sense of coming to you and crying on your shoulder is just about over. The only way for us to *depend on each other* will be in the normal manner which is always, and will be in our friendship, a 50-50 effort.

---

* Michael's Carnegie Hall recital.

† The circumstances Michael was referring to were probably financial. He helped pay the rent on his parents' apartment, and his monetary support was handy in sustaining Jeanne's lavish entertaining.

Before signing off, Michael threw in a little jock banter, diluting the serious tone of his letter and revealing that his spirits remained upbeat notwithstanding the tensions that awaited him back in New York. "I'm very happy for you that things are finally beginning to look up in the female department and that you're … enjoying the finest indoor sport. As you said, the best combination at the moment is work and love, so let's both adhere to this."[41]

Five days later he was back at his typewriter. Much to his delight, Lewis had picked up the pace of his corresponding, and Michael responded to this wellspring of news and affection with a gleeful alacrity. "I read [your] letter four times and really enjoyed it," Michael enthused:

> I'll be home in a week from today and as soon as possible I start apartment hunting. I'm so glad that I'm looking forward to it as eagerly as I am and I feel surer every day that it's going to work out well despite all my former misgivings and doubts. There is, however, no question in my mind that it will be difficult at first for me, but like everything else, practice and experience smooth over most difficulties, and I don't see why my project should be an exception to this rule. I know I can count on your help and in some matters, your amazingly perceptive and correct and honest advice.

After predicting Lewis would find his way as a conductor and suggesting "we must drink excessively to that when I get back to New York and preferably in the presence of some young, ripe women, " Michael ended on a note of high optimism:

> The first thing I'll do when I land at La Guardia is to call you and the second is to get my car out of storage and get on the freedom road, both physically and mentally and actually. We are going to become even better friends, but on a much higher level. I drink to this, too.
>
> With love from a brother who is for the cause,
> ☐ Mike. ☐ Michael. ☐ Mitch. ☐ Mike the Rabe.
> *Check your preference.*[42]

No sooner had Michael returned home than all talk of apartment hunting speedily evaporated. He may have railed at his parents while on tour, but there was still something comforting about being back in the bosom of the family. Fortified by friendship, Michael was in good cheer and full of advice for Lewis who, with roles reversed, was on tour in England.

It was good to receive your letter this morning and to know for sure that you arrived in the Mother country of the Empire in apparently good spirits and feeling ready to bring even greater laurels to the fantastic collection which the Juilliard first orchestra already has in their scrapbook....

Lew, if you really like a Hill bow enough to buy it, then buy it. But it is a well known fact that these bows have a marked tendency to weaken after a few years of continuous use. True, the fleur-de-lis sticks are easy on the eyes, but I know that you're not in the market for jewelry....

I'm working very well these days and I feel that I'm in excellent shape. I hope this condition will last for a long time and not fluctuate as much as it has in recent years. I really do look forward to our drive up to Meadowmount when you return and I'm sure that we can both still get a great deal from Mr. Galamian. As you have so well proven, it's only one's mental approach that does or doesn't do things for you.[43]

Apartment hunting was not the only topic Michael omitted from his letter. Nowhere was there any mention of his intermittent attacks of stage nerves, centered on his fear that he would fall off the platform. In May in Detroit he had had to play the Tchaikowsky Concerto seated.[44] The reason given for this precedent was that he had a fever, but seated performances would become more frequent in the future.

By now the relationship with Adrienne was in its last gasps. She had found the intensity of his love, the weight of his correspondence, and his restricted interests increasingly stifling. Although Michael had not given up on winning her over, he was on the lookout for a new girlfriend and was happy to accept an invitation to a party from Lewis's brother Joel. It was one of those evenings that found Michael completely at sea. The irony was that the young man who had recently met with President Truman and was a guest at Jack Benny's house, whose birthday was remembered by Elizabeth Taylor and who could captivate thousands of people with his artistry, was completely and painfully adrift when left alone with his peers. Flustered Michael turned to Joel for help. If there's a girl here who you like, he was advised, ask her to go for a walk. Michael wasted little time, blurting out an offer to all the startled guests. An embarrassed silence ensued. Michael's naive take on the evening's events was revealed in a letter to Lewis. "Joel had a 'big blast' (as he calls it) a few nights ago and I was invited. I went, but I had to leave early. I just can't enjoy his kind of party and I'm sure you wouldn't either. Is Joel very young, or am I just square?"[45]

During the summer of 1958, three important events took place in Michael's life. Selective Service Number 5014 36 187, a.k.a. Michael Rabin, was turned down for military service (no reason given);[46] the *Telephone Hour* ended, prompting a warm letter from Wallace Magill acknowledging Michael's important contribution to the success of the program;[47] and Michael purchased a new violin. The first mention of violin hunting surfaced in a letter to Lewis dated July 21 and sent from the Warwick Hotel in Philadelphia. Michael had returned to Robin Hood Dell for a performance of the Paganini D Major Concerto. "Josef Kripps will do the stick waving," he nonchalantly informed Lewis, before adding as a postscript, "I've got the Kubelik del Gesu Guarneri (1735). I really like it and am seriously thinking of buying it. I think it's a great violin."[48]

Named after the famous Czech violinist Jan Kubelik (1880–1940), Sevcik's best-known pupil, the instrument also listed the names Petherick and Townley in its provenance and had most recently been owned by Alexander Hilsberg, concertmaster of the Philadelphia Orchestra. The instrument was on loan to Michael from William Moennig and Son, the Philadelphia luthiers, who had acquired it from Hilsberg. Kubelik had had a grand career at the beginning of the twentieth century, his performances of the virtuoso repertoire giving him the moniker Paganini recidivivus. His musical talent and shrewd business sense had made him a wealthy man, but in the 1930s his fortune had dwindled, and he had been forced to borrow money on his instrument.

The del Gesù was brought to America for sale, where its arrival was eagerly awaited by several prospective buyers. Hilsberg beat his competitors to it by meeting Kubelik's emissary at the gangplank when the ship docked. Moennig was now offering the violin to Michael for the price of $26,500.* By the time Michael went to Chicago for the Ravinia festival, the violin was his. "You may heartily congratulate me!" he proudly informed Lewis:

> As of 4 days ago, I became the *owner* of a Joseph Guarneri (del Gesù) violin dated 1735. The violin is in excellent physical shape, looks well and sounds as only a fine del Gesù can. Lots of power,

---

* The instrument was in an excellent state of preservation, with only a few short cracks near the upper and lower blocks and with a small postpatch. The violin was noted to be relatively thick at the center of the back (5 mm.), which, according to Richard Donovon of Moennig, is common among unaltered work by del Gesù. The length of the instrument was 35.1 cm., making it somewhat shorter than the Amatese ideal, but this was again characteristic of del Gesù. It was 0.2 cm. shorter than the violin Michael was using at the time. Sally Thomas relates that Szigeti and Michael met at Galamian's apartment soon after the purchase. After trying out the violin and observing Michael play, Szigeti expressed his opinion that the length of the violin was a little too short. Although Michael limited himself to one violin, he had a choice of bows: two gold-mounted Vignerons, two silver-mounted Vignerons, and one Hill Fleur de Lys.

but it possesses fine quality as well. When you get back, we must celebrate, for reasons which I am sure are obvious to you. By the way, the violin was formerly owned by the famous violinist, Jan Kubelik.[49]

Michael was understandably excited by his new purchase, although Lewis recalled that the Kubelik had not been his first choice of instrument. Michael had flirted with the Kochanski del Gesù, but that violin was substantially more expensive, and his parents had balked at the price.[50] Given the rate at which Michael was concertizing, the Kochanski would not have been beyond his means, but even if he could have overridden parental objections, other factors would have stood in his way. The violin was closely guarded by the estate of a wealthy expatriate Russian, Rachel Garbat, who had been a close friend of Kochanski. Through a remarkable series of coincidental events, Aaron Rosand managed to purchase it on March 15, 1958, his thirty-first birthday.[51] Four and a half months later, Michael bought the Kubelik. "He was never really satisfied with it," recalls Lewis. "He took it to every well-known dealer worldwide, constantly having it redone."[52] A year after Michael purchased the violin, he instructed Moennig's to replace the bass bar for tonal reasons.[53]

On September 5, 1958, with his Kubelik del Gesù in hand, Michael entered a studio in New York and, over a four-day period, recorded Paganini's first opus, the complete 24 Caprices. His name had been associated with this music from childhood, when news had leaked out from Meadowmount and Galamian's 73rd Street apartment of this wonderboy whose technical ability knew no limits. Eleven of the caprices had been recorded in 1950 for Columbia, but now he laid down the complete work for Angel. The recording would be released the following year and, for many violin aficionados, became the standard by which all subsequent versions would be judged.

It was against the backdrop of this milestone in the history of violin discography that Adrienne finally broke off her relationship with Michael. He had little time to sit around and mope, for within days he was back in Europe on tour. First love had ended in disappointment, as it so often does, but the final denouement could hardly have come as a surprise. Perhaps this explains why Michael's letters to Lewis in the immediate aftermath of his failed romance were often breezy, bright, and playful.

A day after arriving in London, he dashed off a note that hinted at some vague, ill-defined distress. But there was humor in it too. "For some unknown reason I was unusually jittery on the aircraft," he confided, "and didn't sleep a wink during the entire crossing. So as soon as I got into the hotel, I went straight to bed. This is a wonderful way to pass time, especially in England." As a postscript, Michael had written: "Enclosed is a typical English souvenir!" And he had included a small, square piece of toilet paper.[54] The note confirmed Michael's antipathy towards the English. Earlier that year he had written to Lewis with similar sentiments. "I have a definite dislike of that country. One feels a lack of warmth towards those people, and Great Britain as a place, physically, will never inspire me."[55] A number of years would pass before his views mellowed.

Michael's 1958 tour took him behind the Iron Curtain once again, this time to Yugoslavia. His visit to Tito's fragile Balkan coalition came eighteen months after his trip to Czechoslovakia and only a few months following the triumph of his erstwhile fellow-Juilliard student, Van Cliburn, at the Tchaikowsky competition in Moscow.[56] But the political import of these events was lost on Michael. Instead, he had begun ruminating on love's labor lost. "Regarding my feelings in general about things," he wrote from Zagreb, "that still remains too complex, even for me to figure out." And he was back to grumbling again, albeit with a twist of wry humor:

> It is just one week since I flew out of New York, and I'm ready to fly back today…. I don't particularly like it here [Yugoslavia]. The concert halls are honestly impossibly bad and that spoils almost everything for me. But even worse, I feel cut off because newspapers and books in English seemingly don't exist here. The only thing I've been able to get that I can read are two airline schedules, and even that's frustrating, because I can't wait to leave this country. Anyway, my last concert in Yugoslavia is on October 6th. There are only two aircraft a week flying West out of Belgrade! As for my chances of survival, I'd bet 50-50 on it.[57]

What differentiated these letters from earlier correspondence with Bertine and Adrienne were two things. First, Michael had begun looking outwards and was no longer so self-absorbed, and second, even when he lapsed back into despondency, the spells were brief and offset by tinges of humor, ensuring his complaints lacked the intensity of previous years. "I sincerely hope that things will be good for you this season, Lew," he wrote. "Keep up your violin playing. I know you have a hell of a schedule coming up, but I hope you realize that this is all an investment for your future, which I, of all people, predict will be a very bright one."[58]

After a concert in Malaga, Michael returned to London, from where he wrote to commiserate with his friend. "What can I say? Of course I feel badly that your parents' home was burglarized, but I must tell you what immediately came to mind. I thought — what a pity you didn't leave your violin there." There was evidence too that he still hankered after his lost love. "So Adrienne Rosenbaum is in New York," he wrote excitedly:

> Quick! Send me her address! I forgot to send her a New Year's Card! Do you think I should write to her? I wouldn't mind spending a little time with her. See if you can send me her address. *Oiy-oiy!*
>
> I play in London tomorrow night and then I'm off to Holland, Sweden, Norway, England again and Brussels. Oy! Where's Adrienne? You're right about the "couch scene" — We (Adrienne and I) should make it together, literally! Oi, J.C.

The thought of Adrienne notwithstanding, his spirits for the most part remained good. "Things seem to be going well with me. But I've been traveling much too much. Would you believe it that since I left New York, I've already flown 8453 miles? And I'm not even half finished with this tour." After telling Lewis of a visit to Hill's to replace a cracked chin rest, he signed off, "With love from Mike (normal-sized brother). P.S. Whaddayamean? Big Brother — As the English would say, 'Brother is quite enough.'"[59]

The concert Michael was referring to in London was a recital of shortened duration, tailored for television, in which he was accompanied by Patrick Harvey. Leon Pommers may have remained behind in New York, but he still knew how to make his presence felt. "I had a letter from [him]," Michael informed Lewis, "in which he asks me to convey his regards to you! Bubele! He also wrote at some length and in detail about a hot pastrami sandwich with kosher pickles. That bastard! He enjoys making me drool!"[60]

From Göteborg, where he was due to play the Mendelssohn Concerto with Dean Dixon conducting, Michael's letter was an amalgam of loneliness, homesickness, and fatigue. "I plod along," he moaned,

> in the usual manner. Basically, it's just one big maze of hotels, airports and concert halls. Occasionally I get the very rare and short moments of normal living. You know I'm not blasé about fine violins, but my violin ceases to excite me any more. It's really a fabulous instrument, but I'm already used to its wonderful sound. I ought to play for a while on my other one, then I'd really

appreciate this one the way I should. What I really need — Well, we both know what I really need, so there's no need for me to elaborate on the subject.61

But six days later, his cheerful spirits had returned:

I've just done 3 recitals in the last 3 days here in Norway. Finally, I must say that I played fantastically and I look back on those 3 recitals as some of the best work I've done to date. I now have one free day and then two Brahms performances with the Oslo Philharmonic.

Switching topics, he also asked Lewis to find out why Galamian had failed to write to him:

I've written to Uncle Vanya many times, and I'm really surprised not to have heard from him at all. When you see him next time, please be sure to give him my best wishes and tell him I'm playing well.62

Michael's last letter on tour was written from London on November 2. To his delight, he had found sixteen letters waiting for him on arrival at the Cumberland Hotel. "Naturally, yours was the first I read," he informed his friend. Lewis, Galamian, Adrienne, Bertine, and his parents among others had written to him. It was a veritable feast of goodwill all arriving simultaneously, and the effect on Michael was electric. Suddenly, the tour in retrospect took on a rosy glow. "[It] has been just wonderful and I've had *great* musical success." He dispensed advice to Lewis on love: "It's good that you have been able to love another girl, and probably the best thing for you would be to find still another girl." He congratulated his friend on a recent conducting success, empathized with Adrienne, who had confessed she was going through a tough time, and wished Steinhardt well after his win in the Leventritt Competition.63

Not even six performances in six days of the Prokofiev G Minor Concerto that awaited him in Belgium daunted him. Nor did a paltry five days' rest back in New York before he headed out on his next American tour, "the money tour," as he called it. After sixteen letters, a little love, some affection, and the realization that he was not forgotten, no challenge appeared insurmountable.

CHAPTER 11
THE HEIGHTS OF SUCCESS

*B*y the late 1950s, Michael was at the zenith of his career. He was one of six violinists with an EMI* contract, the others being Menuhin, Milstein, Oistrakh, Kogan, and Ferras. His recordings were selling well, he was the owner of the famous Kubelik Guarnerius, and he had never been more in demand on the concert platform. Five days' rest was all his management allowed him on his return from Europe. On November 18, 1958, with Leon Pommers as accompanist and fortified by a good pastrami on rye, he headed south: New Orleans, Baton Rouge, Shreveport, and Dallas were his stops before returning to New York. Mozart, in the form of his Tenth Sonata in B-flat Major, now made a rare appearance on a Rabin recital program. According to Josef Seiger, Michael was never at home in Mozart compositions, despite whatever he had told President Truman. He believed the music did not suit his style and denied him the freedom to do what he wanted on the violin.[1]

No sooner was Michael back on tour than the flow of letters to Lewis resumed. "Somehow, last Friday night was one of the nicest times we've had together. I could just feel it, couldn't you? I was really so pleased that you brought your violin and played with us. I must say, again, that you sounded better than ever."[2] The "us" Michael was referring to was one of those special impromptu evenings of chamber music. Vladimir Ashkenazi was in town for his American debut, a series of four performances of the Prokofiev Piano Concerto No. 2, with Leonard Bernstein and the New York Philharmonic.

---

* Capitol.

Ashkenazi was a year younger than Michael and had recently won the Queen Elizabeth Competition in Brussels. After the matinee on November 28, 1958, at Carnegie Hall, George had invited him back to 110 Riverside Drive for some dinner and a little music. Lewis had been invited too. "We played the Brahms F Minor Quintet," he recalls,

> which Ashkenazi had never played before, and he probably didn't leave out one note when he sight-read it. I couldn't believe it. Michael played first, I played second, and there were a couple of players from the Philharmonic who played viola and cello. And after we played, Michael took Ashkenazi into his room, which was filled with model airplanes, the kind you see in the window of travel agencies, except in those days they were mostly propeller planes. And Ashkenazi began running around the room trying to get the propellers spinning simultaneously. Here was Michael looking at me with this smile as if he couldn't quite believe what he was seeing. There was real irony in that — the child laughing at still another child.[3]

Michael took a break from his American tour and returned to Israel on January 17, 1959. Even before he arrived, a sometimes strained correspondence with Cohen and Haftel started up again. The orchestra management wanted Michael to play a Mozart concerto at a youth concert. While happy to perform, Michael stated his clear preference to stay away from Mozart and suggested Lalo or Tchaikowsky instead. Cohen dug in his heels and got his way. Michael also tried renegotiating his fee but received just a $500 raise. Then he asked for jet transportation but was turned down — the IPO had an arrangement with the national carrier El Al and their planes were still turbo propeller. Negotiations also bogged down over some proposed recitals that Michael was keen to play — he objected to playing in Haifa and did not want a cinema for his Tel Aviv venue. Michael suggested Frank Pelleg as his local accompanist, but these plans fell through too. He ended up performing the Lalo *Symphonie espagnole* six times and the Brahms Concerto once.[4]

Two months after Michael had left the country, he wrote to Abe Cohen and ruefully noted that in his two visits to Israel, he had not managed to perform a single recital. He also inquired about the outstanding balance of $1,445.75 owed to him.[5] Yet despite these frustrating hiccoughs, Michael appeared to enjoy his time in the country. Whether the feelings were reciprocated, however, was another matter. In 1961 he wrote to ask for another invitation but received the cold shoulder.[6] Six years later, his English agents Tillet and Holt made a similar request and also got nowhere.[7] The reluctance of the

IPO management to have Michael return remains mystifying. The concert reviews he had received were very good, and his visits were made during a period in his career when he had never played better. His requests — one hesitates to call them demands given his tendency to back down in any negotiations — were hardly in the prima donna category. Perhaps here the IPO had adopted one of Sol Hurok's maxims: "If they're not temperamental I don't want them. It's in the nature of a great artist to be that way."[8]

IN NEW YORK CITY in late March, Michael, accompanied by Leon Pommers, made a recording for Capitol. The Wieniawski Caprice Op. 18, No. 4; Sarasate's "Zapateado" and "Habanera"; and Elgar's "La Capricieuse" were completed in the first session, and the duo returned in April adding eight more short pieces to the list: Debussy's "La plus que lente," Ravel's "Pièce en forme d'Habanera," Chopin's Nocturne Op. 27, No. 8 (arranged by Wilhelmji), Mompou's "Jeunes filles au jardin" (arranged by Szigeti), Scriabin's "Etude in Thirds" (arranged by Szigeti), Engel's "Sea Shell" (arranged by Zimbalist), Prokofiev's "March from *The Love for Three Oranges*" (arranged by Heifetz), and Suk's "Burleska." The collection, entitled *Mosaics,* was scheduled for release in November. Michael had played these miniatures since childhood and loved this music that dated from an era when violinists were also composers and arrangers. His playing reflected this affinity — only Heifetz among the violinists currently active could rival him in this genre.

At twenty-two years of age, Michael was no longer the wunderkind, but that did not mean George had stopped working quietly behind the scenes to foster his son's career. No sooner had Michael returned from Israel than his father went to bat for him. Plans were afoot for Leonard Bernstein to take the New York Philharmonic Orchestra on a historic tour of Russia and Europe. George approached Bernstein backstage after a television recording and asked if Michael could be the soloist. Bernstein was noncommittal, and with the two men surrounded by a throng of well-wishers, the briefest of discussions ended. Undeterred, George immediately put pen to paper, spelling out his request:

> Dear Lenny,…
>
> Michael has reached the stage in his career now where a helping hand by a person of your position and stature could really put him over the difficult hurdle. You, of all people, are well aware of the difficulties with which a young artist is beset, particularly a young American artist. An opportunity of this kind would surely serve to show the European and Russian audiences that we are able to produce violinists of the first caliber in America.
>
> I am sure a word from you, in this direction, could carry enough

weight, and swing it for Michael, and I sincerely hope that you will give this matter your serious and sympathetic consideration.

Affectionately,

George Rabin [9]

Bernstein, in his scrawled reply, was gracious, stating his preference for touring without soloists and assuring George that he would otherwise have considered Michael, "of whom I am as proud as any other American is."[10]*

Whatever disappointment the Rabins felt at this outcome was diluted by an unexpected honor that soon came Michael's way. He was given a $5,000 Ford Foundation grant, one of ten musicians chosen from 350 countrywide. Other notable winners were the pianists Seymour Lipkin and the cellist Leonard Rose. The winners in turn had to select an American composer to write a work for them.[11] Michael chose Paul Creston.

Born Giuseppe Guttoveggio in New York in 1906, Creston was already the recipient of a number of honors and awards, including a Guggenheim Fellowship and a New York Music Critics' Circle Award. He had completed his first violin concerto three years earlier, although it was by no means certain Michael knew the work, which was already rarely performed. Entirely self-taught, with a unique, albeit conservative, style of composition that made use of lush harmonies and expansive orchestration, he was thought of as a composer of the romantic era working in the twentieth century.[12] This must have endeared him to Michael, whose own penchant for the romantic violin repertoire was already well established. Creston's fame was another factor that may have swayed Michael and Galamian. Toscanini and the NBC symphony had championed him earlier, and by the late 1950s, he was among the most widely performed contemporary American composers.

With a series of high-profile concerts approaching over the spring and summer, Michael turned again to the Tchaikowsky Concerto. The first performance on April 12 with Leonard Bernstein and the New York Philharmonic Orchestra at Carnegie Hall was followed by a July 2 appearance with Thomas Sherman at the Lewisohn Stadium and a July 25 engagement with André Kostelanetz at the Hollywood Bowl.

His reviews ran the gamut from praise to excoriation. On a hot, humid night in New York, he was criticized for a tone that wailed and a left hand that lacked agility.[13] On an equally hot and humid night in Los Angeles, he was lauded for impeccable intonation, trills of lightening speed, brilliant

---

* Orchestra members John Corigliano, Laslo Varga, and John Wummer performed as soloists on the 1959 tour, as did Bernstein himself, playing and directing from the piano.

harmonics, accurate double-stops, and passage work that was smooth and agile.[14] The same divergence in opinion marked his June 24 performance of the Brahms Concerto with the Chicago Symphony Orchestra conducted by Milton Katims before an audience of 15,000 in Grant Park.[15] Michael had by now largely stopped listening to what the critics had to say, even while he still assiduously collected their reviews. If he thought poorly of their musical judgment at times, he could not quibble with one observation from a Chicago journalist: "That Mr. Rabin may suddenly have ballooned into the largest individual now tucking a fiddle under his chin, he's certainly no small artist as we have already learned."[16]

Michael had indeed put on a lot of weight recently. This was not something new. As a child, his girth had intermittently bulged to uncomfortable dimensions. The embarrassment he experienced had left him feeling self-conscious about his weight, and during adolescence, when the scales began creeping upwards again, he had been quick to act and modify his diet.[17] Now, with Adrienne out of the picture and touring with a pianist who shared a liking for rich deli food, Michael was again decidedly beefy. He had not yet "discovered" diet pills. For the time being it was willpower alone that he relied on, and intermittently it would abandon him.

When in Los Angeles over the summer, Michael had paid a visit to Jascha Heifetz. Dropping in on Heifetz unannounced was unthinkable, even if Michael was now himself a celebrated artist. Heifetz's typed reply to Michael's request for a visit was characteristically reserved but nonetheless welcoming, and he gave out his unlisted telephone number.[18] There is no surviving record of Michael's impressions of that meeting or what the two virtuosos spoke about, or whether they even played table tennis, a shared passion. Michael's visit essentially was an act of homage to a man who had been his boyhood hero and whom he still revered. While his admiration for Heifetz the violinist would never waiver — Michael steadfastly refused to play Gershwin for many years, stating that after Heifetz's performances, no one had anything else to say[19] — his opinion on Heifetz the man was kept to himself. A year later when Michael returned to the Hollywood Bowl, Heifetz, unannounced, came to listen and look, taking a box near the stage and observing Michael through large binoculars.[20] Michael was thankfully unaware of his idol's intense scrutiny. Navigating Lalo's intricacies on stage under Jascha Heifetz's binocular gaze was not something to be welcomed.*

---

* Michael had another encounter with Heifetz at a concert. Heifetz had come backstage to greet Michael and found him fussing over his del Gesù, complaining about the sound quality. "Are you sure it's the fiddle?" asked Heifetz.

Little more than a month after visiting Heifetz at his Beverly Hills home, Michael was back in Los Angeles, teaming up with the conductor Felix Slatkin and the Hollywood Bowl Symphony Orchestra for a further series of recordings for Capitol. The repertoire again focused on that unique violinist-composer oeuvre that brought audiences to their feet and left critics reaching for their superlatives while simultaneously looking down their noses at the musical content. The album to be recorded would be called *The Magic Bow* and comprised Massenet's "Meditation" from *Thaïs,* Dinicu's "Hora Staccato (arranged by Heifetz), Kreisler's "Caprice Viennois," Brandl's "The Old Refrain" (arranged by Kreisler), Sarasate's *Zigeunerweisen*, Paganini's "Moto Perpetuo," Rimsky-Korsakoff's "Flight of the Bumble Bee" (arranged by Heifetz), and a second recording of Saint-Saëns's Introduction and Rondo Capriccioso. Michael's pulling power with this emotive, schmaltzy music was considerable, and sales estimates for the United States alone were set at 15,000 records for the first year followed by 12,000 for each of the next two years.[21]

Plans by Capitol for Michael to record the Sibelius Concerto had been cancelled by EMI back in May because of poor projected sales estimates.[22] The reference to the Sibelius remains mystifying. Galamian did not like the work and there is no record of Michael having performed it. Moreover, Walter Legge had earmarked other repertoire for Michael, like a repeat recording of Paganini's D Major Violin Concerto. Recently, *Gramophone* magazine had looked anew at Michael's 1954 Paganini rendition as part of a review of contemporary releases: Ricci, Francescatti, Menuhin, and Kogan were the competition. The verdict was unequivocal:

> Columbia already has the most outstanding recording — that by Rabin which seems more breathtaking each time one hears it. Far more perfect in intonation than Ricci (whose finale nevertheless sparkles deliciously), and more effortless and graceful than Francescatti, who uses the same edition, but a different cadenza. Young Rabin's performance is virtually flawless and leaves one amazed at such technical wizardry. Paganini himself could not have bettered this.[23]

Six years was, however, a long time in the recording industry. Monaural LPs were fast becoming obsolete, and Capitol decreed the time was ripe for their young wizard to recreate his masterpiece in stereo. The Vieuxtemps Concerto No. 4 was slated as the companion concerto, but EMI acquiesced to Michael's preference for the Wieniawski Concerto in D Minor instead.[24] Sales estimates were half those for *The Magic Bow.*[25]

Having completed the *Magic Bow* recording sessions, Michael hurried back to New York, picked up a change of laundry, and set off for his first visit to South America, an eight-day trip to Venezuela. "Caracas is obviously a very wealthy city," he observed in a by now rare letter to Bertine, "and it's certainly one of the most expensive places in the world. It's the kind of place where I'd like to come for the 'vacation de-luxe.'"26 The sold-out audiences loved his playing. "The public, in its overwhelming ovation, didn't know what to clap most for," ran a local review, "whether for his impressive bowing, his digital dexterity, his sparkling sound or his singular invigorating style. But one thing was definitely proved, that Rabin is one of the greatest violinists of our time."27 In October, Michael repeated his success in Mexico.

Two days after leaving Mexico, Michael played the Beethoven Concerto in South Bend, Indiana. It was a performance bedeviled by his phobia. After praising aspects of the interpretation, a bemused critic wondered aloud why Michael had stood behind the conductor. "It was almost impossible to see the artist," he complained, "and the orchestra members had difficulty seeing the conductor. It removed any chance of error on entrance, but it also spoiled the audience's full appreciation of Rabin as guest soloist."28 When Michael repeated the concerto with the Mobile Symphony Orchestra a month later, through sheer willpower he had resumed the soloist's customary position on stage.29

His next stop was New Orleans for a performance of the Brahms Concerto, to be conducted by Alexander Hilsberg, the former owner of the Kubelik del Gesù violin. If Hilsberg, who had taken up the position of Musical Director in New Orleans after leaving the concertmaster's chair in Philadelphia, was impressed by the mellifluous sounds Michael coaxed from his instrument, he must surely have been astonished by where the soloist elected to stand. "Mr. Rabin is the first violinist I can recall that placed himself virtually among the orchestra and not in front of it," noted a local reviewer.30

There seemed little Michael could do to banish the fear, which reared up at unpredictable moments. He had not yet consulted a psychiatrist, for there were quiescent periods that must have lulled him into hoping the anxiety that had arrived so precipitously and mysteriously in New Orleans would vanish in similar fashion. A practical consideration, such as the pace of concertizing, would also have hampered him reaching out for help. South Bend, Ottawa, Oklahoma City, Fort Worth, Mobile, New Orleans, Little Rock, Portland, San Francisco, Spokane, Boise, Twin Falls, Los Angeles, Honolulu, and Maui whirled by in a blur. The search for answers would have meant canceling engagements, something he was loath to consider. There was also the thorny issue of stigma to consider. Seeking help for a burst appendix or a troublesome ulcer was a lot easier than admitting to a fear of falling off the stage. For the time being, therefore, Michael kept his own counsel. Not even Lewis or his management knew of his nascent concerns. Just the contrary. To the family, friend, and teacher back in New York who followed his progress from afar, Michael seemed in good shape. And in many respects he was. His reviews had never been better and photographs invariably captured a happy young man, laughing with his accompanist or smiling with a lei around his neck.

At the start of the new year, a slimmed-down Michael was joined in Chicago and Greensboro by Brooks Smith for recitals that began with Mozart's Tenth Sonata in B-flat Major, followed by Beethoven's "Kreutzer" Sonata. That same January, he performed the Wieniawski Concerto in D Minor in Norfolk, with an eye clearly on his May recording date in London. Michael had missed David Oistrakh's visit to New York the month before, but in February he had an opportunity to meet Russians of a different kind.* Running a fever of 104 degrees, he climbed out of his sickbed in New York and traveled to Denver to join family friend Saul Caston and his orchestra in performances of Mozart's Fourth and Prokofiev's G Minor violin concertos. A Soviet trade delegation was in town, and according to an article in the *Denver Post,* they approached the evening "with typical Muscovite culture consciousness. Their bus drivers and some of those accompanying them on the tour chose to go next door for the finals of the Golden Gloves Boxing tournament."[31] Perhaps the presence of a Prokofiev work on the program swung the scales Michael's way. He was awarded a Soviet Peace and Friendship medal for his efforts.

Ten years had passed since Michael's Carnegie Hall debut with the Vieuxtemps Fifth Concerto. *Musical America* acknowledged this milestone with an article entitled "An Ornament to His Profession." The tribute summarized his career thus far, enumerating his many achievements. It also gave Michael an opportunity to discourse on his life outside of music. Here he embellished a little — his love of cars and airplanes were well known, but adding psychology and philosophy to the list spoke more to aspirations unfulfilled.[32]

In another commemorative gesture, the National Orchestral Association, responsible for Michael's first Carnegie Hall appearance, invited him back. This time, however, Vieuxtemps would give way to Beethoven.[33] On March 1, 1960, Michael celebrated his first decade as a fully fledged concert artist by performing Beethoven's masterpiece, standing square in front of a capacity

---

* While Michael was in Hawaii, Oistrakh had visited New York and had left him a message: "Dear Michael, Best wishes to you. I am very sorry I missed you in New York. Hope to see you soon. David Oistrakh."

audience. The kudos he received befitted a master musician. Even Harold Schonberg was totally won over — at last. "In a decade Mr. Rabin has developed into one of the most impressive technicians before the public," he wrote:

> There may have been doubts about the direction his talent was taking, but there was never any doubt about his ability to play the violin. Last night he played a very spirited Beethoven, one filled with youthful vitality. It was one of the best performances that this listener has heard from Mr. Rabin. The playing was beautifully controlled, musicianly and voluptuous in tone. And the way he tore through the Kreisler cadenzas was positively awesome.[34]

Galamian was almost content. George beamed. Jeanne basked. And Michael? What did he experience as he read the hosannas with his morning coffee? Satisfaction perhaps, or vindication? Joy, even pride? Whatever went through his mind in the concert's triumphant aftermath, there was little time to savor it. He was due to repeat the Beethoven concerto within the week, in Texas. Michael surely must have approached the performance with high expectations of finally having rid himself of his bogey: he had slain the critics, the pressure was off, the venue was out of the way, the Beethoven was under the fingers, and the easygoing conductor, Orlando Barera, was someone he enjoyed performing with. But it was not to be. "One wondered why the 23-year-old Rabin took his position in front of the musical director..." queried one critic, "rather than nearer the audience as soloists generally do."[35] The answer was not to improve the ensemble, as he generously suggested. Rather, the venue was El Paso, the stage the very same one on which Michael had first developed incapacitating dizziness seven years ago. Anxiety obeyed a perverse set of rules.

Michael still did not reach out for help. He did not even tell Lewis or Bertine of his fear. Instead, he bottled up his angst and headed back to Europe. March 19 found him in London. "The jet-flight over to tea-town here was fantastic," he joked to Lewis. "Non-stop in 6 hrs. 10 min. After considerable calculation, it finally dawned on me it *is* faster than a Corvette. Seriously though, it was great."[36]

Michael and Lewis had kept their correspondence going over the past year, but from 1960 onwards it was clear that the relationship had undergone changes. The two friends remained very close, but in the interim Lewis had met Adria Goodkin and was dating her seriously. Gone now from Michael's letters were any references to red-headed dancers and warm women that had peppered his correspondence from two years back.[37] The male bonhomie, which had never approached the coarseness of locker-room banter, was now directed more at music. Michael's letters also revealed a discernible shift in how he viewed himself, notably, a greater awareness of his special gifts and an acceptance that concertizing was inextricably part of his life.* This did not stop him from complaining occasionally, but the vehemence of his earlier outbursts was absent. "It seems that the tour consists of 34 concerts with 5 recitals and 29 appearances with orchestra!" he methodically informed Lewis. "Actually, it works out to 34 concerts in 7½ weeks. Now matter how you look at it, it's a hell of an assignment."38 And that's where the caviling ended, for now.

"Now that the first 8 days of this tour have gone by," he confided from Brussels,

> I am beginning to breathe a bit easier. Psychologically, it's better now that I'm "in the 2nd week" of the tour and no more surprised by the difference here as compared to my country. I am much more at ease this time than on any previous tour of Europe, but everywhere I see huge posters advertising that the quickest way to New York is via the Pan American Boeing 707 jet! Goddam it, I know this only too well, and every time I see one of those posters, I do feel lousy.39

Michael always found starting a new tour difficult, even back in America. He had separation anxiety, not just from New York, but also from the familiarity of his home, even if that was synonymous with a mother who allowed him little breathing space. Quite simply, the itinerant musician with over 300,000 accumulated air miles meticulously calculated and neatly jotted down in his flight log had never overcome feeling homesick.

The Atlantic Ocean should have been the perfect barrier to a domineering mother left behind — the time away a welcome respite from her meddling. Sequestered from her all-knowing, all-seeing eye, Michael had an opportunity to cut loose, spread his wings, and live a little. To be sure, he worked very hard, as he often informed Lewis. "Tonight starts 'my' Tchaikowsky run. Five performances in the next four days.... After Brussels, I'm off to Italy for seven days (6 concerts in 6 cities!). That is what is commonly known as B.S."40 But as the Baedeker-type memoirs of many musicians made clear, life on tour had its compensations. The libertine young Rubinstein,41 the culture-hungry Menuhin,42 the resolutely earnest Stern,43 the raconteur and bon vivant young Kreisler,44 among many others, all shared an ability to enjoy life away from the concert stage. Michael did not. He literally counted the days, hours,

---

* Michael's letters for much of 1959 have been lost. So has Lewis Kaplan's entire correspondence addressed to Michael.

and minutes before he could fly home. Geographical separation did not equate with an emotional distancing from his parents. He was still living at 110 R.S.D. His high-flown plans for greater independence, expressed repeatedly and passionately in letters to Lewis two years earlier, had foundered.

Michael had chosen the European-based American pianist Donald Nold for his recitals. Nold was known to the Rabin family. New Jersey born, he had hoped to study at the old Juilliard in 1947 but needed more specialized tutoring before he felt confident in taking the entrance examination. The person he had turned to for help was Jeanne Rabin. He had visited her for private lessons at the Rabin's apartment on 905 West End Avenue and retained vivid memories of how Jeanne would brusquely send Michael back to practice every time the eleven-year-old boy stepped out of his room. Nold thought highly of Jeanne, both as a pianist and teacher, and credited her with helping him gain admission to Juilliard.

After graduating he had gone to live in Europe. "The only Donald the French knew was Donald Duck," he recollected. "Every time my name was mentioned, people said, 'Le canard, quack quack!' So at the suggestion of a friend, I dropped the last *d* and my name became quite exotic sounding — Doh-nahl." When, many years later, George approached him with a request to accompany Michael in Europe, "Donal" was delighted to accept. "Playing with Michael was marvelous," he recalled. "He was a fantastic violinist, technically secure with a beautiful sound." But he also recalled Michael playing a recital seated because of his resurgent fear of falling. It didn't affect the quality of his playing, but it was the first time Nold, who had accompanied other string players such as Tossy Spivakovsky and Walter Trampler, had played under such unusual circumstances.[45]

While phobic anxiety forced Michael to alter his behavior on stage, it did not slow the momentum of his tour. "Wow! The last week has been a bitch!" he wrote from Göteborg:

> 5 concerts in the last 6 days, 1340 miles of train riding and a bit over 1000 miles of flying. The concert with the orchestra here tomorrow night is already the 13th one of the tour. However, you did guess right. The last 10 days of the tour will be easy with only two concerts and 4 recording sessions.

After dispensing advise to Lewis on what he should be doing musically, commiserating with him on lost work opportunities and offering to introduce him to new work contacts, Michael gave a thumbnail sketch of how things were going in Europe. "4 of the 5 Tchaikowskys were good in Brussels — Orchestra — Fair. Mozart in Rome — Good — Orch, *lousy*. Orch here in Göteborg is Fair — performance tomorrow, then on to Stockholm."[46] Another letter, with an apology for his tardy correspondence, followed from Helsinki. "I'm really so M-F busy that I'm amazed at myself that *everything* goes so well and with a minimum of difficulty, etc."[47]

Ivan Galamian loomed large in his students' consciousness. Michael at twenty-three years of age had ceased regular lessons, but Uncle Vanya, as he was known, was still very much part of his life. "These occasional bits of mental wisdom that you pass on to me from Galamian are fabulous," he enthused to Lewis from Helsinki. "I think that, deep down, he's a very humorous man."[48] Four days later, Galamian and one of his students were again the topic of correspondence. Jaime Laredo had the previous year walked off with top honors at the Queen Elizabeth Competition. At seventeen years of age, he was the youngest winner ever. Now Lewis wrote telling Michael that Laredo was to marry. "I can't even begin to imagine what was I.G.'s reaction to this news," replied an incredulous Michael. "Probably, after he picked himself up off the floor, he screamed out 'Missy, vere eez zee Scotch? Queek!'"[49] Five days later, Michael found more Galamianiana awaiting him in London. "I got the funniest letter *and* birthday card from I.G.," he gushed. "I'm going to save it and show you when I get back. He's so unpredictable, and wonderful."[50]

Michael played six different concertos on tour: Beethoven, Brahms, Tchaikowsky, and the Mozart D Major in live performances, the Paganini D Major and the Wieniawski D Minor in the recording studio. For the most part, he confined himself to a single concerto per concert, except in Lisbon and his favorite city, Oslo. "My concert here tomorrow night (with orch.) is a rather busy one," he disclosed. "I'm playing Beethoven *and* Tchaikowsky! I've been playing so much during the past 6 weeks and am in really good form that even this program doesn't seem such a difficult job."[51]

The critics agreed. Praise followed him wherever he played. The Scandinavians considered him a young master.[52] His Brahms Concerto with the London Philharmonic Orchestra at the Festival Hall in London "was remarkable for its technical assurance and an innate sense of style shown in each movement."[53] The review in the *London Telegraph* went on to extol his "spellbinding legato" in the slow movement and his "exact and splendidly masculine chording" in the finale. Noel Goodwin in the *Daily Express,* reviewing the same concert, took issue with how Michael performed the opening movement but, by the time the last notes of the allegro giocoso had sounded, was won over: "I do not remember hearing it better played since Jascha Heifetz's last visit."[54] To Michael, there could have been no higher praise.

The 1960 tour ended with a recording session in London at the Abbey

Road Studios. Michael had provided EMI with a list of favored conductors for the sessions. First choice was either Walter Susskind or Malcolm Sargent. Thereafter, his preferences in descending order were Barbirolli, Giulini, Galliera, and von Matačić.[55] The latter had been on the podium in Michael's first Paganini recording. He also commanded the lowest fee. EMI approached him first. He was unavailable.[56] EMI then suggested either Fistoulari or Goossens, and Michael chose Goossens, recalling their successful collaboration during his 1952 Australian tour. Much, however, had changed in Sir Eugene's life since then. Concerned about what he perceived as his failing musical powers, Goossens had gone in search of rejuvenation but instead had found black magic, witchcraft, and prostitution. In March 1956, the famed English conductor had been caught trying to smuggle banned books, ritual masks, and 1,166 "pornographic" pictures into Australia. Forced to resign from his position at the Sydney Symphony Orchestra, Goossens had returned in disgrace to England, where attempts at resurrecting his career had been largely unsuccessful.[57] When approached by EMI, his diary had openings.

Michael's 1960 European tour was notable for the brilliance of his playing, a greater depth to his interpretations, two stellar recordings, and away from the glare of the stage lights, a less cloying need for advice and reassurance. "Today I'm 24 years old. Shit — " he wrote to Lewis from Lisbon. "Well, in 13 days (if all goes right) I'll come streaking into Idlewild and no doubt, a Sunday afternoon traffic jam…. I'm anxious to see you, talk with you, and, if I can, help you. We have much to catch up with, and I am anticipating many good times together this summer."[58] Expletive aside, it was another outward-looking letter from Michael, imbued with customary generosity and newfound optimism. A week later, even his opinion of London had softened. "I've got to admit it. London is really beautiful at this time of the year. Spring is bustin' out all over and it smells great. I hope it will be nice in New York when I get back. I imagine that Riverside Drive looks nice now with the trees fully leaved." There were fresh plans to find his own apartment and a hint with a wink of a secret sexual liaison. "I also plan to see my friend on 5th Ave. You know who I mean?! Of course, who else?!!"[59]

Despite the intermittent yet tenacious stage anxiety, Michael's confidence in himself had never been higher. Relaxing in his hotel room overlooking Hyde Park, he reflected on the past few months:

> This tour has been a revelation to me because it's been such a
> pleasure compared to all the previous ones. I'll tell you what I
> mean, in detail, when I see you, but as far as I'm concerned, it's a

most welcome and heartfelt change which, among other things
shows that I can live much better with myself. I suppose all this is
part of that process called growing up.

So dear Lewis, this is the last letter of this tour. I'll call you on
Sunday and we can *talk* and make plans.[60]

Even allowing for the fact that Michael's mood had always turned upbeat
as a tour approached the end, his admission of newfound pleasure in his itinerant life signaled a big shift in attitude. Neither of the friends knew that this
note represented the end of their correspondence — no letters would pass
between them again. In light of subsequent events not that far down the road,
one brief eloquent paragraph, penned a few days earlier from Portugal, takes
on a haunting air. "Seriously Lew, I have a premonition that the 'soaring 60's'
is going to be a great decade for both of us. The most exciting thought is that
we will both become men. What we do, depends only on the efforts we
make ... and maybe, a pinch of luck."[61]

CHAPTER 12
CALAMITY

$\mathcal{M}$ ichael's favorable prognostications for the decade ahead seemed well founded. On his return to America, he purchased a Corvette sports car — a new model was just out, and he chose a silver-gray classic with red trim. He would lavish as much attention on it as he did on his del Gesù. That summer he traveled up to Meadowmount in his pride and joy and spent two weeks there, but not with his parents. Instead, he had taken to staying with Leonard Rose and his family in their rented farmhouse, keen to put some distance between himself and his mother, who, he confided to Rose, was driving him crazy.[1] Lewis joined him for what would be their last summer together as footloose bachelors. Michael also visited Paul Creston to check up on the progress of his commissioned violin concerto — the premiere was coming up in November in Los Angeles. It was a relaxing time and he felt good about life. He did not follow through on his plans to find an apartment. He did not seek help for his phobia.

If there was one concerto that Michael needed little inducement to play, it was Tchaikowsky's. He had played this warhorse so many times there was a risk of staleness setting in, which may have accounted for a perfunctory performance he gave in November for a *Telephone Hour* program portraying incidents in Tchaikowsky's life. Entitled "The Music of Romance," the television program was melodramatic, with a watery-eyed Nadezhda von Meck (portrayed by Helen Hayes) wafting in and out of camera.[2] The whole scene was redolent of a film made fourteen years earlier, in which Jascha Heifetz played the same Tchaikowsky while another moist-eyed woman in the throes of some equally strong emotion drifted into view before fading away.[3] But that's where the similarities ended. If the passions invoked in the two women were comparable, the violin playing was not. Michael's performance, although technically secure, lacked the drive and fiery brilliance of Heifetz. In fairness to Michael, the productions too were of unequal quality. Heifetz had Fritz Reiner along with a full symphony orchestra and the backdrop of Carnegie Hall, whereas Michael had to make do with the makeshift Bell Studio Orchestra and a floridly kitsch stage setup.

In the fall of 1960, the pinch of luck Michael had sought became more elusive. A sequence of four events took place that ran counter to the current of his recent successes. The first incident was by itself trivial, more of a nuisance than anything else. Michael became the subject of an inquiry by the Bureau of Educational and Cultural Affairs, an offshoot of the State Department. It had come to their attention that Michael had traveled in Communist countries and had recently been given a medal by a Soviet trade delegation. The paranoid jingoism of the McCarthy era had by then run its course — Michael had been correct when as a teenager he had predicted the Wisconsin senator's comeuppance — but the fear of Communism persisted. The question therefore arose in the minds of the Washington mandarins: what kind of American was Michael? To those who knew him, his loyalty to the United States was never in doubt. But the State Department wanted to make sure, and they asked for a character reference.

It was all done quite openly. Isidore Halpern, a lawyer and family friend, was asked for his assessment of Michael's patriotic credentials. Izzie, or "Uncle Dudley" as Michael lovingly called him, duly obliged, singing his praises in tune with the prevailing political climate. "I know you are not interested in my opinion of his colossal musical talent," he wrote:

> I can, however, give you a very definite opinion of Michael Rabin as a human being.... His parents are people of great honor, distinction and integrity. They are splendid Americans and a credit to our country.... Michael Rabin and I have had many discussions in fields outside of music. He is thoroughly dedicated to the goals, principles and beliefs of our great country. He is a fine, loyal American.[4]

And so it went. In his note of explanation to Michael, Halpern added, "Mike, I said all these things only because they happen to be true."[5]

The second event, more distressing by far, was the sudden death of Dimitri Mitropoulos, who suffered a heart attack while conducting Mahler's Third Symphony in Milan.[6] He was sixty-four years old. Although the conductor had a long history of heart problems, the news still came as a shock.

Mitropoulos's tenure in New York, which had ended with Leonard Bernstein's succession in 1958, had not always been a happy one. But he had consistently championed Michael and had been the first conductor of substance to offer him engagements with a leading orchestra. Although by the time of his death his influence in New York's musical life had waned a little, with his passing Michael lost one of his staunchest admirers and a powerful mentor.

A third setback was the failure of Creston's Second Violin Concerto to make any lasting impression. Mitropoulos had been on the podium when Michael had premiered the Mohaupt concerto in 1954. For the Creston work, it was Georg Solti and the Los Angeles Philharmonic's turn. The performances took place on November 17 and 18, 1960.[7]* According to Creston's programmatic notes, each of the concerto's three movements had certain defining characteristics; form was important in the first, melody in the andante, and rhythm in the presto. To the critics, the influences of Debussy, Ravel, and Gershwin were clearly discernible without diluting Creston's distinctive voice. When Michael repeated the work on November 28 in Seattle with Milton Katims on the podium, the concerto was greeted by the critics as a true American original.[8]† He played it again on January 27, 1961, in Atlanta, but after that the concerto disappeared off the concert programs.‡ A New York Town Hall performance with the Little Orchestra Society a year later was its swan song before it joined the Mohaupt work in obscurity.

The rapid disappearance of the Creston commission reflected the composer's steady fall from favor. By the middle of the 1960s, his major works were no longer played, his name kept alive by a few hardcore devotees and a small but influential group of composers who had been students.[9] As with the Mohaupt premiere, Michael's performance had been technically excellent and his beautiful, trademark sound had enhanced the work's lyricism. In the months ahead, he tried supporting the concerto in other ways too. When he and Brooks Smith performed at a Lado Benefit concert on December 18 at the Biltmore Hotel, Creston came to talk about the concerto. Michael also participated in a conference comprising many of the other Ford Foundation Grant winners held on August 24, 1961, at Yale University. But in truth, he never retained much affection for either of the concertos he premiered. Michael was not a devotee of twentieth-century music, despite having a varied and often melodic repertoire to choose from. "I would love to play the Walton Violin Concerto," he had professed in his *Musical America* interview,

---

* Saint-Saëns's Introduction and Rondo Capriccioso was also played.

† Wieniawski's Concerto No. 2 was also played.

‡ Ravel's *Tzigane* was also played.

"but it would entail too much work and rehearsal time. I don't play contemporary music for the same reason. Also, I have to play what orchestras demand."[10] This was only partially true. Not even a "cantabile e vibrato" marking could lure him into Elgar's lyrical masterpiece.

The biggest musical disappointment for Michael, however, was the decision by EMI not to release his December recording session. Ten short pieces with piano were slated for vinyl: Dvořák's "Slavonic Dance"(arranged by Kreisler), Kreisler's "Tambourin chinois," Debussy's "The Girl with the Flaxen Hair," Kroll's "Banjo and Fiddle," Sarasate's Introduction and Tarantella, de Falla's "Dance espagnole" (arranged by Kreisler), Schumann's "The Profit Bird" (arranged by Achron), Kreisler's "La Chasse," Chopin's Nocturne in E-flat (arranged by Sarasate), and Wieniawski's "Polonaise Brillante." This repertoire had been approved by EMI's International Classical Repertoire Committee on October 18, 1960.[11] The recording was never released for reasons that remain obscure. The most likely explanation was that EMI was having union trouble. A March 6, 1960, memo from the London office to Capitol Records in Hollywood made mention of brewing labor disputes.[12]

When Michael resumed his American tour in January 1961, he quickly settled into the well-established pattern of previous years. Concertos, recitals ("rectals," as he called them), and letter writing filled his time. A steady stream of correspondence came his way too. There was a brief note from Heifetz thanking Michael for remembering his birthday,[13] an offer from Sylvia Mann to host him during his upcoming Robin Hood Dell performance in the summer,[14] a letter from Josef Krips praising his performance of the Beethoven Violin Concerto,[15] and another from the campaign office of the soon-to-be-built Lincoln Center for the Performing Arts mentioning that they had received a gift in his honor.[16]

Superficially, matters appeared to be proceeding relatively well despite the ongoing, albeit intermittent, stage phobia. When he traveled to Cincinnati in February, his colleague from Meadowmount days, Connie Kiradjieff, noted with surprise that Michael played seated.[17] Such occurrences were more frequent now, but they remained difficult to predict with Michael's preconcert anxiety running the spectrum from mild to disabling. Certain halls in particular filled him with dread, suggesting that the structure and setup of the stage was one trigger for his fear. Milton Katims recalled that when Michael visited Seattle, he refused to set foot on the stage, let alone play, until a tarpaulin was draped over the deep orchestra pit.[18] So intense was his trepidation before a performance with the Brooklyn Philharmonic Orchestra that Rose Branower, one of the orchestra helpers, had to go into the men's washroom where he had taken refuge and coax him out onto the platform.[19]

By now Michael had stopped writing to Lewis. The friendship remained firm, but Lewis had become engaged, and as had happened with Bertine, Michael reacted to this development by distancing himself a little. Perhaps he felt he had burdened his sister and more latterly his best friend by writing so insistently, and that this behavior was now inappropriate. It is possible he no longer felt comfortable confiding his innermost thoughts and feelings to a friend whose main emotional attachment would, from now on, be anchored to someone else. Of course, it did not have to be an all-or-none arrangement. Lewis's pending betrothal did not have to signal the end of a correspondence that Michael had so clearly enjoyed and found helpful. But Michael tended to react like this. Feeling supplanted, he withdrew into himself, unable to reach out and fully celebrate his friend's good fortune. There was never any malevolence in this. It was simply all the old insecurities coming to the fore once again, his happiness for a friend diluted by a personal fear of loneliness.

Lewis married Adria on August 6, 1961, and Michael was one of the ushers. Photographs that show a smiling, dapper Michael in a white dinner jacket and bow tie captured only part of the story. Away from the prying lens, Lewis's father-in-law found a glum Michael lying down, avoiding the festivities. "How would you feel if your best friend was getting married?" was Michael's downcast reply to the older man's solicitous inquiry of what was wrong.[20]

The anguish locked up in those few words revealed that Lewis was more than just a close friend to Michael. He was the one person left to whom he could turn for solace. All those lonely hotel rooms, empty moments on the road, meals taken alone, desolate airport lounges at ungodly hours, and pangs of homesickness had been made just that much more bearable by having someone to confide in, a close, empathic friend who was but a postage stamp away. The two young men had shared much over the past few years: romantic disappointments and troubled relationships with parents, not to mention the challenges and hazards of a career in music. It was a kinship based on shared values and reciprocity, for Michael had not just asked for friendship, he had given it too, generously, freely, and often wisely, as his letters made clear. Now, with Lewis a married man, Michael saw much of that slipping away from him. Who would fill the void? Five years back it had been Bertine, but she had married and started a family. For a few years Adrienne had been his muse and confidant, but she too had found love elsewhere. And then there was Lewis and the one great friendship that would ease, or so Michael had hoped, his belated coming of age.

Michael knew a lot of people. His very public persona and his numerous travels ensured that. But a multitude of acquaintances and a mailbag full of letters from famous colleagues could not obscure the fact he had just one close friend. The correspondence with Francescatti had long since ended, driven more by Jeanne than the fifteen-year-old Michael, and although the two violinists still kept in touch sporadically, when Michael had mentioned his distress to his erstwhile benefactor, the advice he got — delivered with Gallic insouciance — was distinctly unhelpful: "Ah, when I am down, you know, I make a good bouillabaisse and open a bottle of wine and life feels much better after that." All the while, George had remained a loving and loved father and Galamian a concerned and revered teacher, but neither could replicate the camaraderie that Michael shared with Lewis. Galamian in particular was nonplussed by his star pupil's intermittent bouts of unhappiness.[21] And crucially, the relationship with Lewis had been the buffer that partially separated Michael from his mentor and tormentor, as he had referred to his mother. Had Michael possessed greater self-confidence and been less adrift socially, the marriage of his friend could have evoked a wistful nostalgia for the fun times of bygone bachelor days instead of the sadness he now felt. But having leapfrogged prematurely into adulthood, Michael was ill-equipped to deal with the challenges posed by life in the real world. The result was behavior that was often self-defeating.

The marriages of Bertine and Lewis did not presage their withdrawal from Michael. There was an emotional realignment as circumstances dictated, but sister and friend remained close to him, loved him for the kind and gentle man he was, admired him for the great violinist he was, appreciated his humor, and enjoyed being with him. And there was every indication Michael continued to feel the same affection for them. It was simply Michael's insecurity that introduced a certain aloofness into the relationships and made him stop writing. Not only did he worry about intruding when not wanted, observing Bertine and Lewis moving forward in their personal lives must have reinforced just how astray his own was.

The altered circumstances of his relationship with Lewis left Michael contemplating a novel situation — the unpleasant prospect of two months abroad without someone close to write to. He had previously always tried assuaging his loneliness on the road by letter writing, the replies he received an affirmation of the friendship he so craved. His plane was due to depart for Reykjavik on September 14, and he knew from experience that the beginning of any new tour was always a tough time for him, the period during which the anxiety of separation from things most familiar was most acute.

The day before Michael departed for Iceland, Jeanne wrote to Alf Levy in London, telling him that people were "awaiting [Michael's] arrival with great impatience and he will receive a royal welcome."[22] For the Icelandic part of his tour, Michael traveled with the pianist Mitchell Andrews. Over the preceding season, Michael had worked with a succession of accompanists. Los Angeles–based Sidney Stafford joined him when he toured out West. Albert Hirsh, the Texan, did duty when Michael traveled South. Brooks Smith, whose name is best associated with Heifetz, featured prominently too, as did Mitchell Andrews.

Six years older than Michael, Andrews had already built a national reputation. He regularly accompanied Leonard Rose, who was friendly with the Rabin family, and it was through this connection that the introductions were made.[23] Michael's association with Andrews would prove his longest with any pianist, and the two performed together right up until Michael's death. His regular appearance alongside Michael from the beginning of the decade did not signal a falling out between Michael and Leon Pommers. Rather, it reflected the realities of Michael's fast-paced career. The large number of concerts played and the extended periods away from home touring meant that few if any pianists were prepared to commit themselves completely to such a routine. Andrews never toured Europe with Michael, and he was never Michael's exclusive accompanist, the way Seiger had been with Elman or Emanuel Bay with Heifetz. But Michael and Andrews admired one another as artists, and their musical compatibility meshed well with their temperaments, ensuring a long collaboration.

A warm, welcoming letter from the American Cultural Affairs Officer, Lawrence Carlson, outlined Michael's Icelandic itinerary. There would be two concerts in Reykjavik and one in Akureyri, ninety minutes away by plane in the North of the country.[24] Michael's repertoire consisted of Beethoven's Romance in F, Op. 60, followed by the Fauré Sonata Op. 13. After intermission came the virtuoso fireworks. In his concert in Reykjavik on September 18, there was a moment of somber reflection too. Dag Hammerskjöld, the Swedish diplomat and head of the United Nations, had been killed that day in an air crash in the Congo while on a peacekeeping mission. As a mark of respect, Michael dedicated his performance of the Chopin Nocturne in C-sharp Minor (arranged by Milstein) to his memory. The audience stood in silence and remained that way for some time after the performance.[25] It was a gesture such as this, combined with fine playing, that ensured Michael's visit was an enormous success. On the spot, he was asked to return within the month to play at the opening of the University Auditorium, the new home of the Symphony Orchestra of Iceland. The spontaneous invitation created logistical problems. The date in question, October 12, fell between concerts in London and Berlin. But Michael had been moved by the enthusiasm of the audiences and, after checking flight schedules, agreed.

After the recital in Reykjavik, Andrews returned to America while Michael went on alone to Scandinavia for concerts in Oslo, Bergen, Stavanger, and Helsinki. Despite some personal misgivings, the tour had started well. But on October 11, when Josef Seiger met Michael at the Cumberland Hotel in London, he found him down in the dumps.26 The night before, Michael had played the Prokofiev G Minor Concerto with the London Symphony Orchestra conducted by Istvan Kertesz. Seiger, who had been in the audience at the Royal Festival Hall, thought Michael had given a memorable performance, his playing in the andante assai in particular of great beauty. The reviews, however, had been mixed, with neither soloist nor composer escaping reproach. Michael was censured for his choice of tempi,27 Prokofiev for writing a "mortally dull" concerto.28

It was not the critical opinion, though, that had upset Michael. It was his manager, Ian Hunter. Michael complained sadly that Hunter had paid him £150 for the concert, a derisory amount for an artist of his stature. Even allowing for London's dubious distinction as the worst-paid venue in Europe, and taking into account that Michael never commanded the type of fees paid the big-name violinists, the amount was embarrassingly small.* To Seiger, it was further evidence of Michael's innocence in the workings of the world, his poor business sense, and his lack of assertiveness. Schuyler Chapin had reached the same conclusion a few years earlier. After a series of meetings that he had arranged between Michael and the marketing gurus at Columbia Artists, there was a consensus that it would be extremely difficult to promote Michael to the public. "There was a certain naiveté that really couldn't fit any picture," recalls Chapin.29

A frenetic return dash to Iceland helped deflect Michael's dark thoughts. Mechanical problems twice delayed his flight from the United Kingdom. Arriving in Reykjavik at 11 PM, he was rushed to the hotel for a quick change into tails before being shepherded onto the stage for a midnight unrehearsed performance of the Mendelssohn Concerto. He was the hero of the hour. The following morning, with Michael back in the air en route to Berlin, the music critic for the *Morgunbladid* reflected on the night's high drama. "Quite

---

* Among the leading violinists of the day, Heifetz commanded the highest fees, followed by Menuhin, Milstein, Francescatti, Szigeti, and then Michael, some ways behind. Performance fees varied according to venue, type of concert, and the decade of performance. Thus, Michael was paid approximately $1,200 per recital in the USA in the late 1950s. When he toured Iceland in 1961, he received $2,000 for his three concerts, two of which were recitals. His two concerto performances in Mexico in 1971 earned him $2,500. His fees with the New York Philharmonic Orchestra towards the end of his career were $1,750 for three promenade concerts in 1969 and $2,259 for a series of three concerts in 1971, one of which was in Avery Fisher Hall and two at outside venues.

my favorite sister, Bert, whom i've always had great esteem, admiration and love.

With affection—

"Mike"

N.Y.
Jan. 20—
1955

Michael in Australia, 1952.

Above: Michael dedicated this photo to Bertine as he set off on his U.S. tour, January 1955.

Right: Michael in the Braniff Airways hangar, Love Field Airport, Dallas, 1952.

Michael and Zino Francescatti rehearsing the Bach Concerto for two violins, April 1953.

Michael and Sir Adrian Boult, London, January 1957.
Photo copyright EMI Records Limited. Used by kind permission of EMI Records Limited

Michael and Claudio Arrau,
Hollywood, 1953.

Michael's Australian accompanist,
Raymond Lambert, 1952.

From left to right: Jascha Heifetz, Donald Voorhees,
and Michael, *The Telephone Hour* rehearsal,
October 30, 1950.

Left: Mike on his bike, c. 1952.

Below: Michael and Esther Williams on the set of *Rhapsody*, Hollywood, 1953.
RHAPSODY © Turner Entertainment Co. A Warner Bros. Entertainment Company. All Rights Reserved. Courtesy of the Academy of Motion Picture Arts and Sciences

Above: Michael and Paul Badura-Skoda, Australia, 1952. *Photo courtesy of* Musical America *Archives*

Below: Michael and Adrienne Rosenbaum, c. 1956.

Above: Michael rehearsing with Johnny Green and the MGM Studio Orchestra on the set of *Rhapsody* Hollywood, 1953. *RHAPSODY © Turner Entertainment Co. A Warner Bros. Entertainment Company. All Rights Reserved. Courtesy of the Academy of Motion Picture Arts and Sciences*

Below, from left to right: Brian Sullivan, Lily Pons, Eileen Farrell, and Michael, *The Telephone Hour*, May 19, 1955.

Above: Promotional picture for Pan American World Airways, New York, c. 1956.

om left to right: Alf Levy, Michael (the back of his head), Hans May, David Oistrakh, Paul
shman, and David Wise, London, June 1956. *Photo courtesy of Alf Levy*

Michael with George (third and second from right) and members of the New York
Philharmonic Orchestra, November 1951. *Photo courtesy of* Musical America *Archives*

Michael in rehearsal in the late 1960s.

Michael in rehearsal with a student orchestra, Amarillo, Texas, August 1960.

Lewis Kaplan.
Photo by Christian Steiner

June LeBell.
Copyright © ANN BLACKSTOCK 2005

ichael, 1957. *Photo courtesy of* Musical America *Archives*

Wayman Adams painting Michael's portrait, Elizabethtown, NY, c. 1950.

Above left: Michael, c. 1966. Above right: Michael and Mitchell Andrews at Madison Square Garden, April 22, 1969.

Michael, c. 1969.
Photo by Christian Steiner

From left to right: Michael, Morey Amsterdam, Jack Benny, Henny Youngman.

Michael, George, and Jeanne, 1969.
Photo courtesy of Musical America *Archives*

obviously, it is no easy task to be a world-famous musician. We wonder when Mr. Rabin will next get some rest?"[30]

The symbolic importance of Michael's debut with the Berlin Philharmonic Orchestra was not lost on him. Like his debuts at Carnegie Hall back home and the Royal Albert Hall in London, the concert was considered a musical rite of passage, an essential presence in any serious instrumentalist's curriculum vitae. For this auspicious concert that would be conducted by Karl Böhm, Michael reverted to repertoire he felt completely at home in, the Wieniawski D Minor Concerto. By this stage in his career, he knew he had little to worry about violinistically, but some niggling musical insecurities remained. In eschewing the hallowed ground of Beethoven, Brahms, and Mendelssohn, he was playing it safe. The Wieniawski was forgotten music in Germany and he had the field to himself. Had he selected a concerto from one of Germany's cultural icons, comparisons with a roster of violin greats would have been inevitable. The Philharmonic had seen them all, from the venerable Joachim to the boy Menuhin who had played the three Bs — Bach, Brahms, and Beethoven — in a single concert.[31] After consultation with Galamian, Michael had decided not to challenge history.

Two months before he visited Berlin, the infamous wall had gone up. President Kennedy had been in office for less than a year, and it would be another twenty months before he would visit the city and deliver his famous words of solidarity. It was a tense and isolated city that Michael flew into, and while his visit was never overtly politicized, the timing and symbolism of his arrival was not lost on the people. If the Berliners were favorably disposed towards the young American virtuoso for reasons other than music, he would still have to earn their respect with the Wieniawski. For his part, Michael too was eager to create a favorable impression, going so far as to tell an interviewer that his list of favorite composers included Mozart.[32]

The two concerts he gave on October 16 and 17 in the concert hall of the Hochschule der Künste were a great success. *Der Abend* commented on his technical mastery;[33] *Die Welt* noted his brilliant musicianship; glittering, large, and flexible tone; and outstanding technique;[34] *Der Tagesspiegel* was impressed that the solo part had been played so cleanly and with such full tone and regarded Michael as a born violin talent of unnerving virtuosity and rhythmic elan;[35] while *Der Telegraf* praised his rich vibrato and luxurious fullness of sound.[36]

During his five-day visit to Berlin, Michael was joined by pianist Lothar Broddack for a recital recording that was broadcast on October 17. The repertoire included Fauré's Sonata Op. 13, Sarasate's "Zapateado," Ysaÿe's Sonata No. 3, and half a dozen Paganini caprices. His playing, particularly of the virtuoso pieces, deeply impressed the German public, and by the time he departed Berlin, traveling via Frankfurt to Zurich, he had in his pocket an invitation to return the following year for a public recital. After a couple of concerts in Italy, Michael's tour ended at the Tonhalle in Zurich on October 21, where once again Prokofiev did not escape rebuke. "That the [second concerto] is somewhat boring is the composer's fault," wrote one critic.[37]

From Zurich, Michael headed home via London. The inveterate letter writer had largely been silent on tour, but an interview he gave with the *Amarillo Globe Times* later that year provided some clues, albeit indirect, on how he viewed his time abroad. Under the heading "Violinist Champions Domestic Artists," Michael was quoted as saying that the United States "produces more music, more art, more theater, more dance, more in every aspect of the arts today than the Europeans. And it's only a beginning. We're far ahead of them, whether the people here and there will admit it or not. And we are culturally conscious." He exhorted Americans not to feel second class on the cultural front and noted that:

> it is very disappointing to me when some of our symphony conductors resign or are asked to leave and are replaced with foreign people we do not even know…
>
> I would like the American concert audience to stop thinking, feeling and believing, he's European, he must be good.
>
> It's time for them to say, Oh, he's American, he's got to be good.[38]

Michael's passionate espousal of homegrown talent, coming so close on the heels of his recent overseas tour, suggested that the two months in the Old World had not been that enlightening. And his forthright opinions did not stop there. The memory of Ian Hunter's meager fee clearly still rankled, for he went on to criticize those who thought that "an $8,000 artist is eight times better than the performer who makes $1,000 a concert…. if a performer gets $3,000 a performance, some are very prone to say, oh he must be very good, he gets $3,000 a concert." Finally, he touched on the themes of motivation and reward that echoed his own journey from child prodigy to mature artist, suggesting that a greater art consciousness on the part of the public would make worthwhile all "[those] years and years of study and the endless practicing and preparation…. Art would have more purpose."[39] Having delivered his polemic, the following evening Michael stepped onto the Amarillo stage and played a Brahms concerto that was regarded as the local musical highlight of the year.[40]

In November of 1961, Michael finally sold his first "del Gesù." He had bought the instrument believing it to be a del Gesù, and he sold it in good faith as a del Gesù. It was only in subsequent years that the violin's origins were revised and it was attributed to one or possibly two of Guarneri's contemporaries.[41] The buyer was Dr. Ernest Szabados, a Missouri orthopedic surgeon. Parting with the violin was clearly difficult for sentimental reasons more than any other, as the records of William Moennig and Son show Michael had not played the instrument in almost three years, having consigned it in January 1959.[42] Dr. Szabados, sensitive to Michael's feelings, wrote him a thoughtful and generous letter on taking ownership:

> Dear Mr. Rabin,
>
>   Enclosed please find a bank draft for the sum of sixteen thousand five hundred dollars ($16,500) in accordance with your agreement of 2 November '61 in the transfer of ownership of one 1724 Guarneri del Gesu.
>
>   I can appreciate your sentiments in parting with it, however, be assured it is in its proper sanctuary and should you ever become nostalgic for it you will have it available.
>
>   My wife and I will continue to follow your brilliant career and with this current transaction hope to crystallize a true friendship that will last forever.
>
>   Cordially yours,
>   Ernest D. Szabados, M.D.
>
>   P.S. My wife says you play the "Csak egy kis leany" in Zigeunerweisen like a true son of Arpad.[43]

The 1961–62 concert season was the last in which Michael's anxieties and distress did not spill out openly on stage and harm his playing. A live broadcast on November 11, 1961, from the Academy of Music in Philadelphia found him in good form with the Tchaikowsky concerto, and prompted notes of congratulation from Madame Ysaÿe[44] and Eugene Ormandy, the Philadelphia Orchestra's Musical Director.[45] And the reviews from Michael's tour of the Texan towns of Lubbock, Charlotte, Roanoke, Odessa, and Amarillo were all glowing.[46]

On January 3, he was back at Carnegie Hall for his first recital there in four years. Accompanied by Mitchell Andrews, he played sonatas by Fauré, Beethoven (Op. 30, No. 3), and Ben Haim (unaccompanied) and a collection of shorter pieces. His review in the *Times* was excellent. "In looks he does not seem to grow older, although his cherubic face is a bit more fleshy and his slightly receding hairline has given him a larger forehead," wrote Raymond Ericson. "In playing, it is a different matter…. Mr. Rabin performed with exceptional intensity, as if determined to get every ounce of personal expression out of his instrument…. At its best, his playing was extraordinary."[47] Michael's playing also prompted a humorous letter from the voucher of patriotic credentials, family friend and lawyer Isidore Halpern. "I was thrilled by … the criticisms you received," he wrote:

> One aspect gave me particular joy. Ever since I got to know you and read the newspapers the next day, there was one thing everyone conceded — they practically had orgasms raving about your technical ability. One imbecile referring to your playing of Paganini said that you tossed off these phrases with "insulting ease" or some such nonsensical remark. They found fault at times with your interpretation. Note, however, my friend, that the Mongoloid idiots rave about your tone, your interpretation etc. Where the hell do they get the idea that you look like a "cherub?" I guess they don't know you. I, as a blood brother of Mephistopheles, say that you look like his nephew. [48]

When Michael appeared with Josef Krips and the Buffalo Symphony Orchestra in a performance of the Tchaikowsky concerto three weeks later, he was still playing well, although a reviewer felt that "Mr. Rabin's concept seems to be one of mastery without involvement."[49] However, subtle changes away from the stage were discernible. A close scrutiny of his flight log reveals a change in his handwriting. Michael had a very legible script, and in the logbook, he printed as opposed to writing cursive. Up until the middle of February 1962, the entries were error- and smudge-free. The large letters, evenly spaced and of the same height, gently sloping to the right, were matched by the meticulous columns of figures summed up without correction, the hours spent in the air and the mileage covered documented with an obsessive neatness. But on February 13, 1962, the record of a flight from Tulsa to Colorado Springs showed some letters sloping to the right, others to the left. On the next flight, three days later, from Colorado Springs to Denver, the writing had a faint smudge.

By themselves these little signs would have been meaningless, perhaps signifying nothing more than some air turbulence as Michael updated the log while in flight. But in light of subsequent events, these blemishes take on a more ominous significance. In mid-March, just prior to his performance of the Creston concerto in New York, Michael's handwriting reverted momentarily to the fastidiousness of previous pages, but the letters soon started bunching up again. By the end of March, flying from New York to Wilkes Barre, Michael made a mistake adding up the mileage and then roughly corrected it, the very first error to appear in twenty-six pages of columns tightly filled with numbers.

There are no entries in Michael's logbook for six months following the end of his American tour on March 27, so his handwriting no longer provides a rough marker for his degree of fine coordination. Over the summer, his name appeared regularly in the press, and initially there was nothing to suggest anything was amiss. Mention was made of his performance in a charity event for Project Hope at Carnegie Hall,[50] that he had sat on the jury of the Memorial Music Award in association with the Ravinia Festival in Chicago,[51] and that he had joined Josef Krips for a performance of the Brahms Concerto at the Lewisohn Stadium on a humid night during which a peg on his violin slipped, bringing the last movement to an unexpected stop.[52] However, on September 26, during the opening week at Lincoln Center, he was scheduled to appear with Joseph Fuchs, Szymon Goldberg, and Tossy Spivakovsky in a Vivaldi concerto for four violins and string orchestra conducted by Leonard Bernstein. When the soloists appeared on stage after intermission, Michael was absent, his place taken at the eleventh hour by Frank Gullino, assistant concertmaster of the New York Philharmonic. The audience was informed that Michael had taken ill.[53]

It was crisis time in the Rabin apartment. Jeanne was laid up with a slipped disk in her back, immobile from the pain and on enforced bed rest. Her brother had recently had a severe heart attack while traveling in Italy and was now back in the United States in an intensive care unit.[54] And Michael, unable to perform at Lincoln Center for undisclosed health reasons, was due to leave for another European tour in three days. When he boarded his plane on September 29 and resumed documenting his flights, a further deterioration in his handwriting was manifest. Shrunken letters, coarse numbers, and uncertainty over the airline's name characterized his entry for the journey from New York to London.

Michael's first performances were in Germany and problems were soon apparent in his Berlin recital. Difficulties with rhythm, poor intonation, and interpretations that "lay between schmaltz and indifference" were noted. He played so poorly that students at the back of the auditorium whistled their disapproval. What had happened to the master violinist who had impressed Berliners the year before? Was the young man burned out and used up within a year, or was it only a bad day? asked one critic.[55] Michael blamed exhaustion — he had spent the day making a recording with Lothar Broddack for a radio station and had misjudged his stamina. Such an excuse, however, lacked substance. Moreover, tiredness could not account for a sloppy performance of the Tchaikowsky concerto in London on November 4. Anthony Payne's critique entitled "Senza Eleganza" noted: "Rabin seemed off form in the first movement and had trouble with intonation and articulation; moreover, his interpretation left something to be desired … [with] a distressing tendency towards vulgar portamento."[56] The contrast with his London debut performance seven years earlier could not have been more stark.

A reason for this spate of recent professional failings soon became apparent. During lunch with Josef Seiger in London the day after his concert, Michael excused himself to go and take his medication — "the little yellow pills," he called them.[57] The tablets were glutethimide, the generic name for the powerful sedative Doriden. First introduced in 1954 as a substitute for the barbiturates, experience soon taught that their potential for addiction and the severity of their withdrawal symptoms were no different. What made drugs such as Doriden particularly dangerous was that once tasted, they were hard to forget. When hooked, a person could not go more than a day or two without medication before anxiety flared anew, more powerfully than before, and the craving for the drug would commence. Such was the slippery slope of addiction, with larger and larger doses required for the same calming effect. And as the dose escalated, so the side effects became more prominent — impaired coordination and a dulling of the razor-sharp digital dexterity that playing the violin demanded. This is what had befallen Michael over the past six months.

It was probably in the spring of 1962 that Michael had first reached out for help. He was at a juncture in his life where, feeling increasingly troubled by his stage phobia, bereft that Lewis's marriage would dilute their friendship, and dreading the loneliness of months on tour without the support of a confidant, he went to see a doctor. The exact date of his first consultation and the name of the physician are not known, but the treatment given was Doriden. To begin with, he had taken the occasional small dose before a concert to still his fear, and such was his command of the instrument that the side effects were not overtly apparent. But by September 1962, it was clear he was taking larger and more frequent doses, and the effects were disastrous.

Doriden was, however, only part of the pharmacological quagmire that Michael had stumbled into unwittingly. A letter from Jeanne to Alf Levy touched on a second area of concern. "Michael has been in Europe and should be arriving or arrived in London by now," she wrote. "He is giving a recital in the new Philharmonic Hall of Lincoln Center on November 27th. I am sure you will see him in London. He has lost a great deal of weight and he has called several times from Europe and assured me he is feeling fine. He dieted so strenuously I was worried for his well being."[58] What Jeanne did not know was that Michael was taking a second prescription drug, phendimetrazine tartrate, the generic name for Plegine, a dieting tablet. The drug was a brain stimulant and its use was contraindicated in persons with emotional disorders. Among a formidable list of side effects were nervousness, dizziness, and insomnia, the very complaints Michael was taking the Doriden for.

Thus, when Michael set off for Europe in the fall of 1962, he was on two medications with antagonistic properties, the sedative Doriden and the stimulant Plegine. It was an appalling treatment regime that would have raised or lowered his anxiety levels like a yo-yo. Had these prescriptions come from a single physician, there would have been a strong case for medical malpractice, but the evidence suggests Michael was seeing more than one doctor, with each handing out prescriptions unaware of the others' existence. Michael was at that stage quite open about taking Doriden, as Seiger's anecdote makes clear, but the use of Plegine was surreptitious, and not even Jeanne with her all-knowing eye had divined the truth behind her son's rapid weight loss.

If Jeanne was worried about her son's emotional state, she never let on to Levy. But she could not resist passing on a little gossip about someone else's psychological misfortunes. "I hear Heifetz is ill and is having marital troubles and psychiatric treatment. I hate to believe these things, so please don't quote me — I feel so badly about it — I hope it's not true."[59]

Michael of course knew he was not playing well, although there was every reason to believe he had not attributed it to the concoction he was swallowing two or three times a day. He left London the day after the Tchaikowsky debacle and limped through a week in Italy before arriving in Lisbon, from where he sent a note of explanation to his friend the cognoscenti cab driver:

> Dear friend Alf,
>
> Firstly, I love you.
>
> Secondly, I am flying non-stop from here to New York via TWA — I am very sorry not to see you and yours again, but the thought of going home is stronger than anything.
>
> *All* concerts since I saw you last on 5th Nov. have really been up to my own standard and I am so relieved about this, as I'm sure you are. I am *sure* the concert of Nov. 4th was an "off-night." So please don't worry about it now. It was an awful experience, but try to do as I do and that's look ahead to the next time — that will be 1st class.
>
> Much love to you, Alice and David,
> Michael[60]

Michael arrived back in New York on November 17. He had ten days to settle himself before an important concert. He would give the first violin recital at Philharmonic Hall,* part of the newly built Lincoln Center. It was a singular honor, and a large audience made up of the city's musical and political elite had come to assess the soloist and the hall's acoustic properties.

Michael chose a varied program that, had he been playing well, would have ensured his success. But alas, the toxic brew of uppers and downers continued to wreak havoc with the legendary Rabin technique. "With so much going for him in sheer temperament and violinistic technique Michael Rabin gave a curiously perfunctory and even careless performance last night at Philharmonic Hall before a large audience that deserved something better," wrote the critic Ronald Eyer. "Mr. Rabin is only 26 years old, but he is out of short pants now and bidding for the major league. He's got to start paying more attention to his P's and Q's." Michael was taken to task for his performances of the Brahms D Minor Sonata and Bach's Partita in D minor, and aspects of his playing were criticized that until then had been inviolate — intonation and technique. The only work that received praise was the sonata by the American composer Robert Kurka, recently deceased at thirty-six years of age. Eyer's concluding remarks must have been inordinately hard for Michael to hear, coming on top of a life devoted to the most rigorous practice. "A word of unsolicited advice to a potentially great young violinist: stop fooling around with those stamp and coin collections and that hi-fi equipment the biographical note listed as your leisure preoccupations and get back to working on the violin."[61]

Mitchell Andrews was on stage with Michael that evening. "Things went wrong," he recalls, "And it was fairly obvious, I'm afraid. Michael played badly, full of little slips and mistakes. I didn't play my best either and Leonard Rose who was in the audience said to me later, 'Rabin rubbed off on you.' It was a concert better forgotten than remembered, but it was the first recital in that hall." Andrews had developed a great fondness and admiration for Michael as a person and as an artist over the past few years of their collaboration.

> We would rehearse maybe two or three times a week if a concert was just on the horizon, or maybe even a little bit more than that if a tour was coming up soon. We usually started around one or two in the afternoon, so that we could finish around cocktail time and have a drink together. Sometimes we would have dinner

---

* Subsequently called Avery Fisher Hall.

together. So we turned it into something that was very pleasant, both musically and socially. 62

Given the frequency of their meetings, Andrews soon became aware of Michael's pill popping:

> One of them was something that you take when you have a cold. Anyway, he took them in such an enormously large quantity that they became, not lethal, but certainly harmful. The results were that his playing suffered. And then there was the strangeness in Michael falling asleep. He would doze off while you were talking to him.

Andrews also recalled Michael's phobia, which was partly alleviated, but not cured, by the Doriden. "He was always concerned about standing too close to the lip of the platform. He wanted to be sure that the piano was not too far forward so that it would force him to stand in front of it in an area he regarded as the danger zone."63

Galamian, George, Jeanne, and Columbia management were deeply concerned about the rapid deterioration in Michael's playing, not to mention his health. These worries were shared by Elaine Weldon, a contemporary of Michael's. She too had shown a precocious talent for the violin, had studied with Galamian, and could empathize with Michael's antipathy towards his mother given her own battles with a demanding parent. The two prodigies had met in childhood, forming an intense, intermittent friendship sealed by shared interests and challenging formative experiences. By now Michael's addiction was transparent, and Weldon remembers him swallowing fistfuls of tablets and falling asleep during conversations or while smoking a cigarette. Her most disturbing recollection is of Michael having a convulsion, which in time she learned had been triggered by a withdrawal reaction from the sedative medication he was abusing in such large quantities.64

Urged by all who loved him to seek help, Michael, compliant as always, listened and obeyed. But the problem had by now been compounded by a faulty solution, the doctor shopping that generated prescription chaos. In the absence of Michael's medical notes, all that is known from pharmacy records is that he consulted multiple general practitioners, all of whom prescribed sedatives and dietetics for him, often simultaneously. And whatever help he sought always took place in the shadow of time pressure and the next tour looming. The result for Michael was a redoubled sense of foreboding now that his technique was publicly deserting him in the humiliating glare of the stage lights.

It is clear from the spidery handwriting in Michael's log book that nothing changed in the two-week interval between his Philharmonic Hall recital and the start of his 1962–63 American tour. Further trouble was inevitable. "Michael Rabin, Violin, Has Off Day in Recital," was the verdict on his December 19 Boston recital. "Violinists occasionally have a bad day," wrote the critic Margo Miller:

> Yesterday morning it was Michael Rabin's turn … and it was probably one morning he'd wished he'd stayed in bed.
> Close tuning between the violin and piano (his accompanist was Mitchell Andrews) proved nearly impossible throughout the concert. Rabin's attacks, bow to strings, were often insecure. He did not always come off a note cleanly. There were scoops and slides — but why go on? The soloist himself cancelled a performance of the chaconne for violin alone from Bach's D minor Partita.[65]

Mitchell Andrews held a high opinion of Michael's technical prowess on the violin:

> [His] natural facility, both left hand and bow arm, were absolutely remarkable. There was nothing he could not do, to my knowledge. At the same time, his playing had a kind of technical solidity that many other facile violinists could not match. I don't know how else to describe it really, it was rock solid. His playing was consistently astounding.

Now Andrews was witness to the slow and painful disintegration of this prodigious talent, and he felt powerless to intervene. "I really felt that I could not do it because of the drug thing," he recalls:

> Never having had any experience with it myself, I did not know how to approach it or give advice. Bertine and I had conversations about it from time to time. At times Michael appeared so helpless you did not know what to do for him. We were on tour and something small would upset him and he became like a little child, not at all the mature adult that he really was. He needed help. I was a little bit like a big brother to him, and I tried as much as I could to bolster his own worth. But I never knew how to deal with the drugs.[66]

Matters could not continue this way indefinitely. Michael was falling apart emotionally and physically in front of an increasingly bemused public. If 1962 had seemed like one long nightmare to him, in reality it was just the prologue. 1963 was his true *annus horribilis.*

On January 16, he arrived in Bismarck, North Dakota for a recital. An audience of 1,000 braved a bitter-cold night with the temperature dropping to sub-zero to hear Michael, who had been billed as one of the nation's foremost violinists. But he never made it from his hotel room to the concert hall. Pleading exhaustion, he told the concert organizers his schedule had been unduly heavy of late and that if he tried to play, he would drop his bow. He offered to return to Bismark in the spring, at his own expense, to make up the concert. Scrambling for excuses, Michael also mentioned it was the very first time in his career that he had balked at playing, that he had never in his own opinion played a bad concert, and that he did not want to blemish this record in Bismarck. Faced with this logic, the vice president of the local music association could only acquiesce.[67] It would be the first of many cancellations that year. A shaky Michael returned to New York for a few days rest and to celebrate Mitchell Andrews's birthday.

Michael had bought his accompanist a wristwatch as a gift and had had it inscribed: "To Mitchell, a most wonderful friend." Andrews was deeply moved by the gift from a man in crisis. Sensitive to Michael's fragile emotional state, Andrews wrote him a compassionate letter in which he effusively expressed his feelings:

> I only hope I may prove worthy of such a gift — that I may be a truly worthy friend to you. I want this very much Mike. So — thank you, Mike. Thank you for your generous and spectacular gift and thank you even more for your generous expression of your affection. I want to assure you of my own very deep affection for you — to say nothing of admiration — and I sincerely hope our friendship will outlast even the life time of this wonderful watch.
> God Bless you,
> Mitch [68]

Andrews's note was dated February 4, 1963, the very day Michael's misfortunes reached their nadir. Andrews could not have known that even as he posted his thank-you note, his friend was in the middle of a great drama playing out in the skies between California and Michigan. Two nights before, Michael had performed the Paganini D Major Concerto with André Previn in Los Angeles before an audience of 3,500 at the Shrine Auditorium. He had scrapped and muddled his way through a concerto that had been, more than any other, his great showstopper.[69] In the audience was eighteen-year-old Elizabeth Matesky, a friend of Mitchell Andrews and a student of Jascha Heifetz. She had good seats and was looking forward with excitement to her first "live" Rabin performance. What unfolded over the course of the next half hour, however, shocked her. "Michael literally came apart during the Paganini," she recalls. "He began sweating profusely and could not stop shaking. His coordination was terrible and he could hardly make the entrances on cue. It was frightening to witness because it was clear to everyone that he was suffering on stage." Matesky remembers the ripples of unease that began running through the audience. She herself felt deeply upset by what she was witnessing. When the torture was over, she went backstage to say hello but found the door to the green room barred. She overheard someone say, "Rabin is having a nervous breakdown."[70]

Exactly what happened after the performance is unclear, but Michael's account of events was probably accurate:

> I was scheduled for a concert in Kalamazoo the same week of the concert I gave in Los Angeles. After the LA concert I accidentally took an overdose of the medication and didn't wake up for two days. I still had time to get to Kalamazoo, and on the plane I decided to stop the medication completely. Of course I didn't realize that you had to taper off; I suffered withdrawal symptoms on the plane, passed out and woke up in a Michigan hospital.[71]

The little yellow pills had proven a false panacea. Seduced by the rapid calm they brought to his fraught emotions, Michael had inadvertently medicated himself into a stupor. Perhaps he had not been told about the drugs' dark side? Or had he ignored the warnings given? Maybe he had simply run out of a supply? Whatever the reason, the situation had become untenable. His reputation as a preeminent violin virtuoso could no longer be sustained on such a shaky edifice. En route to Michigan, Michael had found out belatedly that Doriden did not linger in the system. After two days in Kalamazoo and a further three in Detroit, Michael flew back to New York and was checked into Mount Sinai Hospital. A great career was in decline.

CHAPTER 13
A CAREER RESURRECTED

There is an aura surrounding the great virtuosos. Composed of admiration intermingled with incredulity at their rare and wonderful talent, fostered by a very public persona, nourished by a recognition of extraordinary accomplishment, the mystique helps set their lives apart from their adoring public. For the most part, the facts, myths, anecdotes, and legends that make up any aura are positive, adding luster to the life. But when careers stall prematurely, when inexplicable lapses and blemishes intrude onto the concert platform and performances are cancelled at the eleventh hour, rumor takes hold. Half truths, innuendos, and misinformation now compete with a musical legacy. A remarkable life is diminished.

This was the fate that now befell Michael. For thirteen years, half his lifetime, he had lived a public life. Not a concert season had gone by without his name and face appearing regularly in the media. And then suddenly, overnight, he disappeared. When Michael reluctantly, hesitantly, stepped across the threshold into the alien, disconcerting uniformity of a hospital ward, he shed the mantle of violin virtuoso, forced by circumstances beyond his control to relinquish the one defining aspect of his life. In Mount Sinai Hospital, he was no longer Michael Rabin, America's virtuoso, the heir apparent to a lineage that stretched back one hundred and fifty years to Paganini. As he gave up his Kubelik del Gesu for a wrist tag with a hospital number and swapped his concerts tails for pajamas, he became just another young nondescript male admitted to the hospital with a drug problem. That is not to say his doctors were oblivious to his reputation as a celebrated musician, but for the greater part of each day and night, Michael was in the company of orderlies and fellow patients who were more likely to associate the name Wieniawski with the owner of the corner delicatessen than with a man whose etudes and concertos helped define the composer-violinist genre.

Michael's emotional difficulties had been building steadily over years, but it had taken his sudden and complete physical collapse to unmask the full extent of his unhappiness. There was no longer any room for maneuver, no place left for alibis and compromise. For the Doriden addiction and dependency did not arrive *de novo,* a chance occurrence surfacing unexpectedly in the midst of a successful career. Michael's abuse of sedatives and appetite suppressants was linked inextricably to a plethora of emotional problems whose origins could be traced back to those early heady years of wunderkind fame. The phobia of falling off the stage was one problem, his festering relationship with his mother another. This complicated miasma of emotions would now have to be addressed if the treatment was to be anything more than a hastily applied Band-Aid designed to simply get him back on stage.

A number of decisions with far-reaching consequences awaited Michael, his parents, and Bill Judd. Some were straightforward, dictated by medical necessity, such as admission to a hospital. But others were more complex, for the implications involved concert managers, orchestras, local musical societies, and recording labels. Michael's performance schedule was heavily booked through 1963 and well into the following year. At what point would he be strong enough, physically and psychologically, to resume his peripatetic existence — if indeed that was what Michael wanted, for had he not threatened previously to walk away from his career? And where would he live once out of the hospital? In his letters to Lewis, he had repeatedly made mention of finding a place of his own, only to falter on the follow-through.

Stopping Doriden was a difficult, uncomfortable task, and while in the throes of withdrawal was not the time for making life-altering decisions. It was, however, clear to those who knew Michael that the remainder of his 1963 tour would have to be cancelled. He was simply in no shape to continue performing. All further decisions were put on hold until detoxification had been completed. Looking back on this period in his life, Michael recalled:

> I suppose I reached bottom in January 1963. All sorts of fears were running through my mind — that I would fall off the stage was just one of many. In actuality, I was beginning to lose control of my extremities. I couldn't write and there were times I was unable

to play a concert. Word started getting around that Rabin was this, Rabin was that—and they were right. The word was that I was not to be depended on....

Basically, it all started because of problems I had. The tendency is to push problems out of your mind, and after doing this for some time I began getting a reaction. Originally this was diagnosed as a stomach disorder. The medication for it made me feel good so I kept taking it. Whenever something bothered me, I would just take the medication and the problem would go away. Pretty soon I began losing control of myself.[1]

Sally Thomas saw Michael sporadically in the months before his admission to the hospital. "Michael had one hang-up in life," she remembers:

He thought people only liked him for his playing, and they didn't like him personally. I liked him personally. We used to go out and play ping-pong. There was a big place on 96th Street and he'd come down in his car and get me and he'd roar up there and play for half the night. The whole basement was filled with ping-pong tables. He was at that time into his drug, which was a sleeping pill.

Soon after the table tennis evening, Sally received a phone call from Michael. He felt lonely, he told her—could she come over for a bit?

He was living with his parents on Riverside Drive, so I went over, and nobody answered when I rang the buzzer. The doormen told me just to go up, and the door to the apartment was open. So I went up and couldn't find Michael. I hung around the living room for a while, and then finally I looked in his room and he was fast asleep on the bed. The room was very Spartan. He loved airplanes as well as cars, and he had a couple of planes and his music cases, maybe a book, his bed and desk, and that was it. Very neat. So I thought he would wake up soon and I went to wait in the living room. The doorbell rang again. I answered it and it was Elaine Weldon. I asked her what she was doing there and she told me Michael had called and asked her to come over too. So we sat and waited and pretty soon Michael woke up. He was perfectly normal and we chatted for a while. And then he said, "I have to go and take my medicine," and he went somewhere and came back and said, "I have to go to bed again," and he fell asleep.[2]

Fellow Galamian alumnus Jaime Laredo, five years Michael's junior, remembers receiving a similar distress call from him. "He sounded very depressed," recalled Laredo. "He needed someone to talk to and asked me to come over." But Laredo was on the way to the airport for an engagement in Pittsburgh. "I felt very guilty, not being able to respond at the time," he divulged, "but no sooner was I back than I phoned him."[3] To Laredo's surprise, Michael sounded very happy. He had no recollection of making the call.*

Lewis too had been aware of the crisis brewing but, like Mitchell Andrews, felt overwhelmed at times by the magnitude of Michael's distress. "He spoke at length with me about the drug he was taking, which I was told was a very common sedative and sleeping pill," he recalls:

> He was taking it in massive doses and I asked him how he got it. Michael was of course well known, and physicians thought they were just being nice to him when he asked, "I know you don't know me very well, but I just ran out of my prescription, would you mind....?" And they would say, "Of course, I'm happy to do it for you." And at that time, you could get prescriptions renewed without further prescriptions, so he had a string of doctors on the go and a string of pharmacists. That was what his drug life was like.[4]

Michael initially saw nothing wrong in taking medication and did so quite openly. But over the course of some months, he resorted to trickery and subterfuge to feed the habit. Bea Seidman recalled that before long, every druggist in the neighborhood knew Michael, who soon took to hiding the pills in his violin case and other places. "Michael was not happy with the life he was leading," she recollected:

> He called himself a traveling salesman. He used to ask us, "What do I do? I travel all around the world in airplanes. Everybody knows me but what do I do? I don't even know how to dance." And we told him, "Michael, this is nothing to be concerned about. When you are back in New York you can always go to Arthur Murray. There is always a place where you can learn." And he said, "But I haven't done any of those things. I never had time and I was never permitted."[5]

The divide between Michael's personal and private lives could not have been more stark. Away from the concert halls of the world and the applause

---

* When taken in large amounts, Doriden causes a retrograde amnesia.

of audiences in thrall to his talent, Michael was lost, a lonely young man who had never outgrown his model plane collection that provided the one bit of decor in his sparsely furnished schoolboy bedroom. The images conveyed by Sally Thomas's description are heartbreaking: the celebrated virtuoso asleep on his bed, alone in the apartment, the front door ajar, his friends waiting patiently for him to wake up, his brief moment of lucidity before drifting back into a Doriden-induced slumber. It should not have been that way. The austerity and isolation of his existence came as a shock to those who were able to glimpse beneath the veneer of his great successes. At twenty-six years of age, Michael could have had the world at his feet, his rare gift the conduit to an independent, privileged lifestyle filled with friends, admirers, financial security, and material pleasures. Instead, seventy times a year, he took his bows, played his Paganini encores, acknowledged the applause of the orchestra members banging their violin bows on their music stands, signed autographs in the green room, smiled back at the sea of admirers, dusted off the rosin, put away his Guarnerius, and stepped out through the stage door into his increasingly unhappy, isolated life.

The easiest and most straightforward part of Michael's treatment in the hospital was being weaned off Doriden. The process took a couple of weeks. Once the immediate medical danger had passed and the bulk of the medication was out his system, there was little need to remain in the hospital. He was discharged, but did not return to his parents' apartment, where he was resentfully paying part of the rent.[6] Instead, on the advice of his psychiatrist and to escape Jeanne's control, he went to live with Elaine Weldon and her mother at their home in Brookville on Long Island. The respite was, however, temporary and within weeks Michael was back in the suffocating bosom of his family.[7] For the first time in his adult life, there were no concerts to play, no *Telephone Hour* broadcasts, no rehearsals with Mitchell Andrews, no music to perform, and nothing to practice.

For Michael, life outside of music was empty. Despite the publicity information put out over the years, he was not an avid reader of philosophy and psychology and, as Sally Thomas's description of his room made clear, he was no bibliophile. Photography had been a passing phase, and chess too. He no longer rode a bicycle, and there was only so much time a man could spend with his model plane collection. His Corvette remained an enduring passion, however, and Michael would drive out to spend time at Josef Seiger's or Elaine Weldon's place on Long Island. Here, he could take advantage of the absence of water restrictions and clean his car while speaking openly of his problems. Seiger remembers Michael complaining about his home situation and how smothered he felt by his mother in particular. The pianist urged Michael to find a place of his own, to break with the past and establish his autonomy.[8] Michael agreed, but did nothing.

Fredell Lack was another visitor during these troubled years. When she visited him at 110 Riverside Drive, Michael insisted they go and sit in his bedroom and closed the door so that his parents would not overhear their conversation. After the debacle of his November recital in Philharmonic Hall, she found him contrite, apologizing repeatedly for his poor playing. He complained bitterly to her about his mother, how bossy she was and the many demands she made on him. He forbade Lack talking to his parents: she was his friend, he insisted, not theirs. To Lack, fourteen years Michael's senior, he seemed like a little brother, late in developing social skills and in need of guidance as he navigated an uncertain course through the challenges posed by everyday life.9

Tension soon escalated in the Rabin household. Michael was no longer touring, and the long, empty days at home meant mother and son had a lot of sparring time. A few weeks after Michael had returned home, Lewis received a call at 3 AM. It was George. In a hushed voice, he asked if Lewis could please come over and help. Michael had run amok and was wrecking the apartment. They couldn't cope. They did not want to call the police, but someone had to get Michael back to the hospital. "So I went," recalled Lewis. "I remember walking with him from 83rd Street through Central Park as the sun came up. We sat on a park bench for a while. Michael resisted the idea of returning to the hospital, but there was no other choice. It was one of the saddest moments of my life."10

Jeanne had for some time turned against Lewis because he too had been urging Michael to get his own apartment, but after her son's explosive outburst, she had to concede that living together was no longer tenable. So intense had been the enmeshment between mother and son that it had taken the implosion of Michael's career and two hospital admissions before separation could take place. Even then, when Michael finally did move out in the summer of 1963, he never went far. His new apartment at 185 West End Avenue was a short walk from the home that held such mixed emotions for him.

One of the many myths that have persisted from this period in Michael's life was that he stopped playing the violin and was forced into retirement for a number of years. This is simply untrue. Despite the turmoil that engulfed the first quarter of 1963, in May he climbed into his Corvette and drove to Atlantic City, where he played in a charity event to raise funds for the Atlantic City Hospital. A warm letter of thanks from the president of the hospital's Board of Governors attested to the success of the evening.11 Two months later, he made his seventh appearance at the Dell in Philadelphia, where he played the Tchaikowsky Concerto to the kind of acclaim reserved for his performances of earlier years: "The purity of Rabin's tone was a delight — perfect intonation and never a hint of scratchiness," read a review from the *Philadelphia Inquirer.*12 His choice of encores spoke to the fact that off the sedatives, he had regained his digital dexterity: Bach and Spalding on the first night, Paganini Caprices 13, 17 and 24 on the second.

Michael's ability to play the violin like few others had not evaporated, irretrievably lost in the chaos of a Doriden delirium. His return to concertizing was inevitable, and he would have taken heart from the two successful forays over the summer. But the road ahead was full of pitfalls. The phobia persisted. The tranquillizers remained seductively within reach. And adding to his worries, news of his emotional collapse had traveled far and fast — offers of engagements were drying up. Michael needed to reaffirm his credibility, not only as a great violinist but also as an artist whom promoters could depend on. For the troubled musician, it was a salutatory lesson in the fickleness of human nature. The painful reality was that a few months of erratic behavior had undercut more than a decade of remarkably successful concertizing. Failing to perform for an audience in Bismarck who had braved bitter cold and paid good money to hear him would neither be forgotten nor forgiven. Michael's travel log revealed that he was never invited to return. The hastily cancelled spring tour of 1963 gave rise to similar discontent elsewhere. Had Michael rebounded quickly from the setbacks of that year, the damage to his career and reputation would have been curtailed. But the malaise ran too deep for the clock simply to be turned back a couple years, the emotional detritus brushed away, and the concertizing to begin as before.

The admissions to Mount Sinai signaled a watershed in his career. They wiped the sheen off his genius. Human frailty exposed so publicly did not mesh easily with the notion of technical infallibility. Once dented, the persona would be hard to reconstitute, and Michael, despite heroic efforts, never quite succeeded. By mid-October, eight months after his hospitalization, he took a few more tentative steps towards resurrecting his stalled career. He played a recital at New York City's Washington Irving High School, where he introduced Beethoven's Sonata Op. 12, No. 1, into his repertoire and, one week later, flew to Wisconsin and performed a recital that included Vitali's Chaconne. "Michael Rabin ... simply refuses to stand still," noted the review in the *Milwaukee Journal.* "He insists on getting better and better, on going higher and higher. Now at 26, he has ascended to a dizzying peak of violin mastery."[13]

These early promising signs, however, were short-lived, and the pared-down comeback tour derailed in January when resurgent anxiety prevented him from playing his Miami recital. His colleague and boyhood acquaintance Erick Friedman was in town and stepped into the breech, performing Michael's program with Michael's pianist, Mitchell Andrews.[14] Andrews recalls that getting Michael back from Florida was nerve-wracking. After what had transpired the year before en route to Kalamazoo, everyone feared a repeat collapse, and Judd had to dispatch a chaperone to ensure a smooth passage.[15] A few weeks later, however, Michael felt confident enough to travel unaccompanied to San Diego, where he performed Prokofiev's G Minor Concerto to critical acclaim.[16]

The ups and downs of early 1964 were a harbinger of what was to come in the years ahead. Unpredictability now dogged Michael's appearances, and questions about his reliability surfaced for the first time. Would he appear for a concert, and if he did, how would he play? Michael, for his part, was down-playing any residual infirmity. By now a year of relative inactivity had passed, and he was desperately keen to get his old career back. On March 9 he wrote to the Levys in London:

> Dear Alice and Al [sic],
>
> Apparently you didn't know, but I have been playing concerts since September, and although this season has purposely been lighter than usual, everything has returned to normal and I've never been in better shape than I am at this time. Next season (1964–65) will return to normal, commercially, but I shall be far better equipped, in every way, to handle myself.
>
> I really can't wait to see you because I have so much to tell you.
>
> In June I'll be playing at 7 of the Festival concerts in the Scandinavian countries and in October — November will be doing another European tour. Then 6 months in the USA, then 1½ months in Africa, etc, etc, etc.…
>
> There is a chance that I'll have a one or two day stopover in London, in June — Either coming from or going to the Scandinavian tour. If so, I'll let you have the details well in advance.
>
> Excuse my brevity, but I'm leaving for the airport now. 10 days in 4 states. Let's keep in touch.…
>
> With love and a hug,
> Mike[17]

Michael's entries in his flight log for this period confirm that his hand-writing was back to the neat, carefully scripted letters of previous years. But it is also clear from the entries that he had been a little parsimonious with the truth in his note to the Levys. He never flew anywhere in March, and there was no ten-day, four-state tour. In April 1964, his only trip was an overnight one to Manchester, New Hampshire, while in May, his sole American ven-ture was a two-day sojourn in Spartanburg en route to Charlotte. And while he was due to play in Scandinavia over the summer, the October "European tour" he referred to was more accurately a visit just to Norway and Finland.

Michael may have lacked arrogance, but this should not be misconstrued as an absence of pride. The thinning of his concert schedule was not easy to accept, and during those months of novel inactivity, he had had plenty of time to reflect, reminisce, and take stock of where he stood in life. In a letter written to Adrienne eight years earlier, he had confided that "not to have concerts is a living hell," and now he was experiencing that uncomfortable reality. Carl Dahlgren, who had taken over as Michael's manager from Bill Judd, urged patience and a more gentle pace of concertizing.[18] But reluctant to lose face any further, Michael had gently padded the extent of his comeback. A follow-up letter to Alf, dated March 24, reinforced this impression. "My plans for October aren't set," he had written,

> so I will have to wait for that news. I do know that as of now, there is [sic] not yet any concerts planned for London. I am still surprised at how marvelously well I am booked *all over* Europe and Scandinavia, but how badly my England affairs seem to be handled. I must stir up Hunter somehow.[19]

On May 28, 1964, Michael left for a two-week tour of Scandinavia with festival performances in Oslo, Bergen, and Copenhagen. It was a fortnight without incident, but his protestations of being in good shape could not disguise his intermittent bouts of moodiness. There were also ominous signs that he had resumed his flirtation with prescription medicines. Bertine challenged him directly on this sore point. "I knew it was going on," she recalls,

> but he would deny it. He once took pills out of my medicine chest—they were not even sedatives—all my pills disappeared after he visited, and he was telling me he wasn't taking pills. And then there were times he would appear sleepy. Once we went to a political dinner and he was falling asleep at the table, his head was drooping, and I remember squeezing his hand under the table with my fingernails because I was embarrassed. And then at that dinner I saw him go into the bathroom with Mayor Wagner, and I was like, "Oh my God, what did he do? I hope he didn't say anything bizarre to the mayor." It would always be trying when we were with him, because I'd never know exactly how he would act.[20]

Michael's period of abstinence lasted probably no more than a few months. But in one sense he had learned a lesson from his mid-air collapse en route to Kalamazoo, and he was now leery of dipping into the bottle before a concert. Furthermore, if his handwriting was the barometer by which substance abuse could be measured, his letters and flight log from 1964 until his death betrayed no signs of the withdrawal-type reaction that had precipitated his hospitalization.

While drug addiction undoubtedly cast a long shadow, Michael's life was certainly not all doom and gloom, and Bertine retains happy memories too of her brother from this time. Irrespective of how he was feeling, Michael never lost the traits of gentleness and patience that epitomized his character. "Once, on Halloween, my children went around to his apartment and they all went trick-or-treating," she recollects. "He loved the kids. You know he was great with children. And they had this wonderful time. And I also recall times we would go across to visit him and he would cook dinner, and it would be so lovely, so nice and normal."21

The impression that Michael had reached calmer waters was reinforced by David Levy's account of his visit to New York in the summer of 1964. David, Alf's nineteen-year-old son, was met at Idlewild by Jeanne with the words, "You must be starving, what do you want to eat?" and promptly driven to 110 Riverside Drive, where he was fed and put up in Michael's old room. "Michael was very friendly, very warm, very sincere," David remembers, "and he had this slightly impish sense of humor. He was pleasant to be with, very polite, extremely polite in fact, you know, a genuinely nice guy." David did not know of Michael's recent emotional difficulties and did not divine anything amiss.

> Someone like him must have been extremely busy, but he was very hospitable and spent the best part of a whole day with me. I met him at his apartment, and he drove me in his Corvette to the World Fair at Flushing Meadows and we had lunch together. He would make little jokes with people, like the man selling tickets or the car-park attendants. And I remember he spent some time chatting up one of the girls working there and afterwards apologized for spending time away from me.

After leaving New York later that summer, David made a point of going to hear Michael play at an open-air concert in Chicago's Grant Park. "He played the Glazunov," he recalls, "and I remember that in the middle of the concert there was a plane going overhead and he looked up while he was playing. And I said to him afterwards, 'Why did you look up, did the plane disturb you?' and he said, "No, I just wanted to see what type it was.'"22 This was hardly the response of an artist short on confidence.

The one place outside of the Americas that remained true in its affection for Michael's artistry, irrespective of the fluctuations in his fortunes, was Scandinavia. The admiration was reciprocal, and it was to Norway, his favorite Nordic land, that he returned for a second time that year. On September 29, before departing New York, he had written to Alf Levy, once again inflating the scope of his tour.23 Michael's ongoing need to embellish indicated that bookings were slow in coming, and he returned from Helsinki in early November to a diary that was virtually empty: a concert in Queens and a brief trip north to Erie were his sole commitments before the Christmas season.

By year's end, it had become apparent that the way back would be far slower than first anticipated. If 1963 was Michael's low point, 1964 was the year he began rebuilding his career — venue by venue, concert by concert — a humbling, trying, and at times frustrating task, given the heights he had previously scaled. And if the comeback was to succeed, there could be no further derailments, which meant that concertizing would have to proceed in tandem with psychotherapy. While an inpatient at Mt. Sinai Hospital, Michael had met a psychiatrist, Dr. Michael Chaplik, and he now began psychoanalysis at Chaplik's rooms on East 83rd Street. There was much work to be done, and although the notes from those sessions have not survived, it is reasonable to suppose that many hours were devoted to the thorny issue of how to disengage from a mother whose emotional hold surmounted geographical separation and percolated resolutely down West End Avenue and up to her son's condominium on the twenty-eighth floor.

An examination of Michael's travels reveals that 1963 was the only year he did not play a concert outside the United States. From then on, the number of his appearances, both national and international, increased slowly but steadily, so that by 1969–70, the extent of his concertizing rivaled that of the 1950s. As he clawed his way back to prominence, the unpredictable behavior and last-minute concert cancellations steadily declined, and the bouts of despondency decreased. Similarly, the phobic anxiety that had compelled him to play sitting began to fade too. There were no more signs of ongoing sedative abuse, no further accounts of embarrassing somnolence. As the ship of his great talent righted itself, he began garnering the kinds of reviews reminiscent of those from ten years back that had proclaimed him as the second coming, after Heifetz.

In the summer of 1965 Michael travelled to Vermont for the first of his two Marlboro visits. This summer retreat, founded in 1951 by Rudolf Serkin and Adolf Busch, among others, was known not just for the quality of the music making but also for cultivating a more relaxed and informal approach to performing, far removed from the pressure-cooker atmosphere of concertizing more familiar to Michael. A warm letter of welcome from Serkin preceded Michael's arrival.

> …It made me happy, and I am looking forward with great pleasure
> hearing you often [sic] and, I hope, making music

together…Which works would you like to study this summer and which to perform? Anything from sonatas to concertos, and if possible, also contemporary works. Do you know the Nonettes [*sic*] by Spohr? Have you played the Schubert Phantasy? Any suggestion would be helpful in planning the summer. I am very happy that you are coming, Michel; please forgive me for being so late in telling you that. Affectionate greetings from your friend, Rudolf Serkin.[24]

Michael played neither of Serkin's suggestions, but he did take the first violin part in Brahms' Quartet in A minor. Laredo recalls that Michael was playing beautifully and appeared in good spirits, although a performance of the Debussy String Quartet had to be cancelled at the last moment after Michael mysteriously disappeared, much to the consternation of second violinist Alexander Schneider and others.[25]*

Later that summer, Michael traveled to Brunswick, Maine, at the behest of Lewis, who had started the Bowdoin Summer Music Festival the year before. "He came as a great favor to me," recalls Lewis, who found Michael in good spirits and playing beautifully.[26] But the friends could spend no more than four days together, as Michael had to leave for a two-week engagement in Mexico starting on July 29. On his return to New York in mid-August, he unpacked his suitcase and put it away. He would not tour again until the following year.

During this five-month hiatus, Michael continued his therapy sessions with Chaplik; visited Galamian; dropped by for meals at his parents' apartment; traveled out to Queens to see Bertine, Ivan, and their children, whom he had taken to calling Donald Duck's three nephews; and practiced the violin. It was not an easy time for him, and the constant hankering after bygone glories and the time when he had had to squeeze two performances into a single day tested his newly acquired if fragile equilibrium, not to mention Dr. Chaplik's therapeutic skills. What made the situation galling was that Michael knew he was playing well, and yet when the advertisements came out for the next music season, his name was no longer in its customary position alongside Heifetz, Milstein, Stern, and Francescatti.

If Michael was dating women during this period, he kept it very quiet. He briefly courted Bernard Greenhouse's daughter, Elena, and his on-off-on-again friendship with Elaine Weldon limped along. She would occasionally attend one of his sessions with Dr. Chaplik. Bertine, however, was never introduced to anyone, and Lewis cannot remember any talk of a serious girlfriend. "He was no Romeo," recollected Lewis. "The biggest problem

---

* Michael would return once more to Marlboro in 1966 and sit second desk behind Jaime Laredo in the Marlboro Orchestra for performances of Bach's Orchestral Suites 2 and 3 conducted by Pablo Casals.

Michael had was how to meet a girl. He had no idea."[27] Suzanne Landry (nee Ames), a dancer at the Metropolitan Ballet, was his neighbor for a couple of years in the mid- to late-1960s and saw him often. "He was a genius," she reminisced, "but fragile, like a child. This dear sweet person, a gentle soul, had never been allowed to grow up. He never ran after women and seemed a loner." Landry recalls that Michael's career was not all that big and that he had time on his hands, which he would use to practice. "I also observed that his mother was not very nice to him. She treated him like a kid, and once I saw her loudly berate him after a concert for not putting on a coat. You'll catch a cold, *Michael.* But he was a big man already."[28]

It was perhaps inevitable, therefore, that as Michael grew older, the absence of any visible women in his life apart from a domineering mother led to rumors of homosexuality. Lewis had been shocked by the coarse comments of Leonard Rose, whose assessment of Michael's emotional malaise was armchair Freudian theory expressed in the vernacular of the gutter. "I'll tell you what I think," Rose confided one day, "Michael can't fuck!" Lewis, however, who understood Michael better than anyone, firmly rejected such misplaced notions. "I know it from everything that I witnessed firsthand," he asserted. "He was very much interested in girls. Very much so."[29] The evidence from Michael's relationship with Adrienne supports this contention. Furthermore, towards the end of Michael's life, when he was more comfortable with intimacy and better able to commit to relationships with women, Rose's blunt diagnosis was proved incorrect.

Michael began 1966 with a brace of concerts in Springfield, Missouri, at the end of January. An ice storm kept much of the audience at home, but mindful of how his cancellation under similar circumstances in Bismarck four year earlier had hurt his career, Michael kept his rendezvous with the Springfield Symphony. These two concerts represented the sum total of his 1965–66 American tour, but whatever despair he had felt at this paltry offering was soon banished as he set off on February 27 for his most far-flung odyssey since visiting Australia fourteen years earlier.

He was due to spend a month concertizing in Southern Africa. Flying via Europe, he fulfilled engagements in Spain, Norway, and Denmark before heading south. In Madrid, his playing created a sensation.

> We have witnessed a prodigious event, we remained with our mouths agape! We listened to a velvety tone of an intense and firm texture, to a violinist whose refinement strained the auditory capacity of our ears. What good are mere words, the emotions overcame us, rising into our throats and leaving us gasping for breath. We shall never be able to forget, those of us who were there who lived through this experience.[30]

Even allowing for some Latin hyperbole, it was obvious that Michael was in top form. The fevered prose was also a welcome reminder of how his extraordinary virtuosity could move an audience. Michael left Spain in triumph and headed for Scandinavia with Prokofiev's Second Concerto. The critical praise he garnered may have lacked the white-hot intensity of the Spanish press, but the gist of their messages was similar: Michael Rabin, by the grace of God, was a very great violinist indeed.[31]

From Copenhagen Michael's route to Johannesburg took him through Zurich, Lisbon, Dakar, Monrovia, Accra, Lagos, and Leopoldville. Mitchell Andrews remained at home, citing his objection to apartheid, and the American Richard Syracuse, a recent prizewinner at the Queen Elizabeth Competition, went in his stead. It is hard to know whether Michael would have accepted this tour if his career had not lost momentum. South Africa in 1966 was not a pariah state, and apartheid had yet to become a cause célèbre in the United States. Consequently there were no cultural boycotts in place, and the decision to visit was considered a personal matter. Isaac Stern repeatedly turned down offers,[32] but Heifetz had toured before the war.[33] Menuhin had made multiple visits, his most recent a decade earlier as part of the Johannesburg Festival, for which event Sir William Walton had written a celebratory overture.[34] Furthermore, violinists like Ruggiero Ricci, Salvatore Accardo, and Aaron Rosand were frequent visitors, so in accepting the invitation, Michael was not breaking rank with his colleagues.

On the other hand, as a teenager he had been appalled by the racial segregation he had seen during his concert tours through the Deep South. He supported the Democratic Party, believed in a strong musicians' union, and loathed Richard Nixon.[35] But his political beliefs never translated into social activism. Michael never stopped performing in Alabama and Louisiana, and while he did not condone apartheid, his thirst for more concerts during a difficult period in his career probably meant he went through little soul-searching before accepting the South African tour.

While in Johannesburg, he spent time with Walter Mony, professor of violin at the University of the Witwatersrand. "His playing was superb," recalls Mony,

> particularly in the Brahms D Minor Sonata. Technically wonderful with a burnished tone. And his performance of a piece I had not heard before, "Sea Murmurs" by Engel [arranged by Zimbalist], was stunning. I asked him where he had found the music, and he told me it was not commercially available. Apparently his copy had been written out by hand.

During a luncheon at Mony's house, they were joined by Vincent Fritelli,

an ex-Galamian student and contemporary of Michael who was now the concertmaster of one of the orchestras soon to perform with Michael. Despite
passing an enjoyable afternoon together, Mony noticed that Michael's high
spirits were transient. "He vacillated between euphoria and despondency.
And he appeared restless, wanting to do things all the time. Michael and
Syracuse were also keen to find out where the nightclubs were. They were definitely two young men looking for some action."36

Michael played recitals in five major cities, and the Brahms Concerto with
three of the country's leading orchestras. All went well until problems resurfaced in a concert at the Great Hall of the University of the Witwatersrand.
Before a packed auditorium, Michael opened the concert with Mozart's
Rondo in G and never returned.37 Exhaustion was cited as the cause, but as
in Germany, the excuse was thin. He had played the same program two nights
previously in East London and had a full day to rest before taking the eighty-
minute flight to Johannesburg. A more plausible explanation was his continued misuse of cold medication that contained the stimulant ephedrine.
When taken in large amounts, a hyperexcitable, euphoric state could ensue,
followed quickly by lethargy and apathy. Neither of these extremes was con-
ducive to good violin playing, and there was still one recital left, in Salisbury,
Rhodesia.* The country was not yet in a state of siege following its unilateral
declaration of independence four months earlier, but the dogs of war were
about in the countryside. Michael flew in, played faultlessly, and took the next
plane out.38 Political trouble of a different sort was brewing in South Africa,
but he would be gone five months before the architect of apartheid, Prime
Minister Hendrik Verwoerd, was assassinated in South Africa's Parliament.

Despite Henry Roth's dissenting view,39 there was a perception among
many critics and colleagues that by the mid-1960s, Michael's interpretative
powers had finally caught up to his formidable technique. "When Michael
returned to the concert stage, there was a new boldness and depth to his
playing," recollects Arnold Steinhardt. "He was back in harness and it was
splendid playing. A Brahms concerto that I heard was particularly memorable."40 For his November 4, 1966, comeback recital at Philharmonic Hall,
his first since the debacle on that stage four years earlier, Michael's choice of
repertoire reflected this hard-won maturity. The program opened with
Stravinsky's Divertimento and was followed by Beethoven's "Kreutzer"
Sonata, which Michael dedicated to the memory of Dimitri Mitropoulos. It
was an unusual gesture, more so as Mitropoulos had been dead six years. But
Michael's return to a major New York stage after such a long and frustrating
absence was an emotional moment for him and, as the dedication made clear,

---

* Now called Zimbabwe.

rekindled memories of past collaborations with the ascetic maestro who had been his champion. After intermission, Michael performed the Debussy Sonata, three Paganini caprices (9, 17, and 24), Sarasate's "Malagueña," and Suk's "Burleska."

The concert was a triumph. "[Rabin] began his career in his early teens knocking 'em dead with Paganini and the like," noted Alan Rich in his column the following morning:

> There were some Paganini Caprices on last night's program, but there were also a spacious, quiet, beautifully lyrical exposition of Beethoven's Kreutzer Sonata, the Debussy Sonata and the witty and subtle Divertimento that Stravinsky fashioned from his ballet "The Fairy's Kiss."
>
> And this was the part of the program that held the real rewards.[41]

In the opinion of the *Musical Leader,* "Michael Rabin's recital got off to a stunning start with Stravinsky's Divertimento. This sparkling composition, performed with superb technique and flair, was followed by Beethoven's 'Kreutzer' sonata, projected with seriousness and strength."[42] Elaine Weldon wrote of Michael's "triumphant return,"[43] while the review in *High Fidelity* warmly declared, "Welcome back, Mr. Rabin."[44]

After the concert, a large crowd gathered in Jeanne and George's apartment to celebrate. "It was a marvelous post-concert party," recalls Andrews:

> Michael and I devised a game. There were so many musicians present we thought we would take a poll and find out, by consensus, who were the two greatest twentieth-century composers — excluding the impressionist school. Michael was very wound up over this, and we found out that he was for Stravinsky and Bartok. But the consensus didn't go that way. Prokofiev was the clear winner.[45]

Given the repertoire Michael performed, his choices were surprising and most likely reflected his high enthusiasm of the moment. For it surely must have been deliciously sweet to bask once more in the warm glow of his hometown's critical approval. Away from the celebrations, however, it did not go unnoticed that there were hundreds of empty seats in the auditorium. Rabin redux may have made it back, but to the public, the frisson associated with his name had faded.

It took an artist of singular charisma to retain his or her popularity after dropping out of sight for years. Vladimir Horowitz had that elusive ingredient, his virtuosity amplified by a personal magnetism that audiences found

irresistible. When forced to take a lengthy break from performing as he bat-
tled depression, his absence, far from hurting his career, lent his return an
almost hallowed status. "Dear Mr. Horowitz," gushed one disciple:

> I was among your fortunate audience at Carnegie Hall on Sunday
> and feel impelled to write to you to personally congratulate you
> on your performance. What a great joy to hear you again!…
>
> For all the years that you had concertized here your appear-
> ances were the highlight of the musical scene and the twelve years
> of your retirement from your adoring public were so bleak and
> barren — there is no one like you!
>
> We all prayed and hoped for your return to good health and
> strength and how you came through yesterday!! What superb
> artistry you displayed! So many of the young pianists who had
> never had the privilege and joy of hearing you except on records,
> were awed, thrilled and speechless.
>
> I am sure I don't have to tell you how your audience responded
> to you and adored every note you played and adored you for
> playing.
>
> To me you looked so wonderfully young and sounded even
> more marvelous than I remembered you before….
>
> I want to thank you again for the great joy and thrill you gave
> us all yesterday and to hope that you will feel disposed and strong
> enough to play again and again and share your genius with us,
> your adoring public.
>
> God bless you.[46]

To Vladimir Horowitz, such praise was not unusual, but what lent this
letter a particular salience was that the besotted fan was none other than
Jeanne Rabin. It is sobering to reflect that she wrote this during a period in
which her son too had been forced to step back from a great career, and yet
she could never bring herself to lavish the same unequivocal praise on him.

Michael and his management hoped the successful return recital would
finally demonstrate to the public and critics that he had completely overcome
the emotional problems that had dogged his career four years back. Having
silenced his doubters, Michael looked forward to receiving, once again, the invitations from the great orchestras and concert halls of Europe that he so hankered
after. But six months on, expectations had not been met. A different approach
was therefore required. If Michael's playing alone could not breathe new life into
his international career, perhaps a series of interviews with journalists would. It
was a calculated risk, for it entailed Michael speaking publicly about matters that
were intensely personal, and the Rabins were a very private family.

The interviews were published in July 1967. Michael spoke with candor of his difficulties being a child prodigy, his problems relating socially, the dangers of his addiction to prescription medication, the last-minute concert cancellations, and his lost years — "an agonizing, almost surrealistic period of aimlessness and escape from reality ... a story told only in whispers in the music world grapevine."[47] Looking back over recent events, he confided how he had had to retrain himself by acquiring skills neglected during his clois-tered years of practicing. "I had to learn that other people were important. Fortunately, I was able to find those who could help me. I discovered the great truth, trite though it seems, that people are wonderful." After speaking about his phobia — "I kept moving back, back, and pretty soon I was crowding the cellists" — Michael let his imagination get away from him when he stated he had received his high school diploma from the Bronx High School of Science, a prestigious academy that boasted a number of Nobel laureates as alumni. This fanciful claim was followed by others that owed much to idealism, whimsy, and a touch of wishful thinking:

> There are Rabin fans who believe that his future may rest in the promotion of good music. Like Leonard Bernstein, [he] has the ability to communicate excitement that great music can create....
> It is Rabin's hope that music can do something about quelling the wave of violence that engulfs so many sections of the country and [the] world.[48]

From 1967 onwards, it is informative to look at Michael's domestic and international careers separately. Within the United States, there were definite signs of a revival, although qualitative differences between the invitations of the fifties and late sixties were discernible. Michael's performance history with the New York Philharmonic Orchestra illustrates this point. In the fifties, he was the soloist in seven separate series of subscription concerts, all at Carnegie Hall during the regular symphony season* On the comeback trail, however, his 1967 (the Mendelssohn Concerto), 1969 (Saint-Saëns's Introduction and Rondo Capriccioso, Sarasate's *Zigeunerweisen* and Introduction and Tarantella), and 1971 (Bruch's G Minor Concerto) performances were all part of summer series, the majority of which took place outdoors, where admission was either free or at a reduced price. This is not to decry the quality of the con-certs, conducted by such luminaries as Wallenstein, Maazel, Kostelanetz, and Copland. But limited as they were to the hot summer months — when musical directors Leonard Bernstein and his successor, Pierre Boulez, plus

---

* This statistic does not include his two-week engagement at the Roxy Theatre.

many of the regular orchestral musicians, were on holiday — these park and promenade concerts never carried the same prestige as regular season events.

Similarly, while the gross number of concerts Michael gave nationwide during this period rivaled those of his heyday, looking beyond simple volume revealed how his profile had slipped. In the advertisements for the National Symphony Orchestra's Washington season of 1968, his name was dwarfed by that of a colleague from his Juilliard days, Van Cliburn.[49] He began sharing concert series with little-known ballet and musical theater artists,[50] and was obliged to accept engagements offered by the big Miami Beach hotels. Here, his name appeared in a showbiz package deal, billed as the "Cavalcade of the Stars," that offered nightly entertainment together with three lavish meals a day, all for $19.50 and "nothing more to spend."[51]

A new phenomenon also began appearing in Michael's itinerary, something that back in the crammed-full decade of the 1950s would not have been possible: he began popping up as a last-minute substitute for indisposed colleagues. Thus in March 1968, he replaced Zino Francescatti in San Antonio; in February 1969, he stood in for Nathan Milstein in Kansas City; and a month later, he took over from Leonid Kogan, whose last-minute preference for New York over Toronto and Ottawa prompted the ire of one Canadian critic: "It seems especially ungrateful of Kogan, who made his North American debut here before he was permitted in the United States. Perhaps Mrs. Kogan wanted to do some shopping."[52] In June 1969, he substituted once more for Nathan Milstein, this time in London and Liverpool. In February 1970, he filled in for Christian Ferras at a Hunter College recital in New York, and in January 1971, with only a few hours notice, he replaced Jacqueline du Pré in New Haven, Connecticut. The reviews were all excellent. Even so, whatever satisfaction came Michael's way was diluted by the galling realization that his only access to some famous stages was now via the route of last-minute substitute for someone whose star had eclipsed his own.

The challenges Michael faced in restoring his career to former heights were magnified when it came to concerts outside the United States. Within the Americas, regular visits continued to Canada, although even here there were uncomfortable reminders of lost ground. "Remember Michael Rabin?" asked one Montreal newspaper.[53] Michael returned to Venezuela once, Mexico twice, and also made a ten-day visit to Colombia, accompanied by Mitchell Andrews, in which they played concerts in Medellin, Bogota, and Cali.

Further afield, the tours to Scandinavia continued, and in June 1969, Michael returned to Berlin for a performance of the Bruch G Minor Concerto.[54] This time, the orchestra was not the famous Philharmonic but the lesser-known Radio Symphony Orchestra conducted by Thomas Schippers, which did not stop Michael from passing off the concert as a return Philharmonic invitation.[55] What could not, however, be fudged was the absence of the *grand* tour that had been a regular feature of his itinerary prior to 1962. And it was the dearth of bookings in England in particular that proved the most frustrating of all. Michael expressed his vexation in a letter to Alf Levy.

> It's really been so terribly long since we have seen each other, and I can't tell you with how much eagerness I'm anticipating our meeting in London next month!
>
> Between concerts in Switzerland and Scandinavia I shall be spending four days in London. As you well know I don't have a concert in London, but I am specifically coming to see the people at the Holt office, and basically to tell them that now I get some action from them, or else I shall finally be forced to find other English representation. I have now certainly proved beyond a shadow of doubt that I am now in even better shape than in the "good old days," and if they can't start booking me in London again, perhaps someone else can. In any event, I shall be in London at the Cumberland Hotel, from March 6th to March 10th.
>
> I have been having spectacularly successful and busy concert seasons here in the United States over the past three years.... Oh, the hell with all this. We can talk much better in person next month. I'll call you when I get into town....
>
> Be well and at peace,... affectionate greetings,
> Michael[56]

Michael got nowhere with Hunter and left London without a firm offer of new engagements. He did, however, enjoy seeing his friends again. "Thank you so much for the lovely evening we spent together," he wrote from Oslo. "I felt at home and the dinner was marvelous and the company so 'haimisch.' I truly hope we won't have to wait for years again until our next visit."[57] This time his wish was realized, but it took Nathan Milstein's misfortune — he was knocked down by a car in Wigmore Street — before Michael was finally invited back to fill in with the Tchaikowsky Concerto at the Royal Festival Hall.[58]

Seven years had elapsed since his last London appearance with the same concerto on the very same stage. The difference now was that Michael, Doriden free, was an artist transformed. A firsthand account of that evening has come from London violinist Robin Brightman, at the time a nineteen-year-old student at the Guildhall School of Music and Drama. "I had been expecting to hear Nathan Milstein play the Tchaikowsky with the Liverpool Symphony Orchestra [*sic*] and Charles Grove [*sic*]," recalls Brightman:

It seems that half the Menuhin School were also expecting to hear him because they were all there. Imagine the disappointment at seeing the school blackboard in the foyer with a chalked announcement that Nathan Milstein was indisposed and his place had been taken by Michael Rabin who was only known to me by a 10/6p record on Music for Pleasure — an offshoot of EMI. I didn't have that recording, but I did buy it the next day, and the last time I looked that edition is now selling for £400!!! The performance was *stunning*. He played an encore, the unaccompanied Kreisler Recitativo and Scherzo. I remember that he stood, at times, with his feet right over the front of the platform, even while he was playing, and I wondered how and why he had had the nerve to do this — one false muscle twitch and he would have been thrown off the platform into the front row. It wasn't long before I found the answer. It was a performance of a lifetime.[59]

Michael had been back in New York a week when, on June 30, 1969, he wrote what turned out to be his last letter to Alf.

It was great seeing you again after all that time…. I particularly enjoyed the evening with you in your home…. Wonderful people, delicious food and an atmosphere of comfortable informality, and genuine hospitality. Thanks so very much for that…. It means a great deal to me and I loved it.

I have a very good Summer season, to be followed by an excellent Winter season starting at the end of September, and when I think of all the standard and new repertoire this involves I realize that although it's now Summer, I've really got my work cut out for me. But it won't be too bad…. I'll take two or three weekends off and my apartment is air-conditioned.

Of course I'll let you know of any plans for London as soon as I hear of them. I hope it will be soon and very good.[60]

This time, however, the meeting was not to be. Michael passed through London in April 1970, on his way back from Finland. Six months later he returned, this time en route to Liverpool for a performance of Max Bruch's *Scottish Fantasy* with the Royal Liverpool Philharmonic and James Loughran. It was the last time he would visit a land and a people he had never really warmed to and yet where, perhaps more than in any place other than New York, he had yearned for the "great success."

CHAPTER 14

THE RABIN SOUND
FALLS SILENT

$\mathcal{M}$ichael's ability to restore, in part, his splintered concert schedule was not matched on the recording front. Here his career remained moribund. He made his last long-playing record in 1960. Four years later, he agreed to EMI's terms for a reduced royalty of 2½ percent for the reissue of his recordings. There would be no further reissues during his lifetime. Matters did not have to end this way, however. Decca and Deutsche Grammophon Gesellschaft had by the mid-sixties expressed an interest in signing Michael to their labels.[1] Had he been more assertive in promoting himself, more proactive in dealing with the companies and suggesting innovative repertoire, his chances of clinching a deal would have been enhanced. But faced with this challenge, something unrelated to the mechanics of violin playing, Michael did not know how to respond. He had no business acumen. Despite years of psychotherapy, when it came to the workings of the world, he remained in many ways artless.

The loss of his recording contract was a painful blow that never dissipated. "I would like to be recording with [my del Gesù]," Michael told an interviewer six months before he died,

> but I was with Capitol Records and they dropped me in 1965. All but two or three of my records have been deleted. I tried to get them to reissue some or to send me the rights to them, but nothing has happened. I guess I can't blame the recording companies for not helping me; the classical business is in trouble, I hear. But it makes

me feel bad. I've reached a certain level of performance, and I'm doing from 50 to 70 concerts a year. For an artist it is important for concerts and recordings to go together…. If I were to start recording again, I'd do the Brahms and Beethoven concertos — I never did record them, and then I'd like to do the music of the great violinist composers of the last century. I think there is a romantic revival. Mr. Schonberg said that there is, so it must be true.[2]

Michael's career may not have returned to the heights of earlier years, but his romantic life had picked up considerably. An offshoot of his performance with the Queens Philharmonic in 1968 was a date organized by the orchestra's conductor, David Katz. The woman in question was the singer June LeBell. "I was singing with David in Queens," recalls June,

and he said that he knew this really nice man who lived across the way from me. I knew of Michael and I had heard him play, but I had never met him. So I asked David what he was like and I remember him saying that Michael used to be short and fat, but that now he was tall and slim. So I agreed to the meeting and we went out on a blind date. It was great and we started going together.

From 1968 until Michael's death, June was known to Michael's friends and acquaintances as his first serious girlfriend. They never lived together, but they spent a lot of time with one another. "He was very funny, very warm," she recollects,

outgoing, kind, but most of all — funny. He loved to joke and had a wonderful sense of humor. He would sort of pick up on things. For example, I remember once he didn't send me a Valentine's day card and I was very upset, and I said something about it, and I got a card a day, for the rest of my life, literally. And they were very funny cards and sweet.

June soon became part of Michael's small inner sanctum, comprising Lewis Kaplan, Mitchell Andrews, and Walter Taub, a physician and fine amateur pianist who lived in Michael's condominium complex. As such, she was witness to his long hours of practice. "He said he hated it, but he did it and he used to joke that he did it because there was nothing else that he knew how to do."[3]

Michael seldom spoke about his period of Sturm und Drang earlier in the decade. "He did tell me the time had been very difficult for him," June confided:

> that he had been in therapy, that he had taken medication, and that he was feeling much better. He went back and saw his psychiatrist every once in a while. The problems were related to his unusual childhood, spending most of his life as a kid in his room practicing. He was open and honest about his past, and I accepted him on face value — the way he was with me rather than the way he had been.

As their relationship developed, Michael introduced June to his family. She met Bertine on a number of occasions and was invited to a family bar mitzvah. "Michael spoke a lot about Bertine and seemed close to her and her three children. He also loved his father a lot," she reminisced:

> George was wonderful. He was a kind, gentle man and smart too. Michael only spoke of him well and in glowing terms. He wasn't so high about his mother, but sometimes he would joke about her, and at times you never knew whether he was joking or being serious when he referred to her as "the mother figure." Michael hated her a lot and he also loved her very much. She was a very good mother at times, but she was overbearing and demanding. However, when I knew Michael, he was quite independent. He seemed like a very normal Jewish boy who had a mother problem.[4]

While June's memories of her boyfriend were predominantly sunny, she was aware of brief periods of sadness. Her observations of Michael over a three-year period help round out the picture of the wunderkind in adult's clothing, increasingly confident in some areas, still feeling his way in others.

> I remember that he would be down a little bit or he would need to be alone. He needed to feel that he had privacy and I wasn't impinging in any way. I think that was a very important thing for him, and that probably came from his upbringing. He would just tell me, "I want to be alone," and I would accept that. We might have plans to do something, and he would back out, saying, "I'm sorry, I just don't want to go out." Things like that.

Many years after the fact, June revealed to Lewis that Leonard Rose had been way off the mark in his blunt assessment of Michael's private life. "Michael wanted to be in a relationship very much," she believes, "but I think he was afraid of a total commitment. We did speak of marriage, but that was towards the very end of his life. We both did not want to live in New York. He loved Phoenix, and also spoke of San Diego." By then Michael had given June the key to his apartment and put her photograph in his violin case, his most public display of affection for a woman since his relationship with Adrienne Rosenbaum twelve years earlier.[5]

It was not surprising given Michael's convoluted and rocky road to adulthood that his private life should have contained certain complexities and imponderables. June loved Michael deeply and he reciprocated the affection, but there were periods of uncertainty and tension in their relationship. When Michael was interviewed by the *New York Times* in mid-1971, he was asked about love, marriage, and whether he had a girlfriend. Given what is now known about his upbringing, his obfuscation becomes understandable. He told the interviewer he had "too many girlfriends" and went on to add the following: "I could get married tonight if I wanted to, but I'm still square or romantic enough to wait to meet the girl I'll get bopped on the head by. I hope it'll happen."[6] When June read the article, she was aghast. "He never mentioned me, and I was furious," she recalls:

> My mother was up from Florida at the time and was staying with me. "Do you really want to break up with him?" she asked and I said "No, but I'm very angry and he should never have said that. It was very nasty — what are my friends going to think of me?" And my mother asked, "Are your friends going to marry him?" Then she picked up the *Sunday Times,* which was big, and she told me to go out and buy a few more, and go over to his apartment, and when he opened the door, to hit him over the head. So I did, and we both laughed, and that was the end of it. I yelled at him, and I said "Why did you say something like that?" and he replied, "It was nobody's business and I didn't want to talk about it." I half believed him and half didn't.[7]

Michael's premature death left it unclear whether he would resolve any ambivalent feelings he privately entertained about marriage. There was, however, a tantalizing clue that he was close to doing so. In December 1971, the month before he died, he travelled to Houston for a performance of the

Glazunov concerto. There he met his friend Fredell Lack at the university and gave a three-hour master class to her students. Lack had never seen Michael looking so happy. At last, he informed her, he was truly in love.[8] It had been a long time in returning.

The Houston master class was a rare event for Michael.* He was first and last a soloist and never sought a reputation as a teacher. Nevertheless, his talent and reputation acted as a magnet to young violinists, who saw him as an exemplar of the virtuoso violinist. Among the handful of students who took lessons with Michael was the violinist Tom Strasser.† He was a twenty-three-year old orchestral musician in Kansas City when Michael came to town and performed the Brahms Concerto and a Kreisler encore. Strasser was overwhelmed by what he heard and there and then asked for lessons. Michael agreed, and for the next six months, right up until the week before he died, the two would meet on a Sunday morning at his apartment and spend three or four hours going through repertoire.

"My first lesson started in an unusual fashion," recollects Strasser. "Michael had just got out the shower and opened the door with nothing but a towel around his waist. I was struck by the incongruity of this famous violinist, who by the way was very hairy, greeting me like this on our first formal contact." Strasser was by his own admission in awe of Michael, the natural way he played the instrument and his monumental control. He regarded Michael more as a source of inspiration than a teacher in the true pedagogical sense. They worked on the Wieniawski D Minor Concerto, Saint-Saëns's Introduction and Rondo Capriccioso, and the fugue from Bach's G Minor Sonata, among other pieces. Michael would play and demonstrate, and Strasser would observe and copy. Michael would play his own records but never complained that his recording career had stalled.[9]

Strasser observed that away from the violin, Michael appeared somewhat childlike—a kind and gentle man, soft-spoken and relaxed. His apartment was neat, orderly, sparse—there was a grand piano, a record player, and a shelf for his violin. There was never any talk of women, and Strasser was never aware of any girlfriends. He was struck by the fact that Jeanne would call her thirty-five-year-old son with the most inappropriate reminders—

---

* Michael's first master classes at the Bowdoin Summer Festivals in the mid-1960s were followed by others at the Universities of Texas/Austin, Arizona, and Houston. There was also a return visit to Bowdoin in 1971 and a class for the Washington State String Teachers Association in Seattle two years earlier.

† Subsequently, Strasser joined the St. Paul Chamber Orchestra as a violist.

"Drink your cocoa, Michael, that type of stuff"—and he never seemed to resent it.10

"Michael was not comfortable with himself," noted Strasser. "He was socially awkward and did not know how to respond to certain things or else gave answers that were not always relevant." At one lesson he was taken aback when Michael asked, "Do you really like the violin?" while at another he was advised to go study with Dorothy DeLay. There were times they would go off and play table tennis. On other occasions, Michael would take Strasser's MG Midget for a spin. Once they went to hear a performance of the Beethoven Triple Concerto played by Barenboim, Zukerman, and du Pré. During these six months, Michael refused payment for the lessons. And throughout it all, Strasser's awe never diminished. "I felt this enormous respect for him and his talent," was how Strasser remembered his teacher. "He inspired wonder rather than affection. But in some ways I felt sorry for him too."11

In 1971 Michael's career nosedived. Michael Ries and his associate Hattie Clark had taken over his management at Columbia Artists after the departure of Bill Judd, who in 1969 had set up his own agency, Judd Concert Bureau.* It was clear from a letter Michael wrote to his parents in March 1970 that he found Ries and Clarke's stewardship ineffectual and he was toying with the idea of leaving them and signing up once more with Judd and his new associate Mary Lynn Fixler.12

Apathetic management, however, was not the central issue holding Michael back. Hard as he tried, he had never fully escaped the fallout from his earlier emotional collapse. With mounting irritation, he tried yet again to forcefully debunk what he perceived as perpetual misinformation and inaccuracies that dogged his career. "By 1965–66 I was back to a full load of 50 or 60 [concerts] and have been ever since," he told the *New York Times*'s Beatrice Berg:

> I can't understand how people got the impression I didn't play for three or four years. I was never in a straight jacket. I never went crazy. I was never in a mental institution. Could you believe it, after eight years I still hear about out-of-town symphony managers who say they've heard I was sick for such a long time that they want to wait a little longer before I play with their orchestras to be sure I'm okay? How long do you have to go on paying for not feeling well?

---

* Arthur Judson had long since departed Columbia Artists Management Inc. Carl Dahlgren had left in 1968 to join Sol Hurok's agency, Hurok Concerts, which left Michael back with Bill Judd.

After speaking about his early years — "Mitropoulos was a beautiful person. He was my god" — Michael returned to the events of 1963:

> You think that perhaps people don't like you and you become a semi-recluse. When you start to have emotional problems like that people don't want to know you and this increases the loneliness. The psychiatric diagnosis was "disassociative [*sic*] reaction." I think that means you become so preoccupied with your new and incorrect reactions that you actually disassociate yourself from what's real. You get to a point where you either have to do something about it or quit the human race....
>
> I don't know why there's all this hush about people admitting they're seeing an analyst or a therapist. When you finally decide to go into therapy I think it is reason to celebrate, not to whisper about.

And then, with this lengthy preamble out of the way, Michael addressed head-on his relationship with his formidable mother.

> The idea that if you're not well emotionally you must hate your mother, has been overdone to the point where it's a not very intelligent joke. I realize that my mother created problems for me that she was unaware of. So did my father and my older sister. But I created problems for them.... My parents gave up a lot for me. Jewish mothers — not only of sons, but of Jewish princesses — are a special breed. They will kill themselves for their children. I don't have to go through the *Portnoy's Complaint* thing. Philip Roth said it better than I can. But I can tell you very simply and honestly that if it hadn't been for my Jewish mother, with her pushing and cajoling and her knowledge of music, I wouldn't be a concert violinist today because I'm not as aggressive as she is....
>
> Needless to say, before therapy it was convenient to blame everything on my parents. But as a result of therapy, I see my emotional hangups and strengths in a much healthier light. I'm closer than ever to my parents and I have a real, true friendship with my sister.[13]

Whether Michael was fudging the truth hardly mattered — the public perception was widespread of a mother-son relationship that was way off-kilter. "Believe me, when you find a prodigy you find an ambitious parent in the background," noted Ruggerio Ricci. "My father was some kind of musical maniac."14

The parents of wunderkinder carry a well-known notoriety. Heifetz, Elman, and Menuhin, to give but three examples, all had fathers who could have kept Ricci Senior company. And yet, there are prodigies who have made the perilous journey to successful adult artist without such conditional and manipulative parental control. Given the magnitude of Michael's talent, there was every reason to believe he could have had his great success via a different route, one that left him happier, better adjusted, and less prone to the allure of sedatives and stimulants. Michael, in his interview with Berg, had shown some impressive insights, but when it came to mother, his vision stayed clouded.

Despite revelations about his health and private life, there remained one area of Michael's life roped off from both personal and public scrutiny — his predilection for prescription medication. In an interview four years earlier, he had spoken about his misuse of sedatives and how his abrupt withdrawal from the drug had precipitated his collapse and hospitalization. But to Berg, Michael backtracked and denied there had ever been a problem, claiming all he had ever taken was something called Milpath to treat the "beginning of an ulcer." In this he was being disingenuous, for Milpath's generic name was meprobamate, a highly addictive sedative closely allied to Doriden and the barbiturates.* In a combative mood, he took umbrage with reports that suggested he had difficulties with substance abuse. "I remember being absolutely wild when I read that," he informed Berg:

> I called my lawyer and asked if I could sue, because they completely misrepresented what I said, but he advised me not to. What's the expression when you have a drug problem — "having a monkey on your back"? The drug problem isn't the monkey on my back. It's the people who still like to talk about it. The only drug in this house is Excedrin for the number 12 headache.15

Vehement protestations and honest disclosure did not, however, march in tandem. Michael's medicine cabinet still held more than Excedrin. Mitchell Andrews recalls that by 1970:

> Michael's playing had come back wonderfully. He had regained all his old skills…. And then one day some little, tiny blemishes happened at a concert, and then there were some more little slips at the next concert. Now Michael never slipped when he was

---

* Milpath was also known as Miltown.

drug-free. Really, he had as unblemished a record as you could ask for. These mistakes went on, and I began to wonder whether he was sneaking the drugs back in, when one Monday morning, the phone rang and it was Bertine asking the same question."16

Michael's accompanist and sister were not the only ones to notice something was once again amiss. On June 19, 1970, Michael travelled to Greensboro and performed a Mozart concerto at the Eastern Music Festival. In the audience was the violist and journalist Suzanne Bilyeu, at the time a music student. "Although the performance went relatively well," she recalls, "Rabin looked a bit out of it and there were a couple of bobbles that one would not have expected from a violinist of his caliber. The following day faculty and student scuttlebutt had it that Rabin was having problems with barbiturates."17 What transpired later that evening has been recounted by Sheldon Morgenstern, the Festival Director and conductor who partnered Michael in the Mozart concerto.

> After the concert we were headed to my car to go to a reception at the home of Leah Tannenbaum, then the board president [of the festival], when Michael fell on the pavement. With some help from a faculty member, the pianist Warren Rich, we were able to get him to Leah's. Her husband, Jack, was a doctor and I quickly told him what had happened. He immediately asked to see Michael's violin. When Jack opened the case and found various drugs he said, "Take Rabin back and get rid of those drugs. If he takes any more tonight he will die." Warren went back with us to the hotel, and by then the drugs were beginning to wear off. Michael walked up to the hotel desk clerk and said, "These guys are trying to hurt me. Please stop them from going to my room." We had no choice but to leave. When I telephoned his room at seven the next morning he had already checked out.18

The absence of prescribing records and medical notes make it difficult to track precisely Michael's medication history. The evidence from his performances, the testimony of Bertine, Andrews, and Morgenstern, and the legibility of his handwriting point towards a five-year period (1965 to 1970) of abstinence from sedatives, although he never swore off the intermittent use of appetite suppressants. Why Michael returned surreptitiously to sedative medication was unclear. By his own admission, he had an addictive personality, and given what is now known about the biological basis to addiction it is no longer necessary to invoke some external event, like frustration over his defunct recording career, as the reason for his recidivism. But there is little doubt that an array of concerns, both social and professional, weighed Michael down at times despite the bracing elixir of being in love. He would deal with these worries by withdrawing from people, backing out of an arrangement with June, or asking for his privacy to be respected. It was during spells like these that the pull of drugs would have been at their strongest. Michael's second period of prescription drug abuse was less severe than his first, but word of renewed problems spread quickly within the music fraternity and contributed to the precipitous decline in the number of concerts he gave in 1971.

The long shadow cast by Michael's drug problem and his inability to confront it not only hobbled his career, it ultimately contributed to his death. On Sunday, January 16, 1972, Tom Strasser visited 185 West End Avenue for his music lesson. Earlier that week, fourteen-year-old Marc Silberger had had his one and only lesson with Michael, working on the Ysaÿe Third Sonata.[19]* Neither student recalled Michael looking unwell. On the following Tuesday evening, Michael went around to Lewis's apartment. "When he arrived," recollects Lewis, "my violin was on the piano. My children were young at the time, and Michael picked up the violin and just diddled for them. I will never forget it. It was amazing. It had such articulation and such projection. Everything that he did had that quality." If, as Efrem Zimbalist claimed, Galamian could teach a table to play the violin, then Michael could make any table sing. But there was something else Lewis remembered from that last evening he saw his friend alive:

> He made some cryptic remarks. He hadn't performed for a while, and he was ready to go out on tour a few days later and rather looked forward to it. He had been complaining about a stomach disorder, and I asked him what the doctor had said. And he looked at me and his words were like stone. "Those goddam doctors ought to know what's wrong with you by looking into your eyes." And I said, "Michael, is it not your stomach?" And he just changed the subject.[20]

The following morning, Michael rose as usual. "He always called me in the morning when he got up," divulged June, "and he'd wake me so that I could go to work. He was in a very good mood, he was very up, and he sounded good. We had plans to dine at Captain Nemo's restaurant on 72nd Street that evening." Michael probably practiced for a while. Around midday

---

* Silberger was a student of Lewis Kaplan, Ivan Galamian, and Dorothy DeLay.

his thoughts turned to lunch, but he never got around to eating it. "I didn't hear from him in the afternoon, which was unusual," remembers June:

> I was at work and phoned Michael several times and there was no answer. By 4:30 or 5:00 I was concerned. I hadn't heard from him, I couldn't reach him, and we were supposed to go out about 5:30 or 6:00 PM, so I went over to his apartment and I rang the bell and banged on the door. Nothing. That had happened once before, but he had been all right then. But this time I couldn't get him. I had keys. I went in and I found him lying under one of those fold-up chairs and there was blood around him. He was bleeding from the mouth and the nose and his eyes were open. I had never seen anybody dead before. Michael was sort of clammy. I immediately called 911 to get help from the police, and I called the doorman downstairs, and that is how we got the doctor [Walter Taub] who lived in the building. I tried to revive Michael but couldn't.[21]

June's memory of that shocking late winter's afternoon retains an eidetic quality, and in her heightened state of emotional arousal, she was able to take in the details of her surroundings with an exquisite clarity. "Michael was in his underwear, white boxer trunks, and T-shirt" she noted,

> which was the way he generally walked around the apartment. His violin was out, the case was out, and I think the violin was in the case, as if he had been playing and he had put it down. There was a can of tuna fish — I don't remember if it was opened or not, but I remember the can, a can opener, and a fork, as if he was about to have lunch. And the desk was pushed, as if he had fallen against it trying to answer the telephone and had slipped. He had just had the floors waxed, and you could almost see one slipper in the living room and the other was in the bedroom. It was as if he had come running out of the kitchen, had slid and flown through the air and hit his head on the wooden seat of the chair. And he had evidently cracked his skull on it. Judging from the fact that he was about to have lunch, I guess he died somewhere between 12:00 and 2:00 PM.[22]

June telephoned Bertine from Walter Taub's apartment to break the news. "Michael is dead," was all Bertine could remember her saying. Together with her husband, she rushed in from Queens. By the time they arrived, the coroner had come and gone, and they found Michael "all wrapped up."[23]

George too had come to the apartment. He appeared very controlled and was worried about breaking the news to his wife without having a doctor present. It was not, however, something that could be delayed, and with all the legal requirements completed, the police gone, and Michael taken off to the mortuary, June, George and Walter Taub made their way over to 110 Riverside Drive bearing the grim news. Jeanne clearly knew something bad had taken place even before the distraught party walked into her apartment, but with a mother's intuition, she only had to look at June's face to divine the worst. "On no, not again, not another one," was her anguished response. Then she began screaming. She did not stop until Dr. Taub stepped in and sedated her with an injection.[24]

No one had informed Galamian that Michael had died. He saw the news for the first time the following morning when he opened the *New York Times.* "All of a sudden I heard him coming down the corridor screaming," recalls Judith Galamian,

> "Did you know? Did you know?" And that's as far as he could get. I came quickly and he was standing halfway down the long hallway in our apartment with a newspaper in his hand. And he could never say Michael was dead. He just went into his room and shut the door and stayed there.[25]

Michael died on a Wednesday* and was buried the following Sunday. The day before the funeral, June sneaked into the funeral parlor to pay her private respects. "Michael wore half a toupee because he was balding," she observed, "and the morticians had put it on backwards so I picked it up and turned it around. And I put something under the pillow, which I assume and hope is still there. At least I had the quiet moment with him before the big public funeral."[26]

Michael's memorial service took place on Amsterdam Avenue, on the Upper West Side of Manhattan, the area where he had lived for his entire life. The large crowd, spilling out onto the pavement, contained many musical celebrities, among them Van Cliburn, Itzhak Perlman, and Michael's management. Jeanne appeared inconsolable. "She just wouldn't stop screaming," recollects June. "The ranting and screaming didn't read true. I'm sure she was feeling those things, but I think it was also her way of becoming the center of attention, which I think is what she wanted all along."[27]

Bertine has virtually no memories from that day — overwhelmed by the magnitude of the tragedy, her mind was a blank that admitted only the

---

* January 19, 1972.

occasional, sketchiest details of what was unfolding in front of her.[28] Even to an observer more removed from the weight of grief, like Arnold Steinhardt, there was something biblical in the outpouring of emotion, the mother's continuous shrieking, doing everything but shredding her clothes as a bygone orthodoxy demanded.[29]

Lewis, who had been on tour when Michael died, was asked by George and Jeanne to put together some music for the memorial service. In the fraught, hurried aftermath of his friend's death, he was joined by Felix Galimir, Walter Trampler, Michael Tree, and Tim Eddy in the adagio ma non troppo from Mozart's G Minor Quintet. Before the musicians could start, an ashen Galimir needed a few moments to compose himself, for he had been shocked by the sight of Michael lying in an open casket, something that was not customary at a Jewish funeral.[30]

To June the grief was compounded by what she saw as the terribly inappropriate funeral arrangements.

> Jeanne got what she wanted — a big musical extravaganza. And Michael really didn't like Mozart. So what did they play? Mozart! Nobody talked about him as a person. They only talked about him as a musician. And that's all fine, but in the eulogies they talked as if he was a violin, rather than a person playing the violin. There was no sense of who he was or what he was about. It made me very angry. Especially the fact they were playing things he didn't even like.[31]

The manner in which Michael left the world epitomized, in many troubling ways, the way he had lived in it. A source of perpetual tension for him had been the challenge of reconciling the life of a soloist courting applause with an inner self that felt uncomfortable among people. Now in death, that most private, intimate, and somber of all occasions, he had once again been unable to escape the very thing his mother sought and that he had shied away from, the social spotlight. As the memorial ceremony had demonstrated, Jeanne may have been saturated with grief, but it had done little to lessen her iron will, and she was not done yet. From the chapel, the cortege made its way to Mount Hebron Cemetery, where Michael was buried in a grave alongside his brother Jay. Sybil Sklar recalled that even as the gravediggers were lowering Michael's coffin into the ground, Jeanne could not resist the impulse to supervise their efforts.[32]

For many of the mourners, the scene was too much to bear: the two Rabin boys, Michael in his freshly dug grave, Jay beneath his well-tended tombstone, united not only in death but in all the aborted hopes and joys that their great talents once had promised. Jeanne certainly had her detractors, but few could fail to be moved by the magnitude of her loss. Unlike in George's case, however, the sympathy that came her way was diluted by the effects of her abrasive personality and the misgivings of many over her role in Michael's misfortunes.

Jan Kubelik. Michael owned and played the Kubelik del Gesù for much of his professional life. *Photo courtesy of Anthony Feinstein*

Yura Osmolovsky, Galamian's assistant and Michael's first professional teacher, 1945. *Photo courtesy of Anthony Feinstein*

Fredell Lack, a Galamian student and Michael's friend and confidante, 1946. *Photo courtesy of Anthony Feinstein*

Ivan Galamian at Meadowmou in 1949. *Photo by Michael Rabin*

Artur Balsam in 1979; he wa Michael's accompanist on his first recordings. *Photo courtesy (Anthony Feinstei*

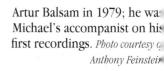

Michael's manager and publicist, Schuyler Chapin, and his wife Betty Steinway in 1953. *Photo by Michael Rabin*

Zino Francescatti in the Rabin home, 1953.
Photo by Michael Rabin

Michael Rabin and Donald Voorhees,
conductor of the Telephone Hour
Orchestra, 1955.

Michael and girlfriend Dorothy
Reichenberger in 1957. *Photo
courtesy of Art Rose*

Leon Pommers, one of Michael's accompanists, c. 1958. *Photo by Michael Rabin*

Michael and sister Bertine in New York City, c. 19[...]

Pianist Richard Syracuse accompanied Michael during his South African tour, 1966. *Photo by Michael Rabin*

Joseph Szigeti and Michael in Geneva, 1967.

CHAPTER 15

EPILOGUE: WITH TIME COMES CLARITY

The rumor mill had not waited for Michael's interment before activating. The obituaries, with their conflicting opinions as to the cause of death, fueled the speculation. The *New York Times* alone put out two different versions.[1] The *New York Post*,[2] *Variety* magazine,[3] and the *Washington Post*[4] stated categorically that he had died of an epileptic seizure, even though there was no history of epilepsy.* *Time* magazine, on the other hand, reported the cause of death as a fractured skull.[5] With theories swirling around, many of them unlikely, rumor took hold. Whisperings of drug abuse resurfaced, and from there it was a short hop to speculative suggestions of an overdose. Bruno Monsaingeon repeated it as fact in his documentary, *The Art of the Violin*.[6] And like the unfortunate stigmata of mental illness, the taint of death by suicide became hard to dislodge. Thirty years later, Sheldon Morgenstern, the conductor who had witnessed Michael's collapse in Greensboro, went on record stating Rabin had killed himself.[7]

The gossip added to the distress of Michael's family, who steadfastly denied he had willfully taken his life. Galamian, no less distraught, was also adamant that death had been accidental. "He did not die of drugs," he told the *New York Times*. "By that time he had stopped the drugs and was playing better than ever. He slipped on a rug and hit his head on a table."[8] This assessment was, however, only partly correct, and it took the pathologist Dr. Michael Baden, who performed Michael's autopsy, to clarify what had happened. At the time, Baden was an up-and-coming New York forensic

---

* Michael's convulsions in the early 1960s were the result of drug withdrawal and did not constitute epilepsy.

pathologist. In the years ahead, he would be called on to re-examine the deaths of President Kennedy and Martin Luther King and give evidence in the O. J. Simpson and Claus von Bülow murder trials, among others.[9] His stellar credentials therefore add weight to his conclusions.

Baden found evidence that Michael had fallen, fractured the back of his skull, and in the process hemorrhaged into his brain. "Rabin's fall was unprotected," confirmed Baden, "and he sustained [the type of injury] that one finds in drinkers who have fallen. A similar situation occurred in the death of Elvis Presley. There is a 'golden hour' during which, if help is at hand, attempts at resuscitation and treatment may change the outcome."[10] But in Michael's case, living alone, the golden hour passed without help, and he slipped slowly, inexorably, deeper into coma until he quietly stopped breathing.

If Baden's autopsy clearly revealed how Michael had died, the question remained why a healthy man in his mid-thirties possessing wonderfully fine coordination had not been able to break his fall. The answer, documented in the coroner's report, was sitting on a table in Michael's apartment — a bottle of barbiturates.* Moreover, more than one doctor had been prescribing the drug.[11] A certain Dr. Feldman had given Michael three grams on October 27, 1971, and a Dr. Stern had given him another three grams on January 18, 1972, the day before Michael died. Laboratory tests confirmed the presence of the barbiturates amobarbitol and secobarbitol,† at levels that were well short of proving fatal.

The coroner's report also mentioned the presence of a bottle of Plegine alongside the Tuinal. The diet tablet had been prescribed on September 14, 1971, by Dr. Walter Taub, Michael's neighbor, friend, and chamber music partner. It was unclear whether Taub knew of the barbiturates, but his prescription meant Michael was back on the potentially toxic stew of sedatives and stimulants that had been his undoing earlier. And there was another worrying detail. Michael's high blood pressure was being treated with Ser-Ap-Es,‡ a medication that potentially enhances the drowsiness induced by barbiturates. Furthermore, Ser-Ap-Es may be associated with a sudden fall in blood pressure on changing posture, which in turn triggers dizziness.

With these pieces of additional information, it becomes clearer what happened on that fatal Wednesday afternoon at 185 West End Avenue. There was no overdose. But the barbiturates Michael took made him drowsy. He lay

---

* Tuinal.

† The two drugs that comprise Tuinal.

‡ Ser-Ap-Es is a combination of reserpine, hydralazine, and hydrochlorthiazide.

down to rest. On rising quickly, perhaps to answer the telephone, his blood pressure probably dipped suddenly, leaving him feeling dizzy and wobbly on his feet. Hurrying unsteadily into the living room and groggy from the barbiturates, he slipped on the waxed floor. With coordination impaired by the sedatives, his head took the full weight of impact. What happened thereafter was documented by Baden in the clinically precise jargon of the forensic pathologist. "Cause of death: Fracture of skull. Contusions and lacerations of brain with intermeningeal hemorrhage."[12]

Michael did not commit suicide. Baden's detailed forensic examination made that clear. It was self-deception, miscalculation, and medical malfeasance that contributed to his accidental death. To be sure, the Excedrin was where he said it had been all along, on the shelf in the medicine cabinet. But mentioning the painkiller in his *New York Times* interview was simply a smokescreen.[13] In failing to acknowledge his ongoing misuse of sedative medication, Michael not only deceived Bertine, Galamian, June, Lewis, his parents, and his many admirers, he ultimately deceived himself. The unforeseen consequence was one of the great tragedies in the history of the violin.

Michael's death left those close to him bereft. George grieved quietly, listening to his son's recordings and spending time with Galamian.[14] For Jeanne, the loss of Michael rekindled the grief associated with Jay, and she never really recovered from this double blow. She had poured her stupendous energy into Michael's career and lived vicariously through him, savoring the fame and glory her limited talent as a pianist denied her. Michael's death was thus more than the passing of a child, it represented the loss of an investment and signaled the end of a way of life that had allowed her access to extraordinary people and legendary places. A little over a week after the funeral, she poured out all her heartache and bitterness in a letter to Alf and his family.

> Thank you for your telegram and letter. What can I tell you? We are shattered beyond words and completely crushed by this unbelievable burden of grief and sorrow. What a tragedy for us to live with — it's unbelievable!
>
> What avail are the messages, telegrams and flowers from the greatest names in music now? Why didn't they contact him when he was alive and make him feel happy, tell him how much they admired him and eased his frustrations about the recordings and all other business matters with which he should never have been concerned or bothered. Now they send these messages to us and tell us what a great loss it is to the world of music, and if possible break our hearts more.

...life seems hardly worthwhile.

He was so attentive to us and so concerned for our well being — it was most unusual, he was all kindness and tenderness for us…. What a great pity he didn't have a chance to make some records which he was anxious to do, which would represent his present maturity and activity!…

At this moment it is very difficult to think clearly let alone do anything. We still cannot grasp the facts [and] it seems incredible that this horrible nightmare really happened.15

Four years after Michael's death, Jeanne died. She had spent the last year of her life in a rehabilitation hospital, a stroke having deprived her of speech. George remarried, to a quiet-spoken woman who said very little. He died in 1993 at ninety-four years of age. It has therefore been left to Bertine, as the sole surviving family member of that generation, to reflect on the complex relationship that bound together her mother and brother.

I had these very angry thoughts when I was young, where I felt my mother used Michael. I'd think she was a frustrated pianist and couldn't make a career of her own, and so I was angry about that and I was angry about a lot of things. Looking back, I think she really loved Michael and thought that she was doing the right thing by making this wonderful career for him. If she could mold him and sculpt him into this violinist, this fabulous violinist which he had all the talent for, then she was doing this for him and this was her gift to him. She wasn't aware of what kind of harm it could be doing at the same time.16

In the months following Michael's death, an article he had written appeared posthumously in *Current Musicology*, 17* concerts were dedicated to his memory, songs were sung in remembrance, a scholarship was offered in his name at the University of Arizona, and a string trio, composed in his memory by Herbert Feldman, was performed at the Carnegie Recital Hall. But if grief held the mourners captive, frozen in time and wedded to past recollections, the business of making music hardly skipped a beat. The year Michael died, Itzhak Perlman's recording of the Paganini caprices, with a

---

* The article, entitled "A Performer's Perspective" (*Current Musicology* no. 14 [1972]: 155–158), reflected Michael's views on the relationship between the performer on the one hand and musicologists, critics, musical "purists," and the government on the other. The article was accompanied by an eloquent obituary from Léonie Rosenstiel, special project editor of the journal and a friend of Michael's.

dedication to Michael, was released on an Angel label.* It was a new land-mark in the annals of great violin playing, a symbolic passing of the bow as it were, for Michael had forged his reputation with Angel and this very reper-toire. Toward the end of 1973, another Galamian pupil, Kyung-Wha Chung, took possession of the ex-Kubelik, ex-Rabin del Gesù.[18] Piecemeal, Michael's modest estate was dispersed.[19]

Given the brevity of Michael's life and the relative paucity of recordings he made, many of which had been deleted by the time he died, there was a risk his legacy would soon be forgotten. Limited mention was made of him in the collected biographies of master violinists. His name appeared from time to time in the *Strad* magazine, and on the fiftieth anniversary of his birth, Henry Roth provided a synopsis of his life and reviewed his recorded output.[20] All agreed he had possessed a special ability — he was a phenom-enal violinist and a fine artist — but his premature passing, the absence of a Beethoven or Brahms concerto in his discography, and some residual doubts about the depth of his musical vision meant the final accolade of great musi-cian was withheld.

As the years passed, his presence was fading. Michael's name did not appear in the 1980 edition of the *Grove Dictionary of Music*, potentially sig-naling his final decline into obscurity.[21] But that did not happen. When the next edition of Grove's appeared two decades later, a few years after the reissue of his complete recordings by EMI Electrola GmbH, the company's German subsidiary, his name had resurfaced.[22]

In a life stripped bare, nearly all is revealed. Secrets are outed, hidden truths exposed, and where confusion and uncertainty once ruled, hindsight now offers some clarity. The great triumphs, longed-for successes, and prodi-gious work ethic are laid out, stretching over three decades, testimony to an extraordinary talent. Alongside can be found all the mistakes, errors, wrong turns, lapses, misguided love, and overweening parental ambition that pro-duced such despair. Michael Rabin faced two great challenges during his short life. The first, accomplished with rare distinction, was to master the violin. The second was to navigate out of the choppy waters he had been steered into unwittingly as a child. In this he never quite succeeded. If this imbues his life with a tragic quality, there is something heroic in it too. For he never ceased battling to find himself and reach a greater personal happiness, even as he kept his rare, sometimes faltering gifts in the glare of public scrutiny.

---

* The complete dedication read: "I would like to dedicate this album to the memory of my dear friend and colleague, Michael Rabin. In preparing for the recording, his influence was a constant source of inspiration to me."

Thirty years after Michael's death, the disconcerting exercise of second-guessing history takes on less bite. Personal memory shifts, fades, and is ultimately extinguished as a generation passes. What remains is a sound, unique and immutable, a reaffirmation of beauty and wonder transcending human frailty.

ACKNOWLEDGMENTS

I WAS SIX YEARS OLD when I first became aware of a violinist named Michael Rabin. In an effort to foster my enthusiasm for a newly acquired half-size violin, my father began purchasing long-playing records. Heifetz, Milstein, Oistrakh, and Stern were names that entered my lexicon early, but none impressed me quite like Michael's. I wish I could state that it was a precocious musical insight that allowed me to discern at such a tender age some unique quality in Michael Rabin's artistry. But the reason for my attachment was more mundane. What to my child's eye differentiated Michael from a phalanx of other virtuosos was his obvious youth. To a boy struggling to learn the violin, nothing was quite so impressive as another boy who had done just that and, moreover, done it so successfully that his young face adorned the cardboard record sleeves stacked neatly inside our family's hi-fi cabinet. It was the solidarity of youth that first bound me to the phenomenon that was Michael Rabin.

Long-playing records were central to my childhood in South Africa. They were my one link to the great violinists who had, by now, stopped visiting the land of apartheid. And as I gradually and painfully fell in love with my violin, it was my modest record collection that helped cement my attachment. Few if any recordings gave me as much pleasure as Michael's coupling of the Paganini and Glazunov concertos. That luscious sound, the startling technical control, the sheer exuberance of his playing — here was a boyhood hero to equal my favorite soccer players.

I was fifteen years old when Michael died. I was informed by the obituarists that his star had long since waned. Not to me it hadn't. Not to a teenager a world away at the southern tip of Africa in thrall to a boyish image and a sound forever young.

MANY PEOPLE GAVE GENEROUSLY of their time and expertise in helping me with this book. It is no exaggeration to say that the book as I initially conceived it could not have been written without the help of Bertine Lafayette, Michael Rabin's sister. Not only did she allow me unfettered access to her collection of letters, concert reviews, and photographs, but she made her home available to me whenever circumstance demanded, graciously giving up her dining room as I scattered documents, albums, and memorabilia in my search for the facts that made up her brother's busy life. On each visit I was given a delicious lunch, abundant coffee, and a warm, enthusiastic welcome that helped make my many trips to New York eagerly anticipated.

The unusual talent of a wunderkind influences many lives, and families often make extraordinary sacrifices to accommodate the genius in their midst. As I got to know Michael Rabin better through long conversations with his sister, I became aware of how their lives were inextricably linked, the closeness of their bond during childhood ensuring that the trajectory of Michael's career carried her, too, along into areas both wonderful and difficult. Opening up her heart and private papers to the biographer has represented a continuation of this journey for the most loving and devoted of sisters.

I also wish to acknowledge Bertine's husband, Ivan Lafayette, whose dining room table I laid siege to on my visits. On many occasions Ivan found me happily ensconced in his home when he returned from a day at the office, and I was always made to feel welcome.

My thanks also go to Lewis Kaplan, Michael's great friend, whose wisdom and enthusiasm were indispensable to me. There were many times when, finding myself at an impasse, I reached out to Lewis for direction and clarification. Without fail, his patience, courtesy, unrivaled knowledge of his friend's career, and deep understanding of "violin" life in America over the past four decades were invaluable to me.

It is also impossible to understand the last few years of Michael's Rabin's life without appreciating the pivotal place occupied by June LeBell, his final, deepest, and most enduring love. I am grateful to June for illuminating the happy years Michael shared with her and for speaking with such candor about his death.

Michael's cousin Douglas Seidman was tireless in answering questions and providing me with the early histories of the Seidman and Rabinowitz families. Norman Robbins and Judy Brodsky added their recollections of their Rabinowitz relatives, as did Sybil and Pamela Sklar for the Seidman family.

Many colleagues, friends, acquaintances, and "Rabin aficionados" shared their thoughts, memories, and memorabilia with me and are likewise due my thanks: Adrienne Lewis (nee Rosenbaum), Mitchell Andrews, Josef Seiger, Arnold Steinhardt, the late Erick Friedman, Schuyler Chapin, Donald Nold, Marsha Silver, Maurice Edwards, Suzanne Landry, Sally Thomas, Judith Galamian, Aldo Parisot, Aaron Rosand, Tony Skey, Charles Beare, Richard Donovan, Robert Bein, Gael Francais, Kyung-Wha Chung, Rose Branower, David Goldbloom, Susanna Salgado, Bernard Greenhouse, Alf and David Levy, Robin Brightman, David Schoenbaum, Michael Waiblinger, Elizabeth Matesky, Sylvia Mann, Robin Bushman, Jack Heller, Leonard Stehn, Walter Mony, Suzanne Bilyeu, Mark Goldenberg, Chaim Taub, Léonie Rosenstiel, Conny Kiradjieff, Jochen Brusch, Adria Kaplan, Ling Silberger, Tom Strasser, Harry Wagschal, Joseph Roche, Milton Katims, Dennis Rooney, Charles Libove, Eric Wen, Jaime Laredo, Carl and Katie Dahlgren, Art Rose,

Dorothy Reichenberger, Dr. Elaine Weldon Ph.D., Victoria von Arx, Richard Syracuse, Michael Kellman, Jon Samuels, Jacob Harnoy, Paul Rosenthal, Fredell Lack, John Maltese, and the late Peter Schenkman.

Michael Baden, M.D., who undertook Michael's postmortem examination, was helpful in explaining his findings to me, thereby crucially and finally debunking the notion that Michael had committed suicide.

I also would like to acknowledge the assistance of a past editor of the *Strad* magazine, Naomi Sadler, and her predecessor, Joanna Pieters; the assistant music librarian at the Irving S. Gilmore Music Library at Yale University, Suzanne Lovejoy; and a number of archivists: Jeni Dahmus (the Juilliard School), Richard Wandel (New York Philharmonic), Avivit Menahem (Israel Philharmonic Orchestra), Kathleen Sabogal (Carnegie Hall), and Steve Lacoste (Los Angeles Philharmonic).

The photographs of Michael in the Columbia 30th Street Studios, New York City, are part of the Frederick and Rose Plaut Archives, housed in the Irving S. Gilmore Music Library at Yale University. Jeanne Rabin's letter to Vladimir Horowitz may be found in the papers of Vladimir Horowitz and Wanda Toscanini Horowitz, also at the Irving S. Gilmore Music Library at Yale University. I am grateful to Yale University for permission to quote from the letter and reproduce the photographs. The photographs of Michael on the film set of *Rhapsody* in Hollywood appear courtesy of the Academy of Motion Picture Arts and Sciences. Publicity photographs that coincided with Michael's recording contract with EMI and its subsidiary Capitol Records (1954–1960) are produced by kind permission of EMI Records Limited. The excerpt from a letter by Leonard Bernstein to George Rabin has been reprinted by permission of the Leonard Bernstein Office, Inc.

I would like to thank those who provided access to letters that appear in the text: Bertine Lafayette for letters written to her by Michael, Jeanne, and George Rabin; Lewis Kaplan for letters written to him by Michael Rabin; Alf Levy for letters written to him by Michael and Jeanne Rabin; Michael Waiblinger for letters written by Michael Rabin to Zino Francescatti; and Adrienne Rosenbaum for letters written to her by Michael Rabin.

In compiling Michael Rabin's discography I am indebted to Bob Trenholm for sharing his encyclopedic knowledge of classical music recordings with generosity, patience, and an infectious enthusiasm.

Dawn Nicolson, one of my research assistants at Sunnybook Health Sciences Centre in Toronto, was at times asked to step away from her job of analyzing brain MRI images of patients with multiple sclerosis and traumatic brain injury to assist me with this biography. Whether she was traveling to the Library of Congress in Washington or the Reference Library in Toronto, the assistance she provided was invaluable, filled as it always was with good cheer. The assistance of Colleen Barry, my secretary at the Sunnybrook campus, is likewise gratefully acknowledged.

To John Cerullo, Carol Flannery, Gail Siragusa, Jessica Burr, and Clare Cerullo at Amadeus Press, my thanks for bringing this work to fruition so elegantly. To Joanna Dalin, my copy editor, thank you for patiently sorting out the devil in the details. Jenna Young skillfully chose and arranged the photographs.

To those I have failed to mention, my apologies for any oversights and my appreciation for the help. Every effort has been made to trace copyright for photographic material used. Any omissions in this regard are entirely inadvertent, and apologies are likewise offered.

This book was written on weekends and evenings, after my medical office had closed and my research commitments were taken care of. This meant I often had to purloin time that would otherwise have been spent with my wife, Kally, and children, Pippa, Saul, and Clarrie. I am the most fortunate of men in having a family that not only tolerates this type of behavior, but supports it with an unfailing patience and affection.

Toronto, April 2010

NOTES

CHAPTER 1

1. Saul Bellow, *It All Adds Up: From the Dim Past to the Uncertain Future; A Nonfiction Collection* (New York: Viking, 1994), 234–235.
2. *New York Times,* November 23, 1977.
3. George Gershwin and Arthur Francis, "Mischa, Jascha, Toscha, Sascha" (Warner Bros. Music, 1932).
4. Douglas Seidman, interview with George Rabin, April 5, 1990.
5. Judy Brodsky, interview with author, New York City, January 15, 2003.
6. Douglas Seidman, interview with George Rabin.
7. Judy Brodsky, interview with author.
8. Douglas Seidman, interview with George Rabin.
9. Boris Schwartz, *Great Masters of the Violin* (New York: Simon and Schuster, 1983), 501–503.
10. Margaret Campbell, *The Great Violinists* (London: Granada, 1980), 296–297.
11. Philip J. Haythornthwaite, *The World War One Sourcebook* (London: Brockhampton Press, 1992), 307.
12. A. J. P. Taylor, *The First World War: An Illustrated History* (London: Hamish Hamilton, 1963), 129.
13. Laurence Ivan Seidman, interview with George Rabin, New York City, September 29, 1989.
14. Martin Gilbert, *First World War* (Santa Rosa, CA: Stoddart, 1994), 477–479.
15. Douglas Seidman, interview with George Rabin.
16. Douglas Seidman, correspondence with author, February 8, 2004.
17. Laurence Ivan Seidman, interview with George Rabin.
18. ibid.
19. Laurence Ivan Seidman, interview with Bea Seidman, February 12, 1983.
20. Norman Robbins, interview with author, New York City, September 24, 2003.
21. United States Government Census, 1930.
22. Laurence Ivan Seidman, interview with Bea Seidman.
23. Department of Health of the City of New York, standard certificate of death, 1932.
24. Bertine Lafayette (nee Rabin), interview with author, New York City, December 20, 2000.

CHAPTER 2

1. Bertine Lafayette (nee Rabin), interview with author, New York City, December 20, 2000.
2. Norman Robbins, interview with author, New York City, September 24, 2003.
3. Bertine Lafayette, interview with author.
4. ibid.
5. *New York Times*, November 25, 1951.
6. Bertine Lafayette, interview with author.
7. Laurence Ivan Seidman, interview with Bea Seidman, February 12, 1983.
8. Sybil Sklar, interview with author, Larchmount, New York, June 18, 2003.
9. Pamela Sklar, interview with author, Larchmount, New York, June 18, 2003.
10. ibid.
11. Bertine Lafayette, interview with author.
12. Fredell Lack, interview with author, November 2003.
13. Paul Rosenthal, interview with author, October 2003.

14. Elizabeth Green, *Miraculous Teacher: Ivan Galamian and the Meadowmount Experience* (self-published, 1993), 13–61.
15. ibid.
16. Judith Galamian, interview with author, New York City, August 2001.
17. Bertine Lafayette, interview with author.
18. Professional Children's School report cards, 1944–1946.
19. Green, *Miraculous Teacher,* 13–61.
20. Bertine Lafayette, interview with author.
21. ibid.
22. ibid.
23. Erik Erikson, "Development as a Lifelong Process" in R. L. Atkinson, R. C. Atkinson, and E. R. Hilgard, eds., *Introduction to Psychology,* 8th ed. (New York: Harcourt, Brace Jovanovich, 1983), 96–99.
24. Michael Kellman, telephone interview with author, June 29, 2010.
25. Bertine Lafayette, interview with author.
26. ibid.

CHAPTER 3

1. Chaim Taub, telephone interview with author, January 8, 2004.
2. Lewis Kaplan, telephone interview with author, January 8, 2004.
3. Elizabeth Green, *Miraculous Teacher: Ivan Galamian and the Meadowmount Experience* (self-published, 1993), 13–61.
4. Flyer for Michael Rabin's debut recital at Temple Beth-El, Providence, RI, on April 9, 1947 (possession of Bertine Lafayette).
5. George Rabin, telegraph to Michael Rabin (Western Union Telegraph Company), April 22, 1947.
6. *Providence Review,* April 24, 1947.
7. *The New Oxford English Dictionary* (Oxford: Clarendon Press, 1993).
8. *Montreal Gazette,* October 31, 1947.
9. Bertine Lafayette (nee Rabin), interview with author, New York City, December 20, 2000.
10. *Providence Sunday Journal,* November 14, 1947.
11. *Montreal Standard,* January 15, 1948.
12. Humphrey Burton, *Yehudi Menuhin* (Boston: Northeastern University Press, 2000), 64–69.
13. Samuel Applebaum and Henry Roth, *The Way They Play* book 5 (Neptune, NJ: Paganiniana Pub. Inc., 1978), 229.
14. Rhode Island Symphony Orchestra program, December 1, 1948 (possession of Bertine Lafayette).
15. *Pawtucket Times,* December 4, 1948.
16. *Woonsocket Call,* December 6, 1948.
17. Flyer for Michael Rabin's Rhode Island series of concerto performances, December 1948 (possession of Bertine Lafayette).
18. Margaret Campbell, *The Great Violinists,* London: Granada Publishing, 1980), 224.
19. Charles Libove, telephone interview with author, May 22, 2000.
20. Michael Rabin's bar mitzvah invitation, 1949 (possession of Bertine Lafayette).
21. *Violin and Violinists,* August—September 1949, 248.
22. *National Federation of Music Clubs Junior Magazine* 1, October 9, 1949.
23. ibid.
24. Green, *Miraculous Teacher,* 13–61.
25. Fredell Lack, telephone interview with author, November 19, 2003.

CHAPTER 4

1. Bertine Lafayette, interview with author, New York City, October 23, 2002.
2. *Great Oaks from Little Acorns: A concert for young people* (Carnegie Hall program), February 11, 1950 (possession of Bertine Lafayette).
3. *New York Herald Tribune,* February 12, 1950.
4. *New York Times,* February 12, 1950.
5. *Alerta, Havana,* April 6, 1950.
6. *New York Times,* April 10, 1950.
7. *Havana Post,* April 10, 1950.
8. *Havana Post,* April 9, 1950.
9. June LeBell, interview with author, New York, June 1, 2000.
10. Michael Rabin, postcard to Bertine Rabin from Havana, Cuba, April 8, 1950.
11. N.W. Ayer Radio News, April 9, 1950.
12. *Journal-American,* April 18, 1950.
13. Publicity information for Michael Rabin, Columbia Artists Management (Mitropoulos's quote dated April 28, 1950, and Szell's quote dated May 25, 1950).
14. ibid.
15. N.W Ayer Radio News, July 5, 1950.
16. Hy Gardner Newsreel (American Press Clippings Inc.), May 21, 1950.
17. Josef Seiger, telephone interview with author, January 7, 2004.
18. Michael Rabin, letter to Zino Francescatti, June 5, 1950.
19. Michael Rabin, letter to Zino Francescatti, July 28, 1950.
20. N.W. Ayer Radio News, May 24, 1950.
21. *Newsweek,* August 21, 1950.
22. *New York World Telegram and Sun,* October 30, 1950.
23. ibid.
24. Zino Francescatti, letter to Michael Rabin, August 8, 1950.
25. Michael Rabin, letter to Zino Francescatti, August 11, 1950.
26. *New York Times,* November 24, 1950.
27. *New York Herald Tribune,* November 25, 1950.
28. J. Abresch (NY) photographer, photograph of Michael Rabin dedicated by Rabin to Ivan Galamian, November 24, 1950 (copy in possession of author).

CHAPTER 5

1. Bertine Lafayette, interview with author, New York City, October 23, 2002.
2. Erick Friedman, telephone interview with author, June 18, 2000.
3. Jack Heller, telephone interview with author, November 12, 2003.
4. Bertine Lafayette, interview with author.
5. ibid.
6. ibid.
7. Judy Brodsky, interview with author, New York City, January 15, 2003.
8. Lewis Kaplan, interview with author, New York City, May 4, 2000.
9. Claude Kenneson, *Musical Prodigies: Perilous Journeys, Remarkable Lives* (Portland, Oregon: Amadeus Press, 1998), 42.
10. Michael Rabin, letter to Zino Francescatti, February 17, 1951.
11. The Bohemians club, program for dinner in honor of Dimitri Mitropoulos, Waldorf Astoria hotel, Sunday February 25, 1951 (possession of Bertine Lafayette).
12. *Cleveland News,* April 5, 1951.
13. Michael Rabin, letter to Zino Francescatti, March 26, 1951.
14. *Cleveland News,* April 6, 1951.

15. *Cleveland Press,* April 6, 1951.
16. Zino Francescatti, letter to Michael Rabin, March 8, 1951.
17. Michael Rabin, letter to Zino Francescatti, March 26, 1951.
18. Michael Rabin, letter to Zino Francescatti, May 2, 1951.
19. ibid.
20. Kenneson, *Musical Prodigies,* 44.
21. *New York Post,* May 15, 1951.
22. Michael Rabin, letter to Zino Francescatti, June 8, 1951.
23. *New York Daily Mirror,* May 21, 1951.
24. Michael Rabin, letter to Zino Francescatti, May 2, 1951
25. Michael Rabin, letter to Zino Francescatti, June 8, 1951
26. *Chicago Daily Tribune,* July 6 1951.
27. *Philadelphia Evening Bulletin,* October 17, 1951.
28. N.W Ayer Radio News, November 29, 1951.
29. *St. Louis Globe-Democrat,* November 9, 1951.
30. *New York Times,* November 25, 1951.
31. ibid.
32. *New York Times,* November 30, 1951.
33. Josef Seiger, telephone interview with author, January 7, 2004.
34. Schuyler Chapin, interview with author, New York City, January 8, 2002.

CHAPTER 6

1. Lewis Kaplan, interview with author, New York City, May 4, 2000.
2. ibid.
3. Zino Francescatti, letter to Michael Rabin, March 15, 1952.
4. Lewis Kaplan, interview with author.
5. *Toronto Telegram,* December 10, 1951.
6. *New York Times,* April 20, 1952.
7. Bertine Lafayette, unpublished letter to the *New York Times,* April 22 1952.
8. Richard Donovon, correspondence with author, October 7, 2003.
9. Josef Seiger, telephone interview with author, January 7, 2004.
10. Humphrey Burton, *Yehudi Menuhin* (Boston: Northeastern University Press, 2000), 160–161.
11. Michael Rabin, letter to Bertine Rabin, June 20, 1952.
12. *Sydney Sunday Telegraph,* June 29, 1952.
13. *Sydney Morning Herald,* June 26 1952.
14. *Adelaide Mail,* June 28, 1952.
15. *Sydney Bulletin,* July 2, 1952.
16. *Australian Broadcasting Weekly,* July 5, 1952.
17. *Australian Broadcasting Weekly,* July 19, 1952.
18. *Tempo,* July 1952.
19. *Canon* 6, No. 1 (August 1952): 30.
20. *Canon* 6, No. 1 (August 1952): 28.
21. *Sydney Herald,* August 21, 1952.
22. Ambrose Bierce, *The Devil's Dictionary* (New York: Dell Publishing, 1991), 27–28.
23. *Adelaide Advertiser,* July 15, 1952.
24. *Radio Call,* July 16, 1952.
25. *Argus,* July 15, 1952.
26. *Sydney Sun,* July 15, 1952.
27. *Australian Musical News,* September 1952.
28. *Sydney Sunday Sun,* July 20,1952.
29. *Melbourne Herald,* July 24, 1952.

30.   *Australian Musical News,* August 1952.
31.   *Sydney Sun,* July 16, 1952.
32.   Bertine Lafayette, interview with author.
33.   *Sydney Sunday Sun,* July 6, 1952.
34.   *Woman,* August 4, 1952.
35.   *Etude,* August 1952, 9–11.
36.   *Christian Science Monitor,* July 19, 1952.
37.   Michael Rabin, letter to Bertine Rabin, August 29, 1952.
38.   *Melbourne Herald,* August 4, 1952.
39.   *Adelaide Sunday Mail,* September 14, 1952.
40.   Michael Rabin, letter to Bertine Rabin, August 29, 1952.
41.   Michael Rabin, letter to Bertine Rabin, September 22, 1952.
42.   Michael Rabin, letter to Bertine Rabin, October 24, 1952.

Chapter 7

1.   Michael Rabin, postcard to Bertine Rabin, February 4, 1953.
2.   Michael Rabin, postcard to Bertine Rabin, February 9, 1953.
3.   *Canon* 6, No 1 (August 1952): 28.
4.   *Los Angeles Times,* February 20, 1953.
5.   *New York Tribune,* March 23, 1953.
6.   *New York Times,* March 23, 1953.
7.   *Chicago Tribune,* April 1, 1953.
8.   *Film Bulletin,* February 22, 1954.
9.   Michael Rabin, letter to Bertine Rabin, April 27, 1953.
10.   *New York Post,* March 12, 1954.
11.   *Newsweek,* March 8, 1954.
12.   Elizabeth Taylor, telegram to Michael Rabin, May 2, 1954.
13.   Michael Rabin, letter to Bertine Rabin, October 16, 1953.
14.   David Schoenbaum, personal communication with author, October 27, 2003.
15.   Jack Heller, telephone interview with author, October 15, 2003.
16.   Michael Rabin, letter to Bertine Rabin, October 19, 1953.
17.   Michael Rabin, letter to Bertine Rabin, October 22, 1953.
18.   Michael Rabin, letter to Bertine Rabin, October 24, 1953.
19.   Jeanne Rabin, letter to Bertine Rabin, October 25, 1953.
20.   Michael Rabin, letter to Bertine Rabin, November 23, 1953.
21.   Michael Rabin, letter to Bertine Rabin, November 26, 1953.
22.   Jeanne Rabin, letter to Bertine Rabin, November 27, 1953.
23.   Michael Rabin, letter to Bertine Rabin, November 26, 1953.
24.   Michael Rabin, letter to Bertine Rabin, November 30, 1953.
25.   Michael Rabin, letter to Bertine Rabin, November 22, 1953.
26.   Michael Rabin, letter to Bertine Rabin, December 7, 1953.
27.   ibid.
28.   Michael Rabin, letter to Bertine Rabin, January 17, 1954.
29.   ibid.
30.   Ronze-Neveu M. J., *Ginette Neveu: La fulgurante carriere d'une grande artiste* (Paris: Pierre Horay, 1952), 128.
31.   Boris Schwarz, *Great Master of the Violin,* (New York: Simon and Schuster, 1983), 356.
32.   *Chicago Tribune.* October 30, 1953.
33.   Humphrey Burton, *Yehudi Menuhin* (Boston: Northeastern University Press, 2000), 342.
34.   Michael Rabin, letter to Bertine Rabin, January 23, 1954.
35.   ibid.
36.   *Seattle Daily Times,* January 26, 1954.

37. Michael Rabin, letter to Bertine Rabin, February 3, 1954.
38. Michael Rabin, letter to Bertine Rabin, February 15, 1954.
39. Michael Rabin. Letter to Bertine Rabin. February 23, 1954.
40. ibid.
41. Bertine Lafayette, interview with author, New York City, December 20, 2000.
42. ibid.
43. Jack Heller, telephone interview with author.
44. *New York World-Telegram,* April 30, 1954.
45. *New York Times,* April 30, 1954.

CHAPTER 8

1. George Rabin, letter to Bertine Rabin, July 5, 1954.
2. Anthony Feinstein, "Psychosurgery and the Child Prodigy: The Mental Illness of Violin Virtuoso Josef Hassid," *History of Psychiatry* viii (1997): 55–60.
3. *Musical Times,* October, 1953.
4. *London Times,* September 25, 1954.
5. *London Times,* September 30, 1954.
6. *London Times,* October 5, 1954.
7. Jeanne Rabin, postcard to Bertine Rabin, October 3, 1954.
8. Michael Rabin, letter to Bertine Rabin, October 15, 1954.
9. ibid.
10. Jeanne Rabin, letter to Bertine Rabin, October 8, 1954.
11. Jeanne Rabin, letter to Bertine Rabin, October 22, 1954.
12. Michael Rabin. Letter to Bertine Rabin. November 24, 1954
13. *Corriere della Sera,* November 9, 1954.
14. *New York Times,* December 4, 1955.
15. Jeanne Rabin, postcard to Bertine Rabin, November 7, 1954.
16. Columbia Artists Management, letter to Jeanne Rabin dated April 19, 1955, containing English translations of reviews from eight Rome newspapers and journals, all dated November 18, 1954; the reviews are from *Momento, Guistizza, Unita, Il Popolo, Pase, Globo, Messaggero,* and *Il Tempo.*
17. Michael Rabin, letter to Bertine Rabin, November 24, 1954.
18. Michael Rabin, letter to Bertine Rabin, December 7, 1954.
19. Jeanne Rabin, letter to Bertine Rabin, December 11, 1954.
20. Michael Rabin, letter to Bertine Rabin, December 7, 1954.
21. *London Times,* December 13, 1954.
22. *Violin and Violinists,* March–April 1955.
23. Michael Rabin, letter to Bertine Rabin, December 20, 1954.
24. The Columbia Gramophone Company Ltd., memorandum, February 8, 1955 (EMI archival material).
25. Michael Rabin, letter to Bertine Rabin, December 20, 1954.
26. Jeanne Rabin, letter to Bertine Rabin, December 22, 1954.
27. Michael Rabin, letter to Bertine Rabin, December 20, 1954.
28. Jeanne Rabin, letter to Bertine Rabin, December 22, 1954.
29. John Barbirolli, letter to George Rabin, January 7, 1955.

CHAPTER 9

1. Schuyler Chapin, interview with author, New York City, January 8, 2002.
2. *Wichita Eagle,* February 3, 1955.
3. Michael Rabin, letter to Bertine Rabin, March 2, 1955.
4. Schuyler Chapin, interview with author.

5. Michael Rabin, letter to Bertine Rabin, March 12, 1955.
6. Claude Kenneson, *Musical Prodigies: Perilous Journeys, Remarkable Lives* (Portland, Oregon: Amadeus Press, 1998), 168–172.
7. *Toronto Globe and Mail*, October 14, 2003.
8. Kenneson, *Musical Prodigies*, 226–229.
9. *Miami Daily News,* February 12, 1955.
10. The Albert Leonard Jr. High School, interview with Michael Rabin, New Rochelle, New York, April 29, 1955.
11. *New York Times,* June 23, 1955.
12. Lewis Kaplan, interview with author, New York City, May 4, 2000.
13. Ivan Galamian, letter to Michael Rabin, October 22, 1955.
14. Peter Schenkman, interview with author, Toronto, February 8, 2000.
15. *Gramophone,* October 1955.
16. *New York Times,* December 4, 1955.
17. *New York Times,* December 30, 1955.
18. Michael Rabin, letter to Bertine Rabin, November 10, 1955.
19. Adrienne Lewis (nee Rosenbaum), interview with author, New Haven, Connecticut, September 10, 2003.
20. Michael Rabin, letter to Adrienne Rosenbaum, January 3, 1956.
21. Michael Rabin, letter to Adrienne Rosenbaum, January 6, 1956.
22. Michael Rabin, letter to Adrienne Rosenbaum, January 20, 1956.
23. Adrienne Lewis, interview with author.
24. *New York Times,* February 3, 1956.
25. *New York Times,* June 23, 1955.
26. Michael Rabin, letter to Adrienne Rosenbaum, March 5, 1956.
27. *Time,* December 10, 1951.
28. *New Orleans Times Picayune*, February 22, 1956.
29. Adrienne Lewis, letter to author, October 21, 2003.
30. *Chicago American,* April 6, 1956.
31. *Chicago Sun Times,* April 6, 1956.
32. Sally Thomas, interview with author, New York City, March 14, 2002.
33. Michael Rabin, letter to Adrienne Rosenbaum, April 17, 1956.
34. Adrienne Lewis, interview with author.
35. A series of favorable nationwide reviews appeared in *Providence Journal,* May 1956; *New Jersey Music and Arts Journal,* June 1956; *San Francisco News,* May 1956; *Boston Post,* May 20 1956; *Boston Daily Globe,* May 1956; *High Fidelity,* June 1956; *Dayton Daily News,* May 30 1956.
36. Dario Soria, letter to Messrs. Olof, Bicknell and Legge, November 6, 1956 (EMI archival material).
37. Alfred Levy, interview with author, London, July 12, 2000.
38. *New York Times,* December 4, 1955.
39. Alfred Levy, interview with author.
40. *Artist Life* (newsletter), Angel Records, 1956.
41. *Philadelphia Daily News,* July 17, 1956.
42. Lewis Kaplan, interview with author.
43. Adrienne Lewis, interview with author.
44. ibid.

CHAPTER 10

1. Adrienne Lewis (nee Rosenbaum), interview with author, New Haven, Connecticut, September 10, 2003.
2. *Washington Post,* December 9, 1956.

3. *New York Times,* December 23, 1956.
4. Michael Rabin, letter to Adrienne Rosenbaum, January 2, 1957.
5. Alfred Levy, interview with author, London, July 12, 2000.
6. Michael Rabin, letter to Adrienne Rosenbaum, January 13, 1957.
7. Michael Rabin, letter to Adrienne Rosenbaum, January 15, 1957.
8. Michael Rabin, letter to Adrienne Rosenbaum, January 26, 1957.
9. Michael Rabin, letter to Dorothy Reichenberger, February 8, 1957.
10. Alexis Johnson, letter to Michael Rabin, April 26, 1957.
11. Michael Rabin, letter to Adrienne Rosenbaum, January 13, 1957.
12. Michael Rabin, letter to Adrienne Rosenbaum, January 15, 1957.
13. Michael Rabin, letter to Adrienne Rosenbaum, February 5, 1957.
14. *Indianapolis Times,* March 10, 1957.
15. Bertine Lafayette, interview with author, New York City, October 23, 2002.
16. *Musical America,* February–March 1957.
17. Michael Rabin, letter to Adrienne Rosenbaum, April 16, 1957.
18. Michael Rabin, letter to Adrienne Rosenbaum, undated.
19. Michael Rabin, letter to Adrienne Rosenbaum, April 23, 1957.
20. *Toronto Daily Star,* May 11, 1957.
21. Lewis Kaplan, interview with author, New York City, May 4, 2000.
22. *Jerusalem Post,* June 29, 1957.
23. Sylvia Mann, letter to Michael Rabin, January 24, 1957.
24. *Jerusalem Post,* June 12, 1957.
25. Isaac Stern, *My First 79 Years,* (New York: Knopf, 1999).
26. Israel Philharmonic Orchestra, correspondence to and from Michael Rabin (a series of letters held in the orchestra's archives).
27. Josef Seiger, telephone interview with author, January 7, 2004.
28. *New York Times,* October 20, 1957.
29. *Saturday Review,* September 28, 1957.
30. *New York Times,* December 1, 1957.
31. J. D. Bicknell, letter to Leo Kepler, February 6, 1958.
32. Leo Kepler, letter to J. D. Bicknell, February 27, 1958.
33. Walter Legge, letter to F. M. Scott (Album Repertoire Director, Capitol Records Inc.), April 17, 1958.
34. Gwen Mathias, EMI interdepartmental memorandum, June 10, 1958.
35. *New York Times,* January 18, 1958.
36. *Sarasota Herald Tribune,* January 20, 1958.
37. Michael Rabin, letter to Lewis Kaplan, January 23, 1958.
38. Michael Rabin, letter to Lewis Kaplan, February 16, 1958.
39. Michael Rabin, letter to Lewis Kaplan, February 26, 1958.
40. Michael Rabin, letter to Lewis Kaplan, March 1, 1958.
41. Michael Rabin, letter to Lewis Kaplan, March 6, 1958.
42. Michael Rabin, letter to Lewis Kaplan, March 11, 1958.
43. Michael Rabin, letter to Lewis Kaplan, July 1, 1958.
44. *Michigan Daily,* May 6, 1958.
45. Michael Rabin, letter to Lewis Kaplan, July 21, 1958.
46. Armed Forces physical examination, Certificate of Acceptability, May 22, 1958.
47. Wallace Magill, letter to Michael Rabin, January 25, 1958.
48. Michael Rabin, letter to Lewis Kaplan, July 21, 1958.
49. Michael Rabin, letter to Lewis Kaplan, August 3, 1958.
50. Lewis Kaplan, interview with author, New York City, December 19, 2000.
51. Aaron Rosand, correspondence with author, February 1, 2004.
52. Lewis Kaplan, interview with author, December 19, 2000.

53. Richard Donovan (Associate, William Moennig and Son), letter to author, October 7, 2003.
54. Michael Rabin, letter to Lewis Kaplan, September 23, 1958.
55. Michael Rabin, letter to Lewis Kaplan, March 11, 1958.
56. Howard Reich, *Van Cliburn* (Nashville, TN: Thomas Nelson, 1993).
57. Michael Rabin, letter to Lewis Kaplan, September 27, 1958.
58. ibid.
59. Michael Rabin, letter to Lewis Kaplan, October 15, 1958.
60. Michael Rabin, letter to Lewis Kaplan, November 2, 1958
61. Michael Rabin, letter to Lewis Kaplan, October 22, 1958.
62. Michael Rabin, letter to Lewis Kaplan, October 28, 1958.
63. Michael Rabin, letter to Lewis Kaplan, November 2, 1958.

CHAPTER 11

1. Josef Seiger, telephone interview with author, January 7, 2004.
2. Michael Rabin, letter to Lewis Kaplan, December 3, 1958.
3. Lewis Kaplan, interview with author, New York City, May 4, 2000.
4. Israel Philharmonic Orchestra, correspondence to and from Michael Rabin (a series of letters held in the orchestra's archives).
5. Michael Rabin, letter to Abe Cohen, April 9, 1959.
6. Michael Rabin, letter to Zvi Haftel (of the Israel Philharmonic Orchestra), March 20, 1961.
7. Tillet and Holt, letter to Zvi Haftel, April 24, 1967.
8. Harlow Robinson, *The Last Impresario: The Life, Times and Legacy of Sol Hurok* (New York: Viking Press, 1994).
9. George Rabin, letter to Leonard Bernstein, March 5, 1959.
10. Leonard Bernstein, note dated March 30, 1959.
11. *New York Times,* March 10, 1959.
12. Monika Slomsky, *Paul Creston: A Bio-Blibliography* (Westport, CT: Greenwood Publishing, 1994).
13. *New York Herald Tribune,* July 3, 1959.
14. *Los Angeles Examiner,* July 27, 1959.
15. *Chicago American* and *Chicago Tribune,* June 25, 1959.
16. *Chicago Tribune,* June 25, 1959.
17. Bertine Lafayette, interview with author, New York City, December 20, 2000.
18. Jascha Heifetz, note to Michael Rabin, June 1, 1959.
19. Josef Seiger, telephone interview with author.
20. *Los Angeles Mirror,* July 27, 1960.
21. EMI, memorandum to Capitol Records Inc., October 27, 1959.
22. EMI, internal memorandum, May 1959.
23. *The Gramophone,* September 1958.
24. EMI, internal memorandum, December 31, 1959.
25. EMI, internal memorandum. October 14, 1959.
26. Michael Rabin, letter to Bertine Lafayette, September 19, 1959.
27. *El Universal,* September 23, 1959.
28. *South Bend Tribune,* October 19, 1959.
29. *Mobile Register,* November 17, 1959.
30. *New Orleans States-Item,* November 18, 1959.
31. *Denver Post,* February 10, 1960.
32. *Musical America,* January 1, 1960.
33. National Orchestral Association press release, February 27–28, 1960.

34. *New York Times,* March 2, 1960.
35. *El Paso Times,* March 7, 1960.
36. Michael Rabin, Letter to Lewis Kaplan, March 19, 1960.
37. Michael Rabin, letter to Lewis Kaplan, October 29, 1958.
38. Michael Rabin, letter to Lewis Kaplan, March 19, 1960.
39. Michael Rabin, letter to Lewis Kaplan, March 25, 1960.
40. ibid.
41. Arthur Rubinstein, *My Young Years* (New York: Random House, 1973).
42. Yehudi Menuhin, *Unfinished Journey* (London: Macdonald and Janes, 1977).
43. Isaac Stern, *My First 79 Years* (New York: Knopf, 1999).
44. Amy Biancolli, *Love's Sorrow, Love's Joy* (Pompton Plains, NJ: Amadeus Press, 2003).
45. Donald Nold, telephone interview with author, January 14, 2004.
46. Michael Rabin, letter to Lewis Kaplan, April 9, 1960.
47. Michael Rabin, letter to Lewis Kaplan, April 19, 1960.
48. ibid.
49. Michael Rabin, letter to Lewis Kaplan, April 23, 1960.
50. Michael Rabin, letter to Lewis Kaplan, April 28, 1960.
51. Michael Rabin, letter to Lewis Kaplan, April 23, 1960.
52. *Aftenposter* (Oslo). April 23, 1960.
53. *London Daily Telegraph,* April 18, 1960.
54. *London Daily Express,* April 17, 1960.
55. Capitol Records Inc., memorandum to EMI-UK, February 1, 1960.
56. EMI-UK, memorandum to Capitol Records Inc., March 8, 1960.
57. *Guardian* (London), October 29, 2003.
58. Michael Rabin, letter to Lewis Kaplan, May 2, 1960.
59. Michael Rabin, letter to Lewis Kaplan, May 9, 1960.
60. ibid.
61. Michael Rabin, letter to Lewis Kaplan, May 2, 1960.

Chapter 12

1. Art Rose, letter to author, June 21, 2010.
2. *Great Violinists of "The Bell Telephone Hour" (1959–1964),* DVD (Video Artists International, 2002); and *New York Times,* November 6, 1960.
3. Bruno Monsaingeon, writer and director, *The Art of Violin: The Devil's Instrument,* DVD (NVC Arts/ Warner Music Vision, 2001).
4. Isidore Halpern, letter to Frederick Colwell (the Department of State), November 11, 1960.
5. Isidore Halpern, letter to Michael Rabin, November 21, 1960.
6. *New York Times,* November 3, 1960.
7. *Los Angeles Times,* November 18, 1960.
8. *Seattle Daily Times,* November 29, 1960.
9. Monika Slomsky, *Paul Creston: A Bio-Blibliography* (Westport, CT: Greenwood Publishing, 1994).
10. *Musical America,* January 1, 1960.
11. EMI, internal memorandum, October 18, 1960.
12. EMI-UK, memorandum to Capitol Records, March 8, 1960.
13. Jascha Heifetz, letter to Michael Rabin, February 15, 1961.
14. Sylvia Mann, letter to Michael Rabin, May 15, 1961.
15. Josef Krips, letter to Michael Rabin, March 20, 1961.
16. Clarence Francis (Chairman of the Campaign Committee, Lincoln Center for the Performing Arts Inc.), letter to Michael Rabin, April 28, 1961.

17. Connie Kiradjieff, telephone interview with author, January 13, 2004.

18. Milton Katims, letter to author, August 2, 2001.

19. Marsha Silver, telephone interview with author, December 23, 2003.

20. Lewis Kaplan, interview with author, New York City, May 4, 2000.

21. ibid.

22. Jeanne Rabin, letter to Alf Levy, September 12, 1961.

23. Mitchell Andrews, interview with author, December 21, 2000.

24. Lawrence Carlson, letter to Michael Rabin, September 6, 1961.

25. *Morgunbladid,* September 19, 1961.

26. Josef Seiger, telephone interview with author, January 7, 2004.

27. *The Strad* 72 (November 1961).

28. *London Daily Telegraph,* October 10, 1961

29. Schuyler Chapin, interview with author, New York City, January 8, 2002.

30. *Morgunbladid,* October 13, 1961.

31. Humphrey Burton, *Yehudi Menuhin* (Boston: Northeastern University Press, 2000), 94

32. *Der Kurier,* October 16, 1961.

33. *Der Abend,* October 17, 1961.

34. *Die Welt,* October 18, 1961.

35. *Der Tagesspiegel,* October 18, 1961.

36. *Der Telegraf,* October 18, 1961.

37. *Neue Zürcher Nachrichten,* November 8, 1961.

38. *Amarillo-Globe Times,* December 4, 1961.

39. ibid.

40. *Amarillo-Globe Times,* December 8, 1961.

41. Robert Bein, letter to author, December 17, 2003.

42. Richard Donovan (Associate, William Moennig and Son), letter to author, October 7, 2003.

43. Ernest Szabados, letter to Michael Rabin, November 15, 1961.

44. Madame Eugene Ysaÿe, letter to Michael Rabin, November 15, 1961.

45. Eugene Ormandy, letter to Michael Rabin, November 27, 1961.

46. *Charlotte News,* November 28, 1961; *Lubbock Avalanche Journal,* November 19, 1961; *Odessa American,* December 3, 1961; and *Amarillo Daily News,* December 6, 1961.

47. *New York Times,* January 4, 1962.

48. Isadore Halpern, letter to Michael Rabin, January 8, 1962.

49. *Buffalo Evening News,* January 22, 1962.

50. *New York Times,* May 29, 1962; and Project Hope, New York Committee, letter of thanks to Michael Rabin, June 4, 1962.

51. Michaels Memorial Music Award of the Ravinia Festival Association, letter of thanks to Michael Rabin, May 31, 1962.

52. *New York Times,* August 1, 1962.

53. *New York Times,* September 27, 1962.

54. Jeanne Rabin, letter to Alf Levy, October 30, 1962.

55. Joachim Hartnack, *Große Geiger unserer Zeit* (Munich: Rütten u. Loening, 1967), 288–291.

56. *Music and Musicians,* December 1962, 53.

57. Josef Seiger, telephone interview with author.

58. Jeanne Rabin, letter to Alf Levy, October 30, 1962.

59. ibid.

60. Michael Rabin, letter to Alf Levy, November 16, 1962.

61. *New York Herald Tribune,* November 28, 1962.

62. Mitchell Andrews, interview with author.

63. ibid.

64. Elaine Weldon, telephone interview with author, June 25, 2010.
65. *Boston Globe,* December 20, 1962.
66. Mitchell Andrews, interview with author.
67. *Bismarck Tribune,* January 18, 1963.
68. Mitchell Andrews, letter to Michael Rabin, February 4, 1963.
69. *Los Angeles Times,* February 4, 1963.
70. Elizabeth Matesky, telephone interview with author, February 10, 2004.
71. *New York Newsday,* July 12, 1967.

CHAPTER 13

1. *New York Newsday,* July 12, 1967.
2. Sally Thomas, interview with author, New York City, March 14, 2002.
3. Jaime Laredo, telephone interview with author, June 21, 2010.
4. Lewis Kaplan, interview with author, New York City, December 19, 2000.
5. Laurence Ivan Seidman, interview with Bea Seidman, February 12, 1983.
6. Lewis Kaplan, interview with author, December 19, 2000.
7. Elaine Weldon, telephone interview with author, June 25, 2010.
8. Josef Seiger, telephone interview with author, January 7, 2004.
9. Fredell Lack, interview with author, November 19, 2003.
10. Lewis Kaplan, interview with author, New York City, May 4, 2000.
11. James Mason (President, Board of Governors, Atlantic City Hospital), letter to Michael Rabin, May 23, 1963.
12. *Philadelphia Inquirer,* July 3, 1963.
13. *Milwaukee Journal,* October 13, 1963.
14. *Miami Herald,* January 13, 1964.
15. Mitchell Andrews, interview with author, December 21, 2000.
16. *San Diego Union,* February 5, 1964.
17. Michael Rabin, letter to Alf and Alice Levy, March 9, 1964.
18. Carl Dahlgren, interview with author, Durango, Co., July 29, 2010.
19. Michael Rabin, letter to Alf Levy, March 24, 1964.
20. Bertine Lafayette, interview with author, New York City, October 23, 2002.
21. ibid.
22. David Levy, interview with author, July 12, 2004.
23. Michael Rabin, letter to Alf Levy, September 29, 1964.
24. Rudolf Serkin, letter to Michael Rabin, no date.
25. Jaime Laredo, telephone interview with author, June 21, 2010.
26. Lewis Kaplan, interview with author, May 4, 2000.
27. ibid.
28. Suzanne Landry, telephone interview with author, September 22, 2003.
29. Lewis Kaplan, interview with author, May 4, 2000.
30. *Madrid Pueblo,* March 21, 1966 (translation in the possession of Bertine Lafayette).
31. *Arbeiderbladet,* March 26, 1966.
32. Isaac Stern, letter to author, February 3, 1981.
33. Artur Weschler-Vered, *Jascha Heifetz* (London: Hale, 1986), 96.
34. Humphrey Burton, *Yehudi Menuhin* (Boston: Northeastern University Press, 2000), 142.
35. June LeBell, interview with author, June 1, 2000.
36. Walter Mony, telephone interview with author, March 25, 2004.
37. Benny Feinstein, interview with author, June 2, 2004.
38. *Rhodesia Herald,* April 26, 1966.
39. *The Strad* 97, no. 1153 (May 1986): 45–47.
40. Arnold Steinhardt, telephone interview with author, November 18, 2003.

41. *New York World Journal Tribune,* November 5, 1966.
42. *Musical Leader* 12, no. 6 (December 1966).
43. *Columbia Owl,* November 16, 1966.
44. *High Fidelity,* January 1967, MA−15.
45. Mitchell Andrews, interview with author.
46. Jeanne Rabin, letter to Vladimir Horowitz, May 10, 1965.
47. *New York Newsday,* July 12, 1967.
48. *Newark Sunday Times,* July 30, 1967.
49. *Washington Post,* April 1, 1968.
50. *New York Times,* October 22, 1967.
51. *New York Times,* January 7, 1968.
52. *Toronto Globe and Mail,* March 12, 1969.
53. *Montreal Star,* February 26, 1969.
54. *Berliner Zeitung,* June 16, 1969.
55. *Miami Herald,* July 28, 1969.
56. Michael Rabin, letter to Alf Levy, February 17, 1968.
57. Michael Rabin, letter to Alf and Alice Levy, March 18, 1968.
58. *London Daily Mail,* June 19, 1969.
59. Robin Brightman, letter to author, October 11, 2003.
60. Michael Rabin, letter to Alf and Alice Levy, June 30, 1969.

CHAPTER 14

1. Josef Seiger, telephone interview with author, January 7, 2004.
2. *Philadelphia Inquirer,* June 27, 1971.
3. June LeBell, interview with author, June 1, 2000.
4. ibid.
5. ibid.
6. *New York Times,* June 6, 1971.
7. June LeBell, interview with author.
8. Fredell Lack, interview with author, November 19, 2003.
9. Tom Strasser, telephone interview with author, March 1, 2003.
10. ibid.
11. ibid.
12. Michael Rabin, letter to his parents, March 24, 1971.
13. *New York Times,* June 6, 1971.
14. *New York Times,* January 18, 1976.
15. *New York Times,* June 6, 1971.
16. Mitchell Andrews, interview with author, December 21, 2000.
17. Suzanne Bilyeu, letter to author, November 21, 2003.
18. Sheldon Morgenstern, *No Vivaldi in the Garage* (Boston: Northeastern University Press, 2001), 139−40.
19. Ling Silberger, letter to author, November 12, 2003.
20. Lewis Kaplan, interview with author, New York City, May 4, 2000.
21. June LeBell, interview with author.
22. ibid.
23. Bertine Lafayette, interview with author, New York City, October 23, 2002.
24. June LeBell, interview with author.
25. Judith Galamian, interview with author, New York City, August 11, 2001.
26. June LeBell, interview with author.
27. ibid.
28. Bertine Lafayette, interview with author.

29.   Arnold Steinhardt, telephone interview with author, November 18, 2003.

30.   Lewis Kaplan, interview with author, May 4, 2000.

31.   June LeBell, interview with author.

32.   Sybil Sklar, interview with author, Larchmount, New York, June 18, 2003.

CHAPTER 15

1.   *New York Times* (National and Late City editions), January 20, 1972.

2.   *New York Post,* January 20, 1972.

3.   *Variety,* January 26, 1972.

4.   *Washington Post,* January 21, 1972.

5.   *Time,* January 31, 1972.

6.   Bruno Monsaingeon, writer and director, *The Art of Violin: The Devil's Instrument,* DVD (NVC Arts/ Warner Music Vision, 2001).

7.   Sheldon Morgenstern, *No Vivaldi in the Garage* (Boston: Northeastern University Press, 2001), 139–40.

8.   *New York Times,* November 23, 1977.

9.   Biographical entry on Dr. Michael Baden, available online at http://www.practicalhomocide.com/bio/bioBADEN.htm.

10.   Michael Baden, telephone interview with author, June 17, 2003.

11.   Department of Health of The City of New York, standard certificate of death (no. 156 72 101354), January 20, 1972.

12.   ibid.

13.   *New York Times,* June 6, 1971.

14.   Bertine Lafayette, interview with author, New York City, October 23, 2002; and Judith Galamian, interview with author, New York City, August 11, 2001.

15.   Jeanne Rabin, letter to Alf, Alice and David Levy, February 3, 1972.

16.   Bertine Lafayette, interview with author.

17.   *Current Musicology,* no. 14 (1972): 15–158.

18.   Kyung-Wha Chung, telephone interview with author, March 23, 2004.

19.   Seth Rubinstein (lawyer), letter to Bertine Lafayette (including Michael Rabin's estate tax return), November 15, 1972.

20.   *The Strad* 97, no. 1153 (1986): 45–47.

21.   *The New Grove Dictionary of Music and Musicians* (New York/Oxford, UK: Oxford University Press, 1980).

22.   *The New Grove Dictionary of Music and Musicians* (New York/Oxford, UK: Oxford University Press, 2001), 705.

This discography has been arranged chronologically. Michael Rabin's first three recordings were made for the American Columbia label. These same recordings were distributed in England on the Dutch label Philips (with different covers).

Thereafter, he was signed by EMI and his recordings appeared in the US on the Angel label and in the UK on the Columbia label with different covers and catalogue numbers. This reference to two separate Columbia labels in the Rabin discography can appear confusing and is explained by the fact that anti-trust laws had earlier forced EMI to sell its American Columbia label while allowing it to keep its UK label.

In 1957 EMI merged their Angel label into their recently acquired Capitol Records subsidiary. Rabin's last four recordings were made for Capitol Records and issued in both Mono (P prefix) and Stereo (SP prefix).

In 1972, the year of Rabin's death, EMI Records posthumously reissued the out-of-print *Magic Bow* LP on their mid-price Seraphim line and re-titled it *In Memoriam* (S-60199).

COMMERCIAL RECORDINGS

For the purpose of this discography, only original US and UK LP numbers have been quoted, with the exception of a couple of Dutch-pressed Philips records for the UK market.

MICHAEL RABIN: PAGANINI, CAPRICES, OP. 1 (recorded in 1950)

(LP) Columbia Masterworks ML 2168; 10" LP (USA) / Philips S 06616 R; 10" LP (Dutch pressing)
(CD) *Michael Rabin: The Early Years*; Sony Classical MHK 60894 (USA) (released in 1999)

Paganini, Niccolò: Caprice in E major (Andante), Op. 1, No. 1
Paganini, Niccolò: Caprice in A minor (Agitato), Op. 1, No. 5
Paganini, Niccolò: Caprice in E major (Allegretto), Op. 1, No. 9
Paganini, Niccolò: Caprice in C major (Andante—Presto), Op. 1, No. 11
Paganini, Niccolò: Caprice in B-flat major (Allegro), Op. 1, No. 13
Paganini, Niccolò: Caprice in E-flat major (Moderato), Op. 1, No. 14

Paganini, Niccolò: Caprice in G minor (Presto), Op. 1, No. 16

Paganini, Niccolò: Caprice in E-flat major (Sostenuto—Andante), Op. 1, No. 17

Paganini, Niccolò: Caprice in C major (Corrente—Allegro), Op. 1, No. 18

Paganini, Niccolò: Caprice in A major (Amoroso), Op. 1, No. 21

Paganini, Niccolò: Caprice in A minor (Tema con Variazioni), Op. 1, No. 24

MICHAEL RABIN PLAYS (recorded in 1952)

(with Artur Balsam, piano)

(LP) Columbia Masterworks AAL 30; 10" LP (USA)

(CD) *Michael Rabin: The Early Years*: Sony Classical MHK 60894 (USA) (released in 1999)

Dvořák, Antonin: Slavonic Dance in E minor, Op. 72, No. 2

Wieniawski, Henryk: Etude-Caprice in A minor, Op. 18, No. 4

Sarasate, Pablo de: Finale from Concert Fantasy on Themes from Bizet's *Carmen*, Op. 25

Kreisler, Fritz: "La Chasse" in the Style of Cartier

Engel, Carl: "Sea-Shell" (arr. Zimbalist)

Kroll, William: "Banjo and Fiddle"

MICHAEL RABIN: "ZIGEUNERWEISEN" / PERPETUAL MOTION (recorded in 1953)

(with the Columbia Symphony Orchestra conducted by Donald Voorhees)

(LP) Columbia Masterworks AL 38; 10" LP (USA) / Philips 409 007 AE; 7" EP (Dutch pressing)

(CD) *Michael Rabin: The Early Years*; Sony Classical MHK 60894 (USA) (released in 1999)

Paganini, Niccolò: Moto perpetuo in C major, Op. 11

Nováček, Ottokar: Caprice, Op. 5, No. 2, "Perpetuum mobile"

Sarasate, Pablo de: *Zigeunerweisen*, Op. 20

MICHAEL RABIN: PAGANINI, CONCERTO NO. 1 AND GLAZUNOV, CONCERTO (recorded in 1954)

(with the Philharmonia Orchestra conducted by Lovro von Matačić)

(LP) Angel 35259 (USA) / Columbia 33CX 1281 (UK)

(CD) *Michael Rabin: 1936–1972*; EMI Classics CMS 7 64123 2 (part of a 6-CD set—Germany) (released in 1991)

(CD) Remastered and reissued as *Michael Rabin: The Studio Recordings 1954–1960*; Testament SBT6 1471 (UK) (released in 2011)

Paganini, Niccolò: Violin Concerto No. 1 in D major, Op. 6

Glazunov, Alexander: Violin Concerto in A minor, Op. 82

MUSIC FROM THE TELEPHONE HOUR (recorded live in Carnegie Hall in 1955)

(with the Bell Telephone Orchestra conducted by Donald Voorhees)

(LP) Telephone EB 3020; 10" LP (USA)

(CD) *Michael Rabin Collection, Volume 2* (Doremi DHR 7951/3; 3 CDs) (Canada) (released in 2009)

Mendelssohn, Felix: Violin Concerto in E minor, Op. 64 (3rd movement)

Massenet, Jules: Elégie: "O doux printemps d'autrefois" (with tenor Brian Sullivan) was also recorded at the time, but was not included on this LP. It has since been released on the Doremi set, Volume 2.

(Also featured on the LP are *Telephone Hour* performances by Sullivan, Iturbi, Farrell, and Pons.)

MICHAEL RABIN: SONATAS FOR VIOLIN SOLO (recorded in 1955)

(LP) Angel 35305 (USA)

(CD) *Michael Rabin 1936–1972*; EMI Classics CMS 7 64123 2 (part of a 6-CD set—Germany) (released in 1991)

(CD) Remastered and reissued as *Michael Rabin: The Studio Recordings 1954–1960*; Testament SBT6 1471 (UK) (released in 2011)

(CD) *Michael Rabin*; EMI Classics CDM 5 67020 2. Contains the Bach and Ysaÿe sonatas remastered in 1999 (USA) and released in the same year together with the complete *Mosaics* album.

Bach, Johann Sebastian: Sonata for solo violin No. 3 BWV 1005 in C major

Ysaÿe, Eugene-Auguste: Sonata for solo violin No. 3 in D minor, "Ballade", Op. 27, No. 3

Ysaÿe, Eugene-Auguste: Sonata for solo violin No. 4 in E minor, Op. 27, No. 4

MICHAEL RABIN: TCHAIKOWSKY, VIOLIN CONCERTO / SAINT-SAËNS, INTRODUCTION AND RONDO CAPRICCIOSO (recorded in 1956)

(with the Philharmonia Orchestra conducted by Alceo Galliera)

(LP) Angel 35388 (USA) / Columbia 33CX 1422 (UK)

(CD) *Michael Rabin 1936–1972*; EMI Classics CMS 7 64123 2 (part of a 6-CD set—Germany) (released in 1991)

(CD) Remastered and reissued as *Michael Rabin: The Studio Recordings 1954–1960*; Testament SBT6 1471 (UK) (released in 2011)

Tchaikowsky, Pyotr Ilyich: Violin Concerto in D major, Op. 35
Saint-Saëns, Camille: Introduction and Rondo Capriccioso, Op. 28

MICHAEL RABIN: WIENIAWSKI, CONCERTO NO. 1 AND BRUCH, "SCOTTISH FANTASY" (recorded in 1957)

(with the Philharmonia Orchestra conducted by Adrian Boult)

(LP) Angel 35484 (USA) / Columbia 33CX 1538 (UK)

(CD) *Michael Rabin 1936–1972*; EMI Classics CMS 7 64123 2 (part of a 6-CD set—Germany) (released in 1991)

(CD) Remastered and reissued as *Michael Rabin: The Studio Recordings 1954–1960*; Testament SBT6 1471 (UK) (released in 2011)

Bruch, Max: *Scottish Fantasy*, Op. 46
Wieniawski, Henryk: Violin Concerto No. 1 in F-sharp minor, Op. 14

MICHAEL RABIN: MENDELSSOHN, VIOLIN CONCERTO / RAVEL, "TZIGANE" / SAINT-SAËNS, HAVANAISE (Saint-Saëns recorded in 1956 / Mendelssohn and Ravel recorded in 1957)

(with the Philharmonia Orchestra conducted by Adrian Boult and Alceo Galliera)

(LP) Angel 35572 (USA) / Columbia 33CX 1597 (UK)

(CD) *Michael Rabin 1936–1972*; EMI Classics CMS 7 64123 2 (part of a 6-CD set—Germany) (released in 1991)

(CD) Remastered and reissued as *Michael Rabin: The Studio Recordings 1954–1960*; Testament SBT6 1471 (UK) (released in 2011)

Mendelssohn, Felix: Violin Concerto in E minor, Op. 64 (Adrian Boult)
Ravel, Maurice: *Tzigane* (Rhapsody for violin and orchestra) (Adrian Boult)
Saint-Saëns, Camille: Havanaise in E major, Op. 83 (Alceo Galliera)

MICHAEL RABIN: PAGANINI, CAPRICES, OP. 1 FOR UNACCOMPANIED VIOLIN (recorded in 1958)

(LP) Capitol (Stereo) SPBR 8477 / (Mono) PBR 8477 - 2 LPs (USA)

(CD) *Michael Rabin 1936–1972* (the Mono version was issued in this set); EMI Classics CMS 7 64123 2 (part of a 6-CD set—Germany) (released in 1991)

(CD) Remastered and reissued as *Michael Rabin: The Studio Recordings 1954–1960*; Testament SBT6 1471 (UK) (released in 2011)

(CD) EMI 67462 2 (Mono Remastering—2001) / EMI 5 67998 2 (Stereo Remastering—2003)

Paganini, Niccolò: Caprice in E major (Andante), Op. 1, No. 1

Paganini, Niccolò: Caprice in B minor (Moderato), Op. 1, No. 2

Paganini, Niccolò: Caprice in E minor (Sostenuto—Presto), Op. 1, No. 3

Paganini, Niccolò: Caprice in C minor (Maestoso), Op. 1, No. 4

Paganini, Niccolò: Caprice in A minor (Agitato), Op. 1, No. 5

Paganini, Niccolò: Caprice in G minor (Lento), Op. 1, No. 6

Paganini, Niccolò: Caprice in A minor (Posato), Op. 1, No. 7

Paganini, Niccolò: Caprice in E-flat major (Maestoso), Op. 1, No. 8

Paganini, Niccolò: Caprice in E major (Allegretto), Op. 1, No. 9

Paganini, Niccolò: Caprice in G minor (Vivace), Op. 1, No. 10

Paganini, Niccolò: Caprice in C major (Andante—Presto), Op. 1, No. 11

Paganini, Niccolò: Caprice in A-flat major (Allegro), Op. 1, No. 12

Paganini, Niccolò: Caprice in B-flat major (Allegro), Op. 1, No. 13

Paganini, Niccolò: Caprice in E-flat major (Moderato), Op. 1, No. 14

Paganini, Niccolò: Caprice in E minor (Posato), Op. 1, No. 15

Paganini, Niccolò: Caprice in G minor (Presto), Op. 1, No. 16

Paganini, Niccolò: Caprice in E-flat major (Sostenuto—Andante), Op. 1, No. 17

Paganini, Niccolò: Caprice in C major (Corrente—Allegro), Op. 1, No. 18

Paganini, Niccolò: Caprice in E-flat major (Lento—Allegro Assai), Op. 1, No. 19

Paganini, Niccolò: Caprice in D major (Allegretto), Op. 1, No. 20

Paganini, Niccolò: Caprice in A major (Amoroso), Op. 1, No. 21

Paganini, Niccolò: Caprice in F major (Marcato), Op. 1, No. 22

Paganini, Niccolò: Caprice in E-flat major (Posato), Op. 1, No. 23

Paganini, Niccolò: Caprice in A minor (Tema con Variazioni), Op. 1, No. 24

MOSAICS (recorded in 1959)

(with Leon Pommers, piano)

(LP) Capitol SP 8506 / P 8506 (USA and UK)

(CD) *Michael Rabin 1936–1972*; EMI Classics CMS 7 64123 2 (part of a 6-CD set—Germany) (released in 1991)

(CD) Remastered and reissued as *Michael Rabin: The Studio Recordings 1954–1960*; Testament SBT6 1471 (UK) (released in 2011)

(CD) *Michael Rabin*; EMI Classics CDM 5 67020 2. This release contains the *Mosaics* album remastered in 1999 (USA) and released that year together with the Bach / Ysaÿe sonatas for unaccompanied violin originally recorded in 1955.

Chopin, Frédéric: Nocturne in D flat major, Op. 27, No. 2
Wieniawski, Henryk: Etude-Caprice in A minor, Op. 18, No. 4
Mompou, Federico: "Jeunes filles au jardin" (No. 5 from *Scènes d'enfants*)
Scriabin, Alexander: Etude, Op. 8, No. 10 in D-flat major, (arr. Szigeti)
Debussy, Claude: "La plus que lente," L.121
Sarasate, Pablo de: Habanera, Op. 21, No. 2 (from *Spanish Dances*)
Elgar, Edward: "La Capricieuse," Op. 17
Engel, Carl: "Sea-Shell" (arr. Zimbalist)
Sarasate, Pablo de: Zapateado, Op. 23, No. 2 (from *Spanish Dances*)
Ravel, Maurice: "Pièce en forme d'Habanera"
Prokofiev, Sergei: March (from *The Love for Three Oranges*, Op. 33)
Suk, Josef: Burleska, Op. 17, No. 4 (from *Four Pieces*)

THE MAGIC BOW (recorded in 1959)

(with the Hollywood Bowl Orchestra conducted by Felix Slatkin)
(LP) Capitol SP 8510 / P 8510 (USA and UK)
(CD) *Michael Rabin 1936–1972*; EMI Classics CMS 7 64123 2 (part of a 6-CD set—Germany) (released in 1991)
(CD) Remastered and reissued as *Michael Rabin: The Studio Recordings 1954–1960*; Testament SBT6 1471 (UK) (released in 2011)
(CD) *Rabin*; Medici Arts MM023-2. Contains the Saint-Saëns, Sarasate, Dinicu, and Paganini pieces from *The Magic Bow* plus the Paganini / Wieniawski concertos from the album recorded in 1960. All these works were remastered in 2008 (Germany) and released the same year.

Kreisler, Fritz: "Caprice Viennois," Op. 2
Dinicu, Grigoras: "Hora Staccato" (arr. Heifetz)
Massenet, Jules: "Méditation" (from *Thaïs*)
Sarasate, Pablo de: *Zigeunerweisen*, Op. 20
Paganini, Niccolò: Moto perpetuo in C major, Op. 11 (arr. Kreisler)
Brandl, Johann: "The Old Refrain" (arr. Kreisler)
Rimsky-Korsakov, Nikolai: "The Flight of the Bumble Bee" (from *The Tale of Tsar Saltan*)
Saint-Saëns, Camille: Introduction and Rondo Capriccioso, Op. 28

MICHAEL RABIN: PAGANINI, CONCERTO NO. 1 AND WIENIAWSKI, CONCERTO NO. 2 (recorded in 1960)

(with the Philharmonia Orchestra conducted by Eugene Goossens)

(LP) Capitol SP 8534 / P 8534 (USA and UK)

(CD) *Michael Rabin 1936–1972*; EMI Classics CMS 7 64123 2 (part of a 6-CD set—Germany) (released in 1991)

(CD) Remastered and reissued as *Michael Rabin: The Studio Recordings 1954–1960*; Testament SBT6 1471 (UK) (released in 2011)

(CD) *Rabin*; Medici Arts MM023-2. Contains the Paganini and Wieniawski concertos together with the Saint-Saëns, Sarasate, Dinicu, and Paganini pieces from *The Magic Bow*, all remastered in 2008 (Germany) and released the same year.

Paganini, Niccolò: Violin Concerto No.1 in D major, Op. 6
Wieniawski, Henryk: Violin Concerto No. 2 in D minor, Op. 22

PREVIOUSLY UNRELEASED RECORDINGS ON CD

The year in parentheses after each individual work indicates when it was recorded.

MARLBORO FESTIVAL: 40TH ANNIVERSARY (released in 1990)

(CD) Sony Classical SMK 45892 (USA)

Bach, Johann Sebastian: Orchestral Suite No. 2 in B minor, BWV 1067 (1966)
Bach, Johann Sebastian: Orchestral Suite No. 3 in D major, BWV 1068 (1966)
(Michael Rabin was a member of the Marlboro Festival Orchestra conducted by Pablo Casals.)

PHILADELPHIA ORCHESTRA CENTENNIAL COLLECTION: HISTORIC BROADCASTS AND RECORDINGS (1917–1998) (released in 1999 on disc no. 11 as part of a 12-CD Centennial Collection Set)

(CD) POA 100 - 7 (USA)

Tchaikowsky, Pyotr Ilyich: Violin Concerto in D major, Op. 35 (stereo broadcast from 1961)
(with the Philadelphia Orchestra Broadcast conducted by William Smith)

MICHAEL RABIN COLLECTION, VOLUME 1 (released in 2000)

(CD) DOREMI (Legendary Treasures) DHR 7715 (Canada)

Paganini, Niccolò: Caprice in E-flat major (Sostenuto—Andante), Op. 1, No. 17 (arr. for violin and orchestra) (1950)
(with the Bell Telephone Orchestra conducted by Donald Voorhees)

Fauré, Gabriel: Violin Sonata No. 1 in A major, Op. 13 (1961)
Beethoven, Ludwig van: Violin Sonata No. 8 in G major, Op. 30, No. 3 (1962)
(with Lothar Broddack, piano)

ANDRÉ CLUYTENS: RARITIES (released in 2007)

(with the Kölner Rundfunk-Sinfonieorchester conducted by André Cluytens)

(CD) Archipel ARPCD 0298 (EU)

Prokofiev, Sergei: Violin Concerto No. 2 in G minor, Op. 63 (1957)

THE MICHAEL RABIN LEGACY: UNISSUED RECORDINGS 1950–1956 (released in 2007)

(CD) Tahra TAH 632-633 (2 CDs—France)

Mendelssohn, Felix: "Auf Flügeln des Gesanges" (On the Wings of Song) Op. 34, No. 2 (1950)
Paganini, Niccolò: Caprice in E-flat major (Sostenuto—Andante), Op. 1, No. 17 (arr. for violin and orchestra) (1950)
Mendelssohn, Felix: "May Breeze," Op. 62, No. 1 (from *Songs Without Words*) (arr. Kreisler) (1950)
Dvořák, Antonin: Slavonic Dance in E minor, Op. 46, No. 2 "Dumka" (1951)
Kroll, William: "Banjo and Fiddle" (1951)
Godowsky, Leopold: "Alt Wien" (No. 11 from *Triakontameron*) (arr. Heifetz) (1951)
Kreisler, Fritz: Caprice Viennois, Op. 2 (1951)
Lalo, Edouard: *Symphonie espagnole* Op. 21 (1st movement) (1951)
Wieniawski, Henryk: Etude-Caprice in A minor, Op. 18, No. 4 (1952)
Wieniawski, Henryk: Polonaise brillante in D major, Op. 4 (1952)
Chopin, Frédéric: Nocturne in C-sharp minor, Op. 27, No. 1 (arr. Milstein) (1952)
Falla, Manuel de: Spanish Dance No. 1 from *La vida breve* (arr. Milstein) (1952)

Sarasate, Pablo de: *Zigeunerweisen*, Op. 20 (1952)

Brandl, Johann: "The Old Refrain" (arr. Kreisler) (1953)

Sarasate, Pablo de: Concert Fantasy on themes from Bizet's *Carmen*, Op. 25 (3rd and 4th movements) (1953)

Debussy, Claude: "La fille aux cheveux de lin" (from Preludes, Book 1, No. 8) (arr. Hartmann) (1954)

Moszkowski, Moritz: "Guitarre," Op. 45, No. 2 (1954)

Elgar, Edward: "La Capricieuse," Op. 17 (1954)

Wieniawski, Henryk: Violin Concerto No. 1 in F-sharp minor, Op. 14 (1954) (with the Los Angeles Philharmonic conducted by Alfred Wallenstein)

Glazunov, Alexander: Violin Concerto in A minor, Op. 82 (1954) (with the New York Philharmonic Orchestra conducted by Dimitri Mitropoulos)

Brahms, Johannes: Violin Concerto in D major, Op. 77 (3rd movement) (1955)

Mendelssohn, Felix: Violin Concerto in E minor, Op. 64 (3rd movement) (1955)

Tchaikowsky, Pyotr Ilyich: Violin Concerto in D major, Op. 35 (1st movement) (1956) (with the Bell Telephone Orchestra conducted by Donald Voorhees)

MICHAEL RABIN: BRUCH, VIOLIN CONCERTO / VIRTUOSO PIECES FOR VIOLIN AND PIANO (released in 2009)

(CD) Audite 95.607 (Germany)

Saint-Saëns, Camille: Havanaise in E major, Op. 83 (1962) (with Lothar Broddack, piano)

Bruch, Max: Violin Concerto in G minor, Op. 26 (1969) (with the RIAS-Symphonie-Orchester conducted by Thomas Schippers)

Kroll, William: "Banjo and Fiddle" (1969)

Wieniawski, Henryk: Etude-Caprice in A minor, Op. 18, No. 4 (1969)

Tchaikowsky, Pyotr Ilyich: Meditation, Op. 42, No. 1 (from *Souvenir d'un lieu cher*) (1969)

Sarasate, Pablo de: Concert Fantasy on Themes from Bizet's *Carmen*, Op. 25 (1969)

Sarasate, Pablo de: Malagueña, Op. 21, No. 1 (from *Spanish Dances*) (1969)

Sarasate, Pablo de: Habanera, Op. 21, No. 2 (from *Spanish Dances*) (1969)

Sarasate, Pablo de: Zapateado, Op. 23, No. 2 (from *Spanish Dances*) (1969) (with Lothar Broddack, piano)

MICHAEL RABIN COLLECTION, VOLUME 2 (released in 2009)

(CD) DOREMI (Legendary Treasures) DHR 7951-3 (3 CDs—Canada)

Wieniawski, Henryk: Violin Concerto No. 1 in F-sharp minor, Op. 14 (1950)
  (with the National Orchestra Association conducted by Charles
   Blackman)

Brahms, Johannes: "Contemplation" ("Wie Melodien zieht es mir"), Op.
   105, No. 1 (arr. Heifetz) (1951)
Kreisler, Fritz: "Caprice Viennois," Op. 2 (1951)
Saint-Saëns, Camille: Introduction and Rondo capriccioso, Op. 28 (1951)
  (with the Bell Telephone Orchestra conducted by Donald Voorhees)

Bach, Johann Sebastian: Double Concerto in D minor, BWV 1043 (1st
   movement) (1952)
  (with Zino Francescatti and the Bell Telephone Orchestra conducted by
   Donald Voorhees)

Wieniawski, Henryk: Violin Concerto No. 1 in F-sharp minor, Op. 14 (1st
   movement) (1953)
  (with the Los Angeles Philharmonic conducted by Alfred Wallenstein)

Mohaupt, Richard: Violin Concerto (1954)
  (with the New York Philharmonic Orchestra conducted by Dimitri
   Mitropoulos)

Mendelssohn, Felix: Violin Concerto in E minor, Op. 64 (3rd movement)
   (1955)
Massenet, Jules: Elégie: "O doux printemps d'autrefois" (with Brian
   Sullivan, tenor) (1955)
  (with the Bell Telephone Orchestra conducted by Donald Voorhees)

Paganini, Niccolò: Caprice in A minor (Agitato), Op. 1, No. 5 (1961)
Paganini, Niccolò: Caprice in E major (Allegretto), Op. 1, No. 9 (1961)
Paganini, Niccolò: Caprice in B-flat major (Allegro), Op. 1, No. 13 (1961)
Paganini, Niccolò: Caprice in E-flat major (Moderato), Op. 1, No. 14
   (1961)
Paganini, Niccolò: Caprice in E-flat major (Sostenuto—Andante), Op. 1,
   No. 17 (1961)
Paganini, Niccolò: Caprice in A minor (Tema con Variazioni), Op. 1, No.
   24 (1961)
Ysaÿe, Eugene-Auguste: Sonata for violin solo No. 3 in D minor "Ballade",
   Op. 27, No. 3 (1961)
Milhaud, Darius: "Tijuca" (No. 8 from *Saudades do Brazil*) (1962)

Szymanowski, Karl: "La fontaine d'Aréthuse," Op. 30, No. 1 (1962)
(Milhaud and Szymanowski with Lothar Broddack, piano)

Spalding, Albert: *Dragonfly* for solo violin (1962)
Creston, Paul: Violin Concerto No. 2, Op. 78 (1962)
(with the Little Orchestra Society conducted by Thomas Scherman)

Brahms, Johannes: Violin Concerto in D major, Op. 77 (1967)
(with the Chicago Symphony Orchestra conducted by Rafael Kubelik)

Prokofiev, Sergei: Violin Concerto No. 2 in G minor, Op. 63 (1968)
(with the Chicago Symphony Orchestra conducted by Andre Vandernoot)

Bruch, Max: Violin Concerto in G minor, Op. 26 (1969)
(with the RIAS-Symphonie-Orchester conducted by Thomas Schippers)

MICHAEL RABIN COLLECTION, VOLUME 3 (released in 2010)

(CD) DOREMI (Legendary Treasures) DHR 7970 (2 CDs—Canada)

Wieniawski, Henryk: Polonaise brillante in D major, Op. 4 (1952)
Saint-Saëns, Camille: Introduction and Rondo Capriccioso, Op. 28 (1952)
Paganini, Niccolò: Caprice in C major (Andante—Presto), Op. 1, No. 11
(1952)
Paganini, Niccolò: Caprice in G minor (Presto), Op. 1, No. 16 (1952)
Paganini, Niccolò: Caprice in A major (Amoroso), Op. 1, No. 21 (1952)
Scriabin, Alexander: Etude, Op. 8, No.10 in D-flat major, (arr. Szigeti)
(1952)
Godowsky, Leopold: "Alt Wien" (No. 11 from *Triakontameron*) (arr.
Heifetz) (1952)
Kreisler, Fritz: "Tambourin Chinois," Op. 3 (1952)
Ravel, Maurice: *Tzigane* (Rhapsody for violin & orchestra) (1952)
Tchaikowsky, Pyotr Ilyich: October "Autumn Song", Op. 37b, No. 10
(from *The Seasons*) (1952)
(with Raymond Lambert, piano, at Sydney Town Hall)

Engel, Carl: "Sea-Shell" (arr. Zimbalist) (1956)
Mendelssohn, Felix: "Sweet Remembrance," Op. 19, No. 1 (from *Songs
Without Words*) (arr. Heifetz) (1956)
Prokofiev, Sergei: March (from *The Love for Three Oranges*, Op. 33) (1956)
Saint-Saëns, Camille: *Caprice d'après l'Etude en forme de valse* Op. 52, No. 6
(arr. Ysaÿe) (1956)
(with the Bell Telephone Orchestra conducted by Donald Voorhees)

Creston, Paul: Violin Concerto No. 2, Op. 78 (1960)
(with the Los Angeles Philharmonic conducted by Georg Solti)

Mozart, Wolfgang Amadeus: Violin Concerto No. 4 in D major, K. 218 (1960)
(with the Denver Symphony Orchestra conducted by Saul Caston)

Tchaikowsky, Pyotr Ilyich: Violin Concerto in D major, Op. 35 (1964)
(with the Oslo Philharmonic Orchestra conducted by Oivin Fjeldstad)

Glazunov, Alexander: Violin Concerto in A minor, Op. 82 (1968)
(with the Radio-Orchester Beromester, Zurich conducted by Erich Schmid)

Paganini, Niccolò: Caprice in E major (Allegretto), Op. 1, No. 9 (1970)
(WQXR Radio—*The Listening Room*)

MICHAEL RABIN: THE FIRST, LAST AND HIDDEN RECORDINGS
(released in 2012)

(CD) Testament SBT3 1470 (3 CDs—UK)

Lalo, Edouard: *Symphonie espagnole* Op. 21 (1947)
Paganini, Niccolò: Caprice in C major (Andante—Presto), Op. 1, No. 11
(1947)
Paganini, Niccolò: Caprice in E-flat major (Sostenuto—Andante), Op. 1,
No. 17 (1947)
Paganini, Niccolò: Caprice in A minor (Tema con Variazioni), Op. 1, No.
24 (1947)
Paganini, Niccolò: Caprice in A minor (Agitato), Op. 1, No. 5 (1947)
Saint-Saëns, Camille: Introduction and Rondo capriccioso, Op. 28 (1947)
Kreisler, Fritz: "Schön Rosmarin" (1947)
Schalit, Heinrich: Serenade (based on a traditional Jewish folk tune) (1947)
(Lalo, Saint-Saëns, Kreisler, and Schalit with Jeanne Rabin, piano)

Brahms, Johannes: Violin Concerto in D major, Op. 77 (first movement)
(1949)
Bach, Johann Sebastian: Partita for solo violin No. 2, BWV 1004 in D
minor (Allemanda, Corrente, and Giga) (1949)
Kroll, William: "Banjo and Fiddle" (1949)
Paganini, Niccolò: Caprice in A minor (Agitato), Op. 1, No. 5 (1949)
(Brahms and Kroll with Jeanne Rabin, piano)

Dvořák, Antonin: Slavonic Dance in E minor, Op. 72, No. 2 (1961)
Kreisler, Fritz: "Tambourin Chinois," Op. 3 (1961)
Debussy, Claude: "La fille aux cheveux de lin" (from Preludes, Book 1, No.
8) (1961)
Kroll, William: "Banjo and Fiddle" (1961)
Sarasate, Pablo de: Introduction and Tarantella, Op. 43 (1961)
Falla, Manuel de: Spanish Dance No. 1 from *La vida breve* (1961)

Schumann, Robert: "Vogel als Prophet," Op. 82, No. 7 (from *Waldszenen*)
(1961)
Kreisler, Fritz: "La Chasse" in the Style of Cartier (1961)
Chopin, Frédéric: Nocturne in E-flat major, Op. 9, No. 2 (1961)
Wieniawski, Henryk: Polonaise brillante in D major, Op. 4 (1961)
(all 1961 recordings with Brooks Smith, piano)

Carpenter, John Alden: Sonata for Violin and Piano (date unknown)
(with Grant Johannesen, piano)

Brahms, Johannes: Violin Concerto in D major, Op. 77 (1970)
Bruch, Max: *Scottish Fantasy*, Op. 46 (1971)
(with the San Diego Symphony Orchestra conducted by Zoltan Rozsnyai)

INDEX